THE
CAMBRIDGESHIRES
1914 TO 1919

Mrs Adeane decorating the Colours with laurels, 21 May 1919

Cambridge Chronicle photo.

THE
CAMBRIDGESHIRES
1914 *to* 1919

BY

BRIGADIER-GENERAL E. RIDDELL
C.M.G., D.S.O.

AND

COLONEL M. C. CLAYTON
D.S.O., D.L.

With an Introduction by

MAJOR G. B. BOWES
T.D.

Printed and bound by Antony Rowe Ltd, Eastbourne

PREFACE

This volume is an effort to present a record of the war service of the 1st Battalion The Cambridgeshire Regiment during the years 1914–19.

It is based on diaries, letters and notes written by those serving in the regiment, and makes no claim to literary merit. Wherever possible the story has been written as a personal narrative; and our individual responsibility for the several chapters is indicated by the initials of the writer under the chapter-heading. We are fully aware that the course pursued lays us open to the charge of being egoists. We are prepared to accept this risk; we feel that an account of an engagement is more readable when described by an eyewitness than as a bare recital of the sequence of events.

Some ten thousand officers and men were posted to this Battalion during the war. Those who find they are mentioned by name must be modest; their inclusion may well be because we consider them typical of the rest. Those whose names or deeds are omitted must remember that the unknown hero was often the bravest of them all.

We have tried to present a picture of those thousands as we saw them—clean-living, honest people, and typical specimens of the British race. They had their faults, like all humans, but their virtues outweighed their faults many times over.

The appointment of Commanding Officer of an infantry battalion had no glamour attached thereto, but an extra share of hard work and responsibility; Tebbutt, Copeman, Archer and Saint all had the same experience. Like them, we found the load made lighter by the friendship of officers and men. It is in token of that friendship that we offer this book to those who wore the Cambridgeshire Badge in Flanders, Artois and Picardy.

E. R.

M. C. C.

January 1934

ACKNOWLEDGMENTS

We are indebted to the Editor of *The Cambridge Chronicle* for collecting and placing at our disposal a large number of pictures from which four illustrations have been selected; to the Imperial War Museum for permission to reproduce three photographs; to Mr W. H. Swift, for much helpful advice, and for the care and industry with which he prepared the work for the printers, and passed it through their hands; to the Staff of the University Press, for the interest which they have taken in the volume, and for the care which they have devoted to its production; and to past and present Cambridgeshires who have provided material, and by help in other ways have made possible the publication of this work. Lastly, we should like to express the great debt we owe to Major G. B. Bowes for his invaluable advice and assistance in the compilation and publishing of this volume. It is very largely through his efforts that we are enabled to issue the book in its present form.

E. R.

M. C. C.

January 1934

CONTENTS

Contents

PLATES

INTRODUCTION

REGIMENTAL HISTORY FROM 1860 TO 1914

By MAJOR G. B. BOWES, T.D.

THE Cambridgeshire Regiment, T.F., prior to the Great War, had an unbroken history of over fifty years as a military unit composed of civilians. Its forerunner, the 30th Foot (Cambridgeshire Regiment), had its origin in 1702, and as a line regiment it took part with distinction in most of the campaigns of the eighteenth and nineteenth centuries, and existed as a separate corps till 1881, when it became the 1st Battalion East Lancashire Regiment. There were also Volunteer Corps in Cambridgeshire and the Isle of Ely during the Napoleonic Wars. But the continuous history of the Cambridgeshires as a unit of the non-professional citizen army began in 1860 with the formation, as part of the new Volunteer Force, of the 1st and 8th Cambs Rifle Volunteer Corps at Cambridge (where the previous year steps had been taken to form a Rifle and Drill Club), and of the 2nd, 4th, 5th, 6th, 7th, 9th, 10th Cambs R.V.C. at Wisbech, Whittlesey, March, Ely, Upwell, Newmarket and Soham respectively. (The 3rd Cambs. were the Cambridge University Corps, which like the 1st was formed out of the Cambridge Rifle Club.) To these were added later the 17th Essex R.V. at Saffron Walden and the 1st Hunts R.V. at Huntingdon.

On 6 February, 1860, the 1st Cambs R.V.C. enrolled its first members, being one of the earliest corps to be formed in the country, and on 25 May, 1860, under the command of Captain W. P. Prest, received on Parker's Piece its colours, presented by the ladies of Cambridge, a full report of the ceremony appearing in *The Cambridge Chronicle* of the following day. The stewards were found by the newly-formed Cambridge University Corps, an instance of co-operation which continued in later years.

The various Companies were grouped into two Administrative Battalions, the 1st A.B. under Major F. D. Fryer, with H.Q. at March, the 2nd A.B. at Cambridge under Major Viscount Royston, succeeded by Major F. Barlow. Losing successively the Companies at Newmarket, Soham, Upwell and Huntingdon, the whole were merged in 1872 into one unit under the title of 1st A.B. Cambs R.V.; this was changed in 1880 to 1st Cambs R.V. Corps, and in 1887 to 3rd (Cambs) V.B. Suffolk Regiment.

The different corps each had their own uniform, some grey, some green, but shortly after they were merged into one Battalion it was decided to adopt one uniform, and scarlet with dark blue facings and silver lace was approved. Usually these facings are only allowed in the case of a Royal Regiment, but thanks to influence in high quarters the privilege was granted and subsequently confirmed to the Cambridge-shires, who proudly retain them to this day. There was only one uniform for the rank and file, their jackets (like those of the officers) having some of the discomforts but not the full smartness of latter-day tunics; the officers in undress uniform wore a dark blue jacket with 'frogs' and 'barrels', and later many of them also wore mess uniform. In 1897 a scarlet patrol jacket, which served both for drill and ceremonial occasions, was adopted for the officers, and the new pattern mess-kit. In 1906 the Battalion changed to khaki for all ranks, and in 1908 full dress (with scarlet tunics) was introduced for ceremonial and 'walking out'.

The Battalion consisted of 9 Companies, 'A' to 'D' with H.Q. at Cambridge, forming the right half Battalion, 'E' (Wisbech), 'F' (Whittlesey), 'G' (March), 'H' (Ely) with 'I' (Saffron Walden) being the left half, each under a Major.

From 1872 onwards the officers commanding the Battalion were:

1873–80	Colonel J. M. Heathcote, V.D.	
1881–88	„	G. S. Hall, V.D.
1888–97	„	J. H. Peppercorn, V.D.
1898–1902	„	C. T. Heycock, V.D.
1902–1908	„	A. J. Lyon, V.D.

The adjutants were Captains Busbey, W. Hardinge, P. Schreiber, Majors C. H. Gardner, T. D. Dunn, Captains H. Cautley, A. F. Poulton (Suffolk Regiment), A. W. Abercrombie (Connaught Rangers), G. H. S. Browne (Suffolks), F. G. Davies (Suffolks) and R. Martin (Royal Irish).

The officers were mostly drawn from well-known families in the district, sometimes for two generations, and among those who served for a considerable time were included in Cambridge such names as Barlow, Claydon, Clay, Fuller, Fawcett (for many years senior officer of the H.Q. Companies), Liveing, Beales (father and son), Knowles, Bowes (father and son), Basham (father and son), Smith (A. W.), Heycock, Lyon, Papworth, Morley (father and son), Moyes, Rhodes (two brothers), Lilley, Few (two brothers), Peck, Pryor and Apthorpe Webb (Surgeon Captain).

At Wisbech and Upwell: Fryer, Elworthy, Metcalfe, Ollard (four of two generations), Carrick, English (four) and Copeman.

At Whittlesey: Peed, Ground, Weldon (Captain for nearly forty years), Elliott (C. N.) and Webster.

At March: Catling, Dawbarn, Elliott (T.), Grounds, Forrest, Whittome and Sharman.

At Ely: Hall, Horne, Tebbutt and Archer.

Among N.C.O.'s and men the same spirit was seen, often lasting for more than a generation. Large employers of labour contributed their quota in no small measure, such as the Cambridge University Press (which for years provided a whole company under Captain C. J. Clay and his successors), the colleges through their servants, the Post Office, the railways, the timber yards of Wisbech, the small-holders of the Fens, and from smaller firms and individuals the Companies recruited clerks, skilled mechanics, shop assistants and hardy tillers of the soil.

During this period the members of the different Companies, entirely at their own expense, without pay or allowances, continued throughout the year at their headquarter-town to attend drills and practise rifle-shooting. From 1875 onwards for a week during the summer many attended camp as a Battalion, latterly as part of the Harwich Volunteer Infantry Brigade, usually by the sea at such places as Lowestoft or Yarmouth, where the 'denes' afforded space for camp-site, drill and manœuvre. In addition some of the keener officers studied tactics, signalling, etc., one of whom passed every professional examination both junior and senior and was the first officer in England to do so. Later some attended army manœuvres, and the H.Q. Companies took part in field-days with the Cambridge University R.V. and school cadet-corps. As time went on, sections were formed of signallers, cyclists, stretcher-bearers and machine-gunners, each under officers who underwent special training to make themselves and their sections proficient. To quote *The Regimental Gazette*, No. 3 (July, 1916): 'Despite many difficulties real and imagined, despite discouragement and neglect, despite (in shame be it said) ridicule and contempt, the leaders of the Volunteer movement always struggled gallantly "to keep alive the great patriotic spirit which had always been the Soul of the Volunteers". They overcame obstacles and aimed at efficiency till "the country came to see the true value" of their unselfish efforts.'

Their opportunity came early in 1900, shortly after the outbreak of the South African War, when appeal was made to the Volunteer Force to go out as individuals or in units, an appeal which did not fall on deaf ears. Among many other Battalions, the Cambridgeshires responded nobly, and three officers—Captain (afterwards Major) G. F. Whitmore, Lieut. Percy Hudson (now Colonel P. Hudson, C.M.G., D.S.O.) and Rev. W. T. R. Crookham (Chaplain, who served in that capacity till after the Great War—with 43 N.C.O.'s and men went out as a section of the Volunteer Service Company of the Suffolk Regiment, which Captain Whitmore commanded. They took part in some heavy fighting, and in long marches, serving for a time under General French (afterwards Field-Marshal the Earl of Ypres), and won high praise. On their return on 6 May, 1901, they were given a public welcome at Cambridge, attended a thanksgiving service and received the Freedom of the Borough, being afterwards entertained at a public dinner. Four years later, on 12 June, 1905, the Battalion furnished the Guard of Honour for the unveiling by Lord Methuen of the Cambridgeshire War Memorial on the east wall of Great S. Mary's church. On public occasions, such as the Jubilees in 1887 and 1897, the Queen's Funeral in 1901, and the coronation of King Edward VII in 1902, the Cambridgeshires figured officially, and often found guards of honour for the visit of any member of the Royal family. The Head-Quarter Companies held an annual Prize Distribution and Ball, and were specially honoured on several occasions, e.g., by the presence in 1884 of H.R.H. Prince Albert Victor of Wales (afterwards the Duke of Clarence), then an officer in the C.U.R.V., and in 1903 of Sir John French, who had not forgotten those who served under him in South Africa.

On Sunday, 29 March, 1908, the H.Q. Companies attended church parade for the last time as Volunteers under Lieut.-Col. B. W. Beales, V.D. (whose father had been one of the original members enrolled in 1860 and was for many years an officer) at Great S. Mary's church, and there laid up the colours which had been presented in 1860, and which still hang in the chancel. Two days later, after a farewell mess-dinner attended by past and present officers, and in the presence of a large concourse of people on Market Hill, the Regimental buglers sounded the Last Post for the death of the Volunteer Force, and a minute later the Reveille which heralded in the Territorial Force. Colonel Lyon, all the officers, and most 'other ranks' were transferred from the old to the new without a break in their service.

The change-over from the Volunteer to the Territorial Force was much more than a mere change of name. Under the Territorial and Reserve Forces Act 1907, which owed its inception to the foresight and clear thinking of Mr (afterwards Lord) Haldane, then Secretary for War, the citizen army was for the first time organized in 14 Divisions, each with its proper complement of all arms. All officers and men were liable to be called up for permanent service in the United Kingdom in time of national emergency. All ranks received pay and were subject to military law during annual training, and 'allowances' were given for special training. Its administration, except in times of annual training, embodiment, or actual military service, devolved upon the new County Territorial Associations, composed of both civil and military members, which were responsible for clothing, equipment, upkeep of buildings and ranges, and jointly with the units for recruiting. Cambridgeshire and the Isle of Ely were well served by their Association, which, under the chairmanship of Mr C. Adeane, with Major A. J. Pell as Vice-chairman, worked hard to improve the well-being of the units, to increase their numbers, and to arouse and maintain the interest in the Territorial Force of employers and the general public. Under their auspices, a public meeting was held in the Guildhall, Cambridge, on 28 November, 1908, under the presidency of the Mayor, who was supported by leading representatives of the Town, County and University, the principal speaker being Mr Haldane himself. As the result of local efforts also detachments were raised in several villages, which were allotted to the nearest Company.

There being no Cambridgeshire line regiment, the Cambridgeshires shared with a few other Territorial units the honour of being the 1st Battalion of their county Regiment. They were also honoured by having as their Hon. Colonel Lord French, who paid them a visit on 13 March, 1911. On 19 June, 1909, Colonel Lyon with 24 officers and 'other ranks' attended at Windsor, in company with representatives from many Territorial units, to receive from H.M. King Edward VII their new colours. The Battalion consisted of 8 Companies, 'A' to 'D', with H.Q. at Cambridge, and 'E' to 'H' in the Isle of Ely. The training, first under Colonel Lyon, and from 1911 onwards under Colonel L. Tebbutt, T.D., D.L., became gradually more systematic and intensive, with the fifteen days' camp instead of a week, and frequent instruction classes and tactical schemes for officers and N.C.O.'s, who thus fitted themselves for the greater responsibilities which now fell on them. The adjutants at this period were Captains R. Martin (Royal Irish), M. F. Fox (Leinsters) and H. A. P. Littledale (K.O.Y.L.I.) and the duties of Quartermaster were admirably performed by Lieut. H. E. Verrinder, whose unremitting care in matters of clothing, equipment and messing in camp contributed not a little to the well-being of all ranks. In January, 1914, a great recruiting week was held in Cambridge and throughout the county, by which the Battalion was brought up to strength by the addition of 430 recruits of a fine type, and on the outbreak of war it had a waiting list. The three years from 1911 to 1914 laid the foundations of the thorough training and preparation and enhanced *esprit de corps* which bore fruit in abundant measure in the following four years and a half.

And so we come to July 1914, with the 1st Battalion The Cambridgeshire Regiment at full peace strength and with a waiting-list of recruits, assembled 960 strong at Ashridge

Park for Annual Training, a training in field-work and march-discipline which set the seal on fifty-four years of hard work and devoted service.

CAMBRIDGE
Armistice Day 1933

The roll of officers in July 1914 was as follows:

Commanding Officer: Lieut.-Col. L. Tebbutt.

Field Officers: Majors C. E. F. Copeman and G. L. Archer.

'A' Coy: Capt. W. T. Sindall; 2/Lieut. O. N. Tebbutt; 2/Lieut. G. T. G. McMicking.

'B' Coy: Capt. G. B. Bowes; Lieut. F. C. Symonds; 2/Lieut. C. S. de Cerjat.

'C' Coy: Capt. E. T. Saint; 2/Lieut. R. J. Tebbutt.

'D' Coy: Capt. R. E. Sindall; 2/Lieut. T. H. Formby.

'E' Coy: Lieut. M. C. Clayton; 2/Lieut. W. M. West.

'F' Coy: Capt. H. H. Staton; 2/Lieut. E. W. Saunders; 2/Lieut. J. D. Smalley.

'G' Coy: 2/Lieut. J. W. A. A. Ollard.

'H' Coy: 2/Lieut. C. A. H. Keenlyside.

Adjutant: Capt. H. A. P. Littledale, K.O.Y.L.I.

Quartermaster: Hon. Lieut. H. E. Verrinder.

Medical Officer: Lieut. R. Ellis, M.B., R.A.M.C. (T.F.) (attached).

Chaplains:
   Rev. W. T. R. Crookham, Chaplain, 2nd class (T.F.) (attached).
   Rev. F. B. B. Whittington, Chaplain, 4th class (T.F.) (attached).

Chapter I

PEACE

19 *July*—4 *August* 1914

M. C. C.

JULY, 1914, saw the 1st Battalion The Cambridgeshire Regiment assembled at Ashridge Park for their annual training. We were practically at full strength; a successful recruiting effort had filled our ranks. We were very raw, but the material was good; the four Cambridge Companies comprised college servants, printers from the Pitt Press, gas workers, clerks, shop assistants, in fact a sprinkling of all that goes to make up the population of a University town. The other four Companies recruiting from the Isle of Ely were mainly agricultural—smallholders and agricultural labourers, and a good number of railway workers. As a subaltern I commanded 'E' Company, drawn from Wisbech—timber sawyers, solicitors' clerks, men drawn from fruit orchards, a large proportion of the local Post Office staff, in short men from all trades.

Our N.C.O.'s were in the transition stage; the seniors were Volunteers who had stayed on when the Territorial Force was organized out of the Volunteer system in 1908. These N.C.O.'s were men who as Volunteers did their drills and went to camp at their own expense; they excelled in musketry and close order drill, but adopted an attitude of benevolent neutrality when newly joined subalterns fresh from the O.T.C.'s tried to broaden the field of training. They were, however, the backbone of the system; many of them already had sons serving under them, and their fathers' and grandfathers' services dated back to the sixties, when the predecessor of the 1st Cambridgeshire Regiment was formed.

Professional men, farmers, employers of labour and their sons made up the Corps of Officers. We did our attachments to Regular Units and special schools, we attended Army Manœuvres when possible, but the average Territorial officer had all his spare time taken up in recruiting and training his men—and his spare cash in meeting the many expenses 'not recoverable from Army Funds'.

Col. Tebbutt's tenure of command was about to expire; for years he had been a keen military student both at home and on the Continent. His predecessor, Col. Lyon, had commanded at the change over from the Volunteer to the Territorial system, and Col. Tebbutt was the first purely Territorial C.O. in the line of succession. As if to emphasize this fact, he had for four years conducted a strenuous campaign; new drill-halls and equipment, fresh officers and permanent staff, and a completely new outlook on training, especially of officers and N.C.O.'s, had been a few of the results achieved. And now Col. Tebbutt's period of command was drawing to a close; his two elder sons were already gazetted, but he intended his last annual training to be a strenuous one.

The Adjutant (Capt. H. A. P. Littledale, K.O.Y.L.I.) was also something in the nature of an innovation. No longer was a Territorial Adjutancy to be considered a soft job for a Regular officer. Littledale laughingly used to remark that he had never worked so hard in his life. New aspects of training both of officers and men, a complete overhauling of mobilization procedure, a nominal roll, furnished by Company Commanders, of all ranks, showing the occupation in civil life of each man, these and a hundred other subjects stimulated thought throughout the Battalion.

The fortnight's training was pretty thorough; it involved a good deal of marching (how thankful we were afterwards!), the recruits made amazing progress, but all the same camp seemed at the commencement like previous camps. If I were

Lieut.-Col. Tebbutt and Major Copeman

Major Archer, Capt. Littledale and the Band

ASHRIDGE PARK, JULY 1914

asked to fix a date dividing two epochs I think that I should select the Sunday midway through camp. We had of course discussed Press news all the previous week, but it did not seem directly to affect us. We held the customary Church parade on a Sunday morning, the Battalion resplendent in the glory of scarlet tunics against a typical English background of immense beech trees, the band playing the Battalion back on to the parade ground, and then the Dismiss—who could know it was to be the last full-dress parade?

Rumours quickened, Littledale dashed off in a car to Cambridge, bringing back the boxes of Mobilization Orders which had been kept under lock and key at H.Q. I was amazed at the wealth of detail contained therein; I was even told where to buy an extra shirt for a man.

All this, as Col. Tebbutt explained, was 'purely precautionary', but the 'First Precautionary Period' had already arrived: Saint with his 'Special Service Section' departed to guard the Ipswich wireless station.

Annual training finished, on the Sunday we returned home. We knew the suspense could not be long: the next morning my Company clerk commenced typing nominal rolls. I arranged for volunteers with cars to take round mobilization notices when the order arrived.

On 4 August, 1914, at 8.30 p.m. I received a telegram: 'Mobilize, first day of mobilization August 5th—ADJUTANT'. We were at war.

Chapter II

MOBILIZATION

4 August 1914—14 *February* 1915

M. C. C.

WITHIN an hour men were streaming into the Wisbech Corn Exchange; and my fellow-subaltern, Monte West, arrived, his Gladstone bag containing one mess jacket, one boiled shirt, and his shaving kit! By midnight most of the 114 men of my Company had reported; by 6 a.m. 113; the 114th, who had been away from home, arrived later.

At 6 a.m. parties were marched to various shops and fitted out with sundry pairs of boots and articles of clothing. Our train left at 11.30 a.m.; at March we joined up with 'F' and 'G', and picked up 'H' on the same train at Ely. On arrival at Cambridge we found the rest of the Battalion billeting in schools.

Medical rejections were responsible for a number of vacancies in the ranks; they were immediately filled, former N.C.O.'s and men waiting in queues to enlist at every Drill Hall. The Cambridge Companies enlisted a large number of undergraduates from the C.U.O.T.C., and from the same source came officers. These officers were forthcoming under arrangements made in 1912 (to take effect in the event of mobilization) between Col. Tebbutt and Col. H. J. Edwards, commanding the C.U.O.T.C.

'Progress returns' twice daily and constant kit inspections were the order of the day. The officers' swords were sent to be sharpened. The colours were marched under escort (B Company) with band and drums to Great S. Mary's church and handed over for safe keeping to the Vicar and Churchwardens.

The following Saturday morning we entrained for Romford, completing the concentration of the East Midland

Brigade. Our stay lasted just over a week, and then came three days' marching as a brigade to Long Melford, where we stayed eight days. The weather was hot, but the men marched splendidly, bivouacking at night in fields. Only about 1 per cent. of the Cambridgeshires fell out on the march.

At Long Melford I was ordered to move my Company to Ipswich, twenty-six miles distant, to take over guard-duties from the yeomanry. We set off at 3 p.m., arriving at noon next day, and went straight out to guard-duty at night.

The rest of the Brigade had meanwhile moved to Bury St Edmunds, and officers and men were invited to volunteer for service abroad. Those unfit or unwilling were drafted to take over guard-duties, and the 'Ist (Imperial Service) Battalion Cambridgeshire Regiment' was formed at Bury under Major C. E. F. Copeman, Col. Tebbutt having been found medically unfit for active service. The numbers needed to bring us up to establishment were quickly supplied by means of drafts from the depôt at Cambridge.

Training was greatly impeded by the lack of Regular personnel. Littledale crocked up in September, and we were without a Regular Adjutant until a week before we sailed in February 1915. Furthermore, the permanent Staff N.C.O.'s were withdrawn, Cutting only being left as R.S.M. To make things more difficult the machine-gun section and whole Companies were called upon to dig defences on the East Coast.

In September we moved to Stowlangtoft Hall, and here for the first time the Battalion was concentrated under one roof. For weeks at a time we had to be ready to move at one hour's notice. Not only did this hinder training but it bore hardly on the men. The authorities showed little appreciation of the fact that Territorial soldiers had left their businesses, etc., at an hour's notice; on one occasion, during an alarm period, they even refused permission to a sergeant to go home to attend his wife's funeral.

The first Cambridgeshire casualty to appear in the papers

was notified. McMicking was reported prisoner; he had been on holiday in Germany in July, and his efforts to get out of the country were frustrated. Twice he escaped, only to be recaptured, and he died in Holland a few days before the Armistice.

De Winton and Hay, the Brigadier and Brigade Major respectively, worked like Trojans to forward training, but the Divisional Staff mainly contented themselves with criticism and finding fault—at times most unfairly. Col. Copeman, with his zeal for physical fitness, hardened us; Companies could do a three-mile run without a man falling out of his place. Towards the end of the year we tried to make up arrears of musketry, but this again was impeded by a series of 'readiness tests'. Perhaps an hour after Companies had left for their training-grounds a panting cyclist would arrive with a warning order. Back to billets to collect equipment, a march down to the railway-siding, and then a long wait whilst Staff officers argued as to whether No. 1 of the front rank should place his pack on the rack or under the seat of the railway carriage. We moved into Bury when the Hertfordshires left for France in November. Although it was known that we were the next on the list for service abroad, we were always being called out on futile errands. My Company spent nearly a week guarding a railway line during one of these 'wind-up periods', whilst I concentrated on the problem of issuing a 14 lb. pot of plum and apple jam to one hundred men strung out over fourteen miles of bridges and culverts.

Coincident with the reorganization of the Battalion from the old eight-company system to the modern four-company one, came warning orders for France. Algeo of the Dorsets came as Adjutant. We exchanged our circus procession transport for limbers and G.S. waggons, and the Lord-Lieutenant and the County Association came down to bid us 'Farewell'. On 14 February, 1915, we left Bury in three trains and embarked that night at Southampton.

Chapter III

EARLY DAYS

15 *February*—16 *March* 1915

M. C. C.

OUR convoy, guarded by destroyers, safely crossed the Channel, and next morning we disembarked at Havre and trekked up the long hill to No. 6 camp. Two days later we entrained, and arrived at Cassel at noon on 18 February. After detrainment we marched to Terdeghem, our first billets being in farms around the village. We were notified that we were to join the 82nd Brigade of the 27th Division. This formation had been in France since Christmas and consisted of Regular Battalions from India and China with the 9th Royal Scots, Princess Patricia's Canadian Light Infantry and ourselves as additional battalions. We had several days' training under the watchful eyes of various Generals. Plumer, as Corps Commander, and Smith-Dorrien came twice, the latter 'a real human General, who did the men no end of good'. We moved to Boeschepe, whence on 2 March Saint took 'B' Company up to Dickebusch. They were employed in digging in rear of the front line, and both officers and N.C.O.'s performed spells of duty there. Corporal Dewey had the mournful distinction of being the first man to fall in action.

We accompanied our new Brigade when they returned to the line on 10 March. 'A' went straight to Kruisstraathoek, where they found two hundred men that night to carry knife-rests to the front line. Meanwhile 'C' had moved into billets at Dickebusch. 'The village was full of civilians, the male population being employed at nights in digging support trenches.' Twenty minutes after our arrival we marched up to dig in the second line behind Voormezeele. As we moved up in the darkness the whole front was clearly indicated by the display of Verey lights, which rose and fell throughout the night. Rifle-fire was fairly constant; at times it rose to a crescendo, the bullets whistling high over our heads. By 2.30 a.m. we had completed our allotted task to the amazement of the sapper officer, who had not realized that we were an agricultural Company, drawn from the Fens, with hereditary skill in dyking.

On 13 March Ollard took up his machine-gun crew into the front line at St Eloi, whilst 'A' and 'B' moved into support.

The next night I paraded at H.Q. 2nd D.C.L.I. at Dickebusch to accompany them on a tour of instruction in the line. With me were Smalley, Butlin, Seaton and four sergeants. One officer and one sergeant were detailed to accompany each Company. When we came out of H.Q. Smalley found that his Company was already several hundred yards up the road. For no apparent reason I told him to attach himself to my Company, which was just passing, and I raced after the leading Company. As things turned out it proved a momentous decision for me.

We plodded on to Voormezeele; the platoon to which I was attached took the St Eloi road to the Bus House, and then struck across the fields. I had an irresistible inclination to duck; bullets were passing over our heads all the time; occasionally one would hit the sodden ground with a 'plop'. We were getting near the trenches; when a Verey light went up we stood like statues, expecting a burst of fire, but none came in our direction.

We reached the trench, a sandbagged wall of earth about five feet high; the ground was too waterlogged to dig down. Each of these 'grouse butts' held about thirty men. There was no parados, the trench being open to the back and sides. There were a succession of these grouse butts at intervals of about eighty yards; the enemy trenches were on the rising ground about one hundred yards in front.

The sentries stood with their heads over the parapet and fired whenever they thought they saw anything suspicious. Occasionally, and especially towards dawn, firing would increase until taken up all the way down the line: then the storm would quieten again to intermittent shots, but firing never really ceased all night.

Half-way across No Man's Land we had a listening-post of two men which was always withdrawn before dawn. I went out with the platoon sergeant; every time a light went up we dropped flat; the result was that I was wet through by the time I regained the trench. I sat shivering on the fire-step all night, not knowing what to make of it all, and wondering why we volunteered for the task.

With the first pale glimmer of daylight came a roar of musketry down the line. This lasted for some minutes, and then the rest of the 'Stand-to' hour was spent in silence, the men trying to warm their numbed fingers on their hot rifle-barrels.

It was daylight now; I could have a good look round. Through a periscope I surveyed the enemy line—a long continuous sandbagged wall overlooking us everywhere except on the left, where we held the St Eloi 'Mound'. Jenkins, the platoon commander, pointed out to me where Smalley's Company was on the Mound, and I told him that I had exchanged positions with Smalley.

About fifty yards in front were several still forms lying in curious attitudes. They were all Frenchmen with baggy scarlet trousers.

In rear, about five yards behind the trench, were five mounds with crosses carved out of condensed milk boxes, a mute reminder of what was constantly happening. But what struck me as much as anything was the long flat expanse of muddy fields running back a thousand yards to Voormezeele.

I expected to see support trenches but there were none visible; I understood then why reliefs and counter-attacks could only be carried out under cover of darkness.

The platoon commander was freshly commissioned from Sandhurst, and the platoon sergeant a typical Regular N.C.O. wearing both South African ribbons. Most of the men had had several years service, and until a few months previously they had been stationed in Hong-Kong. A corporal had been wounded six months before, when serving with the 1st Battalion, and a grey-haired private explained that he was a reservist recalled to the colours.

I was to return with Sergt. Hemy after dark that night to rejoin the Cambridgeshires. The men plied Hemy with questions. They were genuinely interested in the arrival of a Territorial Battalion. We made the fifth Battalion in the Brigade, the others, besides the 2nd D.C.L.I., being the 1st Leinsters, 1st Royal Irish, and 2nd Royal Irish Fusiliers. There seemed to be a consensus of opinion that Territorial battalions drawn from home would have better stood the cold and damp than these seasoned troops drawn from hot climates. The sergeant told me that bullets were not the worst enemy. Only a few nights before he had counted fifty kilted figures on the road from the Bus House; after forty-eight hours in the mud of the front trench their chilled limbs would not support them, and stretcher parties from the supports had had to carry them back.

Shortly after he had told me that bullets were not the worst enemy, I saw the sergeant peering over the parapet towards the enemy: the crack of a bullet, and he fell lifeless. He was the first man I had ever seen killed. We laid him in rear of the trench; and the reservist hacked a cross out of some firewood and wrote the sergeant's name and number in indelible pencil in readiness for the burial beside the other five after dark.

I felt sick, and it was as well that I did not know that not one but eight fresh mounds would be raised behind the trench before many hours had elapsed.

At 5.30 p.m., whilst I was gazing towards the Mound, I suddenly saw the trench there lifted into the air; sandbags and debris seemed to rain around, and a moment later there came the dull 'boom' of the explosion. At the same instant the whole of the German line opened fire; away by the Mound I saw the enemy advancing. We immediately opened fire on our front. I remember firing my revolver at two men; whether I hit them I know not; in fact I have no clear recollection of what did happen for several minutes. I remember Jenkins telling me to make my way to the right to watch if the enemy worked round, and stopping on the way to tell a red-haired private to follow me. As I shouted to him a burst of machine-gun bullets sprayed his head into pulp from his jaw upwards, and his brains splashed all over me and two other men.

Behind us the enemy was placing a thick and well-aligned barrage. Every ten seconds something like a coffee tin came twirling through the air and fell in the mud behind us before it burst with a shattering report.

I must have looked occasionally to the left, where the main fighting was taking place, but, even immediately afterwards, my mind was a complete blank regarding what I saw there.

When darkness arrived the position was that our trench was intact, though seven out of the thirty men had been killed. Away on our left by the Mound was a serious state of affairs; we had lost six trenches and the village of St Eloi. Ollard and Sergt. Bowyer with their machine-guns in trench S. 9 had materially helped to stop the enemy advance, and had taken on and knocked out an enemy machine-gun.

Saint's 'B' Company had advanced splendidly under heavy fire to occupy a supporting position early in the evening. Unfortunately O. N. Tebbutt was killed whilst reconnoitring towards St Eloi; he was a great loss. Intellectually he was head and shoulders above most men of his age, and a master of detail, and his death cut short a promising career. 'A', 'C' and 'D' spent the night in furiously digging themselves in in fresh support positions in case of a further enemy advance.

Meanwhile a counter-attack during the night by the Royal Irish failed to restore the position, and we in the line were left in the uncomfortable situation of not knowing whether we should find the enemy next morning shooting at our trenches from the rear as well as the flanks.

There was no sleep for anyone that night; we had to keep our eyes skinned for fresh attacks, and scrape up extra defences on our exposed flank. Dawn arrived without any fresh developments, and we slept in reliefs during the day. The reservist made seven more crosses of firewood, but the last ones were very small. No rations of course had arrived, and the supply of wood ran short, but what we missed most was drinking-water.

When darkness came we buried our dead and erected the pitiful little crosses. The return of Hemy and myself to our own unit, which had been 'deferred owing to unforeseen circumstances' the previous evening, could now take place.

I made my farewells, and then we set out. When we had gone fifty yards I told Hemy I had left behind a spare pair of boots.

'Are you going back for them, sir?'

'I wouldn't go back to that trench for fifty pairs' was my reply, and we strode on.

I arrived at Battalion H.Q. in a château behind Voormezeele at the same moment as Ollard, and we were able to contradict in person the report that we were 'Missing, believed killed'. Copeman, wise and understanding, refused to let us make our reports until the morning. A little food and a tot of rum, and we were soon sleeping on the floor.

The next morning I rejoined my Company, which had

spent the night digging. The rest of the officers and sergeants who had accompanied me when we went into the line had been in the thick of it. John Smalley, who had taken my place in the trench on the Mound, was never heard of again; his sergeant was wounded and taken prisoner. Butlin had come through unscathed, but his sergeant had been killed. Seaton's position had been overrun by the enemy. He had fallen into the mud of a shallow trench, several Germans had trodden upon him, and he was very cross. He had the sense to lie where he was until dark; then he recovered and cleaned his glasses and crawled back into our lines.

That night (16 March) we left the château at 10.30 p.m. and marched to Westoutre, arriving at 5.30 a.m. For the first time in the war I knew what it was to be tired out; for the last hour we halted every fifteen minutes, and each time I dropped fast asleep on the stone cobbles.

St Eloi was the first occasion that the 1st Cambridgeshire Regiment was in the line; it coincided with a hostile attack, and our introduction to war was a rude one. I have tried, in the form of a personal narrative, to explain the reactions of one fresh to war. My own feelings appeared to have been shared by the others; we all agreed that war was a bloody business.

Chapter IV

THE FIRST TIME AT YPRES

17 *March*—26 *May* 1915

M. C. C.

OUR stay at Westoutre lasted nearly a fortnight. We were not, however, idle: much training was carried out, and we found parties for digging rear lines of defence. It was whilst employed on one of these that we met an officer who had been in the fighting at St Eloi. He told us that Smalley was not killed when the Mound was blown up, but behaved with great gallantry, until finally he was shot through the head whilst engaged in bringing up a greatly needed box of ammunition.

Longley, our Brigadier, inspected the Battalion and said he was very pleased with our behaviour under fire for the first time. We took part in a Brigade Parade and were inspected by Smith-Dorrien, who, 'rather to our annoyance, singled out the Cambridgeshires for special mention. We felt we deserved a good word, the men had done wonders, but our achievements were modest compared with the four Regular Battalions who had borne the brunt of the fighting'.

St Patrick's day, spent out of the line, with three Irish battalions in the same village, was bound to be exciting, and Ollard's machine-gun section 'ought to have drunk up their rum—it was not safe elsewhere'.

Archer and the four Company Commanders had bussed up to Ypres and spent the night in the trenches at Hooge, where we were to relieve the French on 2 April.

We paraded at 3.30 a.m. and arrived at Ypres about 8 a.m. As we marched into the Grand Place I was struck by the sheer beauty of the Cloth Hall; the sun was shining and the stone-work stood out in all its glory. A few shops were closed, but the majority of them, and all the cafés, were doing a roaring trade. Milk carts drawn by dogs were making their morning calls, and children were hurrying to school.

We were billeted in the Ramparts and the houses nearby. We watched with interest the French cooks at work with their cookers, preparing a meal for their troops when they were relieved.

That night 'B' and the machine-guns went into the line with the R.I.F.'s, 'D' with the Leinsters, whilst 'C' joined the D.C.L.I. in support at Sanctuary Wood. We proceeded up the Menin road to Hooge—still a pleasant village with striped wooden shutters on the houses. Sanctuary Wood, as part of a noted pheasant shoot, was well furnished with tall trees, as were the woods and coverts around. The latter that week were given the names by which they were to be known for the rest of the war: Bodmin Copse after the D.C.L.I., Cam Grove after ourselves, whilst Armagh Wood and Clonmel Copse were also self-explanatory.

The relief was somewhat prolonged owing to language difficulties. 'C' Company took over from a French Company. Their C.O., a tall young bearded subaltern, was excessively voluble; Staton understood him not at all, and I very little. He kept asking whether we were the Company for 'demi-repos', Staton kept assuring him that we were not half-asleep, and it was some time before we found that 'demi-repos' was the equivalent for our 'supports'.

The dug-outs consisted of tents formed of fir-poles and held about eight men. I asked the French officer where the men's latrines were. He looked puzzled for a moment, and then he waved his arm in a magnificent gesture embracing the whole of the wood. He was quite right; our national zeal for sanitation made it necessary for us to dig over large portions of the wood a few days later.

During the whole of this argument his men had been slipping away by two's and three's. The same thing took place in the line; as soon as Saint's Company came up the communication trench, the French heaved themselves over the parados and departed in groups across the fields to Ypres. We were all tired out, and after 'stand to' we slept despite of occasional shells which fell in the wood. The trees were continually being snicked by the bullets from the line, and altogether Sanctuary Wood belied its name. Copeman would not forgo his daily walk, and every morning we used to see him striding along with the inevitable walking-stick. Then one morning I missed him: his old enemy sciatica had caught him, and although he remained in Ypres until the 24th (by that time hardly a nice place in which to endure sciatica), he had to be evacuated to hospital and Archer succeeded him.

The next night I moved up with 'C' into Cam Grove, one hundred yards behind the line; the wood was systematically shelled, but we escaped casualties. Marr arrived from the 2nd Battalion in place of Smalley, and this began Marr's long association with the Battalion. On the evening of 4 April 'C' Company moved into the front line, being interspersed amongst a Company of Leinsters. The lines ran very close together; in places the Germans were only twenty yards away, their snipers were active, and the slightest exposure was dangerous.

Our own trenches were at the foot of the slope and about eight inches deep in liquid mud; on our right were 'A', who had taken over a section of the line from 'B'. Two days later we took over a section on our own, which we held alternately with 'B' for a spell of four days at a time.

The other two Companies were similarly holding the line, and on the whole these were very comfortable trenches. Sited in thick woods, the deep communication trenches allowed access at all times of the day to the front line, and, equally important, the wounded could be easily evacuated. We were too close to the enemy to be shelled, only fifteen yards in places. The lower trenches certainly were rather wet, but the main trouble with 'B' and 'C' Companies' trenches was the activity of German snipers. At one place where the line ran down a slope the whole trench was enfiladed from the left. We did a great deal to obviate this by means of 'flying traverses', but not before a sniper claimed five of our men, nearly all shot through the head.

When we returned, after four days in Cam Grove, Saint had done a good deal more work, but had not discovered the position of the sniper. The next morning he killed another man out behind our trench. Without a moment's hesitation Staton dashed out to bring in the man, and whilst stooping over him was hit by the sniper. The bullet fortunately was a fraction of an inch too high, traversing and depressing the top of his skull. Staton was able to walk down to the dressing-station, but his wound put an end to the active service of an officer who held the affection of his men to a remarkable degree. He was always known as 'The Master' (the C.S.M. was 'The Foreman'); his age would have been justification for his remaining at home, but when his Company needed a lead he was the first to volunteer.

The same day one of our men was sniped some distance behind, on a line running at right angles to the trench; this gave us the needed clue. Algeo supplied the corroboration. I told him of the suspected point, and he impetuously put his head over the parapet to see for himself; a second later a bullet whizzed through his curly hair. Algeo let out a burst of invective and departed, instructing me to deal with the sniper, and incidentally remarking that I was the new Officer Commanding 'C' Company.

Naturally the only way to deal with the sniper was to shoot him, but this taxed our ingenuity. That night we cut a loop-hole through the parapet, only to find when daylight came that a tree obstructed the view. The next night we cut another loophole, and at daybreak I peered through the hole

B C   2

whilst a khaki cap was exposed further down the trench. The sniper rose to the bait; I suddenly spotted him in a little steel 'rabbit hutch' painted like a tree trunk. The crack of his rifle confirmed his position—it was time—he had hit eight of 'C' Company.

All four Companies were getting accustomed to the routine of trench life. The woods were still full of pheasants and rabbits which gave variety to our 'shackles'. Sanctuary Wood was always unhealthy owing to spasmodic shelling, but the view of the average man was that that was entirely a matter for Battalion H.Q. to endure, though we sympathized when we ourselves were there in reserve.

The transport, however, was having a hectic time. Night after night Platt-Higgins came riding up with his limbers, and although the bottle-neck outside Ypres was systematically shelled, as was the Menin Road, they always managed to squeak through.

We had our first dose of lachrymatory gas shells. Saint on coming up to Cam Grove found us weeping. He scoffed at us for a full minute and then commenced dabbing his eyes, and ended by weeping profusely himself.

On 18 April things started to liven up. The 5th Division on our right carried out their carefully arranged attack on Hill 60 and gained the summit. But it was the signal for the enemy to commence the greatest bombardment we had yet experienced. Not only was the whole of our area severely shelled, but the German heavy guns took up the challenge, round after round of heavy stuff falling into the town. Great gaps were torn in the houses and Cloth Hall, and soon the whole of the sky behind us was reddened by the glare of big conflagrations. Platt-Higgins, however, turned up with rations as usual.

Our batteries could do nothing; not only were they outnumbered, but they had arrived at the 'three rounds per gun per day' period.

On 22 April we were fortunate; the great gas attack which enveloped the French, Canadians and British stopped just short of our left flank. All day we were subjected to heavy rifle- and shell-fire but no attacks developed on our front. Copeman, who was still in Ypres, hobbled out to the Potije Road and saw amazing sights—terror-stricken French Colonials swarming back, our own men with blood-flecked lips and fast dimming eyes groping their way to dressing-stations before their sight gave out. Away in front our infantry and gunners were putting up their fight against odds, many of them to succumb to gas before even the enemy could close round them.

We knew little of this at the time; our portion was heavy firing and continual 'stand to's'. The Royal Irish and D.C.L.I. went away to help to stem the break through; 'C' and 'D' Companies now found the Brigade Reserve, and we occupied the line Cam Grove–Clonmel Copse.

Archer informed us that the reason our rations had not arrived was because the enemy had penetrated to within a thousand yards of Ypres; then, for no apparent reason, they hesitated and the Lahore Divisions arrived in the nick of time. We knew that Platt-Higgins would have got through if it had been possible; that night and the night of 26 March, 1918, were the only two in the war that our transport failed to do so.

It was clearly touch and go whether we were going to be cut off; the bottle-neck at Ypres contracted; at night it seemed as though the enemy lights completely surrounded us. Our line had been skinned to provide troops to fill the gap on our left; 'B' Company were informed that they would have to spend eight days at least in the front line trenches.

My 'C' Company were kept in reserve during this period of stress; and we worked like niggers. We were always being ordered off to some danger-point in case of eventualities which fortunately did not arise. At night we worked unceasingly on the construction of a new line running along Observatory Ridge and the eastern edge of Sanctuary Wood.

It was intended to shorten our line; a cord was to be drawn across the deepest part of the Salient. The night of 3 May was fixed for the date of withdrawal. The Leinsters on the right, our 'B' and 'D' in the centre, and the R.I.F.'s on the left, were to withdraw at 10.30 p.m. through the D.C.L.I., and 'A' and 'C' Companies. This force would hold the Clonmel Copse line until the front-line troops were settled in the new line in rear.

During the afternoon, however, the D.C.L.I. were despatched to the help of the 81st Brigade on the left, so 'A' and 'C' had to form the intermediate line.

We took up our positions in readiness. Soon after 10.30 p.m. the R.I.F.'s passed through my Company, all except a few men left behind to keep firing. These were withdrawn at 1.30 a.m. Hopkinson, who was in charge of the rear party of 'B', reported to me that all his men were withdrawn except one who was missing. That individual came panting in half-an-hour later; situated in a lonely traverse he had not heard, or had misunderstood, the order to withdraw. He kept firing his rifle at intervals, and then suddenly became aware that the trenches were deserted and that he alone was facing the German army!

The night wore on, the enemy firing in front had ceased, and we could hear them moving about in our deserted positions. I began to get anxious, dawn was approaching, and my orders were to stay there until I received definite orders to withdraw. Suddenly in the half light I saw Algeo approaching.

'Everything is in order now, Clayton; bring in your Company.'

I checked the Company out of the wood, and Algeo and I walked back; we were the last British to walk up that slope for two-and-a-quarter long years.

The R.I.F.'s were waiting to close the gap in the wire after our passage; I had hardly established myself in a dug-out in

Sanctuary Wood before the whole of the new line opened
fire on the approaching enemy.

Now that the front line was immediately in front of Sanctuary Wood the latter became an extremely unhealthy place.
Our line on Observatory Ridge was shelled continually,
which meant that we received all the 'overs'; both 'A' and
'C' lost several men from this cause.

On the morning of 6 May the enemy recaptured a portion
of Hill 60 with the help of gas. They then turned their
attention to the hard hit 15th Brigade on the left of Hill 60.
Our guns were powerless to help the infantry; high explosives
and shrapnel poured on their line unceasingly; by midday
the fast diminishing survivors were being blinded by tear
gas shells.

About eight hundred yards in rear of Hill 60 and the 15th
Brigade position stood Fosse Wood. This was really an extension of Armagh Wood, which ran along the rear of our new
position to Sanctuary Wood. If the enemy gained an entrance
into Fosse Wood they would be able to work up in rear of the
whole of our new position.

In these circumstances I was summoned in the early afternoon and ordered to secure Fosse Wood, which 'must be held
unless the new line is to be imperilled'. I had only three
platoons of 'C', Marr had taken No. 11 up to Ypres on
fatigue. My Company had been temporarily attached to the
D.C.L.I. The C.O., a great soldier, warned me that it would
probably be a sticky job. 'You must move at once and hold
on, whatever happens.'

We were under cover whilst traversing Armagh Wood, but
as soon as I reached the narrow tongue joining the two woods
I saw that we were bound to be observed both from Hill 60
and by a German plane overhead. I led off with the first
section of No. 9, leaving Saunders and West to regulate the
advance of the remainder by section rushes.

We had not gone fifty yards before we came under machine-gun fire. I cut the rushes down to twenty-five yards at a time; so far we were untouched, but looking back I was horrified to see one platoon bunching together and losing several men thereby.

Several 5·9's were now falling on the edge of the wood. I urged the platoons to hasten and scatter out into the line I indicated. Sergt. Rowe, who had been hit, was beseeching his men to hurry up and get a move on. (I had had him promoted to corporal as far back as 1911.) Luckily there were a number of derelict French trenches which gave a certain amount of cover, the shelling had lessened, a few 5·9's falling about a hundred yards over, and several of them not bursting.

We had completed the first part of our task, the wood was occupied, and it was necessary to formulate some defence scheme. I sent word to Saunders and West to come up to see me; I also summoned Sergts. Jackson, Hurry and Taylor, who were platoon sergeants. I had just opened this informal conference when a 5·9 burst twenty yards away. As we went down flat we heard another coming; it must only have been a second or so but it seemed an age; it grew louder; the wail of the shell developed into a deafening shriek; the ground two yards from me gave a shudder; an instant later came a deafening roar; the ground beside me was flung upwards and outwards, and the air was filled with reeking soil. For several seconds I lay flat on the brink of the newly formed crater, shielding my head from the rain of debris.

When I looked up, Sergt. Jackson, who was on the other side of me, clutched my arm and begged me to see to his leg, which was practically severed. I made a tourniquet with his entrenching tool and puttee; he begged me to stop, but I kept on relentlessly until the blood stopped gushing. I turned round to the others: Sergt. Taylor was past human help, and Monte West asked me in a weak voice to have a look at his shin. I grabbed Taylor's entrenching tool and once more made a tourniquet. But though this stopped the bleeding, it could not save him: Monte died next morning, and by his death I lost one of my closest friends. Saunders was lying with a smile on his face; a tiny piece of shell had gone through his brain; he was past aid; he had joined his lifelong friend John Smalley.

Some men came running up; shelling was now pretty general. I remembered that Sergt. Hurry had been with the other four, so I called and to my relief got an immediate reply; he had a piece of shell through the fleshy part of his leg.

By a cruel piece of bad luck, each of the five to whom I was speaking was hit; I was however unscathed. I went round to the platoons; they were all rather unhappy, for we had already lost thirty men through shells and machine-gun fire. Our stretcher-bearers were hit. I sent back a message telling H.Q. what had happened.

Twenty minutes later I espied Hopkinson coming across with his long loping stride (he was a cross-country Blue). Gill followed with a stretcher party; the worst cases were got away, the others had to stay until dark.

During the night Algeo came down and told me that the position in front had improved and we were to return to the Battalion at Sanctuary Wood. We arrived as it was getting light, and Marr met me. I was standing talking to him when a shell burst on the side of the path. The next thing I remember was Marr pouring out a torrent of abuse at the slowness of the stretcher-bearers. The enemy had no compassion for poor 'C' Company; of the six officers who came out with 'C' a few weeks previously, Sandy Keating was in hospital with a rheumatic heart, the rest were now killed or wounded.

Meanwhile 'A' and 'C' were given twenty-four hours' respite at Brigade H.Q. outside Ypres; the remainder of the Cambridgeshires were sent into the front line. The enemy were now concentrating their attacks on the left of the Menin Road. Corfield and Marr both took out officer's patrols to watch events on behalf of Brigade H.Q. and sent back valuable information. Algeo's diary for 9 May states: 'Situation still critical, 80th and 81st Brigades heavily attacked. Enemy's artillery fire most horrible, their guns hopelessly outnumbering and outranging our own. Marr took out his platoon to the last crossing on the Menin Road, with patrols on either side, to look out for stray Germans coming through the gap in the 81st Brigade'.

On the 10th Algeo reports: 'Artillery fire still heavy but infantry attacks less determined. R. J. Tebbutt wounded whilst on officer's patrol. "D" Company in 2 and 3 trenches heavily shelled, dug-outs and bits of trenches blown in'. The first respirators were issued, little pads to wear over the mouth and nose.

On the 13th the Cambridgeshires were again in Sanctuary Wood as Brigade Reserve, 'shelling horrible and wood stinking dreadfully'. Information was urgently required as to the enemy's intention, and Hopkinson, who spoke German fluently, accompanied by Gill volunteered to try and obtain it. They crept up to the German parapet and lay there for ninety minutes, gleaning scraps of information. Emboldened by this success, the next time they actually clambered into the German line against a sleeping sentry. They were trying to cut off the German's identity disc when the alarm was given, but they got safely away.

Not only did they receive a telegram of congratulation from the Corps Commander, but their exploits were quoted at length in Sir John French's Despatch, and they each received the M.C.

Algeo sums up the period 15—22 May as 'digging, wiring, whizzbangs, and hoping for rest'. Relief came on 22 May, when the Brigade was relieved by the 83rd, and the Cambridgeshires marched by Companies to Busseboom, which was reached at 1 a.m. Seven weeks previously, when the Cambridgeshires had marched into the Salient, vegetation

Machine-Gun Section in trenches in Shrewsbury Forest

Sergt. Pull serving out tea in the trenches

THE YPRES SALIENT, 1915

was still at its winter stage. Anyone with experience of the Salient will agree that seasons there were not marked by changes in vegetation, and coming out after a few weeks in the blasted zone was always rather an experience. 'We awoke to find ourselves in very charming surroundings. Beautiful trees, green trees and nice little streams.' The latter especially were most welcome; 'we were verminous to a degree, and a fresh rig-out of clothing was necessary for all the battalions'.

A few hours after arrival, Plumer and the Divisional Commander went round billets. 'The net result of the inspection was that the Divisional Commander found a man who said he did not know how to use his respirator, but as the G.O.C. was under the impression all the time that he was inspecting the Leinsters it didn't matter much.'

All that night there was a heavy bombardment in the Salient. Next morning orders were received to be ready to move at thirty minutes' notice; this state of affairs lasted for two days, and at last, on 26 May, orders were received to march to Dranoutre. 'The men were quite unfit to march after so long in the trenches, and at least half of the Brigade fell out', but somehow they got to Dranoutre. The Cambridgeshires had left the Salient for the first time.

Chapter V

ARMENTIÈRES—FLIXECOURT

27 *May* 1915—26 *February* 1916

M. C. C.

THE 27th Division was to take over the line at Armentières, 'the softest place in France. Marvellous trenches with every modern convenience. Civilians living in the village behind, and newspapers delivered up the communication trench'.

After Ypres it was a revelation: 'a little light shelling; absolutely peaceful; nothing to report on our front; thank God'. The Cambridgeshires had taken over from the Queen's Westminsters, with all four companies in the line, which was a long one. This was, however, being shortened by digging a fresh trench across a re-entrant.

Officer's patrols went out each night; the enemy was six hundred yards away; Butlin and Bates did a good reconnaissance. On 31 May Algeo reports: 'First casualty—a silly ass lolling about on the parapet. Very difficult to prevent the men from playing the fool under these circumstances'.

The next night, however, the Battalion lost one of its most brilliant and fearless officers. Hopkinson and Gill with two men went out to reconnoitre the German line. They got within twenty yards of the enemy's line and then were fired upon. Hopkinson was hit and left for dead, Gill though badly wounded got away with the two men. Arrangements were made next day to ascertain if the Saxons had taken in Hopkinson, 'but they only shot through our flag'.

Two days later Archer went up to the R.I.F. trenches, which were closer to the enemy, and put out a board saying that we wanted to speak to them. 'We eventually got them with a megaphone, and they told us that Hopkinson was alive—but he was never heard of again.'

Except for trouble from snipers the situation remained quiet; 'peace, perfect peace, except for those who wield the pen. Our lives made loathsome to us by returns of every description called for by Brigade'.

There was a little excitement on 18 June as we blew up three mines in front of Frelinghem. 'Might have been quite a good show if our guns had been allowed to bombard properly, but for reasons not unconnected with the vulnerability of Division H.Q. they were not allowed to do so.'

That was the last note Algeo was to write in the Unofficial War Diary kept at H.Q. He departed to his beloved Dorsets, and the Cambridgeshires lost a fine soldier. His caustic humour and virulent language were but a mask under which he endeavoured to hide his real feelings. He had one great disappointment which he never forgot—when his Battalion sailed away with the B.E.F. in August 1914 he was down with typhoid and could not go with them. Now at last he was to rejoin the shattered remnants of his old Battalion. No one would have cared to predict that he would survive the war; like his friend Hopkinson he was killed whilst on patrol.

Corfield took over as Adjutant but fell a victim to malaria, and was succeeded by 'Guy', or, to give him his proper designation, 'Lieutenant Sir Guy Butlin, Bart.'

The enemy was beginning to liven up. The Cambridgeshires had gained the upper hand over his snipers, and now he tormented them with rifle grenades of a superior type to the British. Casualties were getting more frequent; R. E. Sindall (one of the originals) died of his wounds; the next day (3 July) Crookham, who had only recently come to the Battalion, was mortally wounded by a rifle grenade. Here was one more instance of the 'hereditary nature' of a Territorial Battalion: Crookham's father had been chaplain with

the Battalion both in South Africa and in this war, and at the
time was serving in Egypt.

The rain of rifle grenades continued until the Division was
relieved on 15 July by the newly arrived 12th Division. The
new line was at Bois Grenier. Our arrival coincided with
another sad loss. A stray shell fell on the road as Keenlyside
and Bates were going to the line. Bates was slightly wounded,
but Keenlyside only lived for a few minutes. He had served
in South Africa, enlisting whilst an Oxford undergraduate,
and had mobilized his 'H' Company at the outbreak of war.
He was an outstanding Company Commander. 'D' Company were inconsolable for several days; it also brought home
to us that the originals were going out fast.

The Bois Grenier sector was quiet. Butlin remarks:
'Nothing happening in the trenches, but absolute Hell in the
office'. Archer adds a note: 'A horrid strafe on the lack of
energy of our working-parties. Find much comfort in *Punch*:

> "If all the troops with all the tools
> Should dig for half a year,
> Do you suppose," our Captain said,
> "That we should then be clear?"
> "I doubt it," said the Adjutant,
> Knowing his Brigadier.'

The enemy had commenced sniping. The Battalion took
them on; 'our snipers won the day; after bagging five peri-
scopes we hit the Hun who started signalling the shots'.

A few days out of the line, and September sees the Cambridgeshires holding the line at Rue de Bois; 'very restful,
our rifle batteries strafe our own and the enemy trenches
with delightful impartiality'.

Another of the 'originals' met his death. It was Seaton, 'a
thoroughly conscientious officer, whose duty brought him
from the peace of an academic life to one of bloodshed;
distastefulness of second must have been accentuated by the
first'.

On 9 September the Cambridgeshires were drawn out of the line. The 27th Division was being sent down to take over fresh line from the French and to help break in two 'K' Divisions. A train journey, a march, and new ground on the banks of the Somme.

A spell holding the line, innumerable working-parties, more line, and then on 25 October the French take over our line. A succession of rumours as to the reason for the withdrawal of the 27th Division from the line. General Milne ('Uncle George'), the Divisional Commander, comes to say farewell. The 27th Division is proceeding elsewhere (Salonica) and leaving behind its three extra battalions.

The parting from Regular battalions, who had initiated the Cambridgeshires into the rules of the game, was a wrench; the point, however, which was the chief concern was what was going to happen. They were not long left in doubt—a few days digging in the Seventh Corps line, and then a 'bus move on 30 November to Flixecourt. The Cambridgeshires had fallen on their feet; they were detailed as the Training Battalion for the 3rd Army School.

This tour of duty, which lasted into February, must be briefly dealt with. Training was strenuous; 'not only had we to learn, but we had to teach others. We learned to do all sorts of fancy attacks, etc., for the benefit of the colonels, etc., studying at the School'.

On 14 February, the first anniversary of embarking at Southampton, 'the Relics' dined together. The party consisted of Archer, Few, Butlin, Wood, Platt-Higgins and Bates, R. J. Tebbutt being absent on leave. The tour of duty at Flixecourt finished on 26 February, when the Cambridgeshires entrained for St Omer.

Chapter VI

THE 39TH DIVISION

February—May 1916

M. C. C.

THE 39th Division was one of the last New Army Divisions to be sent across to France. It came minus one infantry Brigade. To meet this deficiency the 118th Infantry Brigade was formed by taking four Territorial battalions which had been serving in France for over a year.

The other battalions chosen were the 4/5th Black Watch, 6th Cheshires, and, by a coincidence, the 1st Hertfordshires, who had formed part of our old Brigade in England. These four battalions regarded themselves in the light of seasoned troops sent to stiffen the fledgling Division.

These feelings were rather jolted when addressed by the new Divisional Commander; 'he spoke of keeping up the "traditions" of the 39th Division, and how the Division had detrained in record time. All very nice but hardly tactful'.

The new Brigades were introduced to trench routine in the Pont du Hem sector, and then the Division was withdrawn for a few days. 'Genl. Haking, the new Corps Commander, discovers that we have one hundred and sixty men who have had no leave since coming to France fourteen months ago; he promises to get leave accelerated. Unfortunately the next day all leave is cancelled.'

On 16 April the Cambridgeshires took over the Festubert line; a certain amount of sniping, and weather very wet and cold. On 25 April comes the cryptic entry by Formby: 'Lt. T. Hope Formby takes on duties of temporary adjutant, a great day in the annals of the Battalion. Fifty men who came out with the Battalion go on leave'.

At the beginning of May a move was made to the Givenchy sector. There was an epidemic of rifle-grenades, and casualties were continuous, anything up to ten per day. The new Division was being subjected to the close attentions of the Corps and Army Staffs. A new Brigadier made his appearance, a game of general post commenced amongst C.O.'s; several of the latter, who had borne the strain of command over many months, were being replaced by Regular officers released from training duties elsewhere.

Archer was amongst the number. 'We did not know who was to be the new C.O. All we knew was that we were losing one whose first thoughts had ever been for the officers and men under his command. He had commanded for over a year through thick and thin—largely thin, and our hearts were sore at losing him.'

Chapter VII

PREPARATION

June—August 1916

E. R.

ON 10 June, 1916, I reported to 118th Infantry
Brigade H.Q., 39th Division, to assume command of
the 1/1st Cambridgeshire Regiment. My old friend
Norris, the Brigade Major, confided to me that I was in for
a stiff job. Subsequent events proved that this estimate of
the value of the 1st Cambridgeshires was hopelessly in-
accurate. Nearly four months later they had made history.

There were still a few hours of daylight, so I made for
Battalion H.Q.

There are no rules governing tactics, only principles: in
consequence, commanding officers cannot be expected to
agree in their interpretation of what should or should not be
done under varying circumstances. Like most 'new brooms,'
I began by sweeping out some of my predecessor's arrangements, and, in their place, directed that my own ideas should
be swept in. What a dull occupation soldiering would be if
it were not for its inexhaustible possibilities! Agreed—but
have we not all suffered from the eccentricities of 'new
brooms'? My new command showed a willingness to suffer
with that patience and cheerfulness which is indicative of a
well-disciplined unit.

Having rearranged Battalion H.Q., I set off with one of
the officers to visit the Companies holding the left section of
Givenchy.

On reaching the front line I made the acquaintance of
Eric Wood, the Captain of the left front Company. I believe
Wood was originally intended for the Church; I liked him

from the first. His men knew what was expected of them, and it was evident that they trusted their leader. Here was one officer I could rely on, and I made a mental note of the fact. All was well with 'B' Company.

The 1st Cambridgeshires was a Territorial Army Battalion recruited from the Fens and the town of Cambridge, with a sprinkling of University men in the ranks. Many of the officers were from Cambridge University.

The fact that the Boche fired a few shells and a number of rifle-grenades into our lines as I wandered through the network of trenches, made me think. What was his game?

It was after dark when I got back to Battalion H.Q. There I found a telephone installed at the side of my bunk, the signallers moved into a shelter near the H.Q., and the officers acquainting themselves with the details of our defence scheme. Willing workers make good soldiers if they are told what is required of them and why the work is necessary.

In the early hours of the morning I was lying on my bed thinking over the events of the day. Suddenly the ground shook. A dull thud-like noise came from the direction of the front line; then the rattle of rifle-fire, the tac-tac-tac of a Lewis gun and the whiz-bang of shells.

Taking the telephone, I rang up 'B' Company.

'Captain Wood's just gone to the front line, sir. Shall I send for him?' said the answering signaller.

It is a bad thing to speak to the man at the wheel, so I replied:

'Tell Captain Wood to speak to me as soon as he can spare the time. Do you know what has happened?'

'No, sir,' said the signaller, 'but I expect the captain has the job well in hand.'

That was good enough for me. Keeping the telephone line open I decided to wait for Wood. A few minutes later I heard his voice:

'The Boche mined J Sap and blew a fair-sized crater. My

B C

3

men occupied the lip before the Boche could get there. Nobody killed; but three men wounded. We are all right now.'

Wood was evidently the good soldier I thought him to be.
I never had reason to change that view.

At dusk we were relieved. It had rained all day. As I
watched the drenched men of my new command file down a
communication trench, one of the officers was reciting a few
lines from the classics. Probably his memory failed him;
anyway he stopped. Whereupon the third man behind him
continued the quotation. I pushed into the trench to find out
what manner of man this private soldier was; for one who
could so glibly compare the rain-sodden hill at Givenchy with
Aganippe, the fountain on Mount Helicon sacred to the
Muses and supplying poetic inspiration, must be a man of
education and imagination. Fate ruled that I should not
speak to him. A stray bullet, probably from a fixed rifle two
thousand yards away, hit him in the back of the neck. He
was dead when we lifted him out of the mud.

'Bad luck', said the adjutant. 'He might have made a
name for himself after the war. He was hopeless as a soldier.'

Nevertheless, I was sorry. There is always a place for brains
in war. This man should have been employed in some other
capacity where his ability might have been of great value.
Thousands of priceless lives were sacrificed in the humble
ranks of our armies. Some, because there was no one to sort
the wheat from the chaff; some because of their dread of the
responsibility which is inseparable from a commission; whilst
others clung to the comrades with whom they had shared dug-
outs and billets, victory and defeat, joy and sorrow, through
weeks or months that seemed to be an eternity. There was a
mistaken idea, running through the minds of so many of our
civilian soldiers, that it was not playing the game to leave the
fighting branches for a safer place on the Staff somewhere
behind the lines.

The regimental officer, being in close touch with his men,

was in a position to recognize individual capabilities and failings. He stuck like glue to all good fighting soldiers, and utilized all the bad fighters he could not get rid of in some menial capacity. These generally drifted away to look after latrines or work in the army laundries, baths, and similar establishments. Had our regimental officer known that his comfort and safety depended on the standard of efficiency of the Staff, he would have been ever on the look-out for suitable men to recommend for Staff employment. Unfortunately, he did not know. And how the devil could he know, with only a few months' service in which to learn all that his professional colleague would take years to grasp?

Consequently, neither the regimental soldier nor the Staff should be blamed for their many deficiencies. The nation as a whole must bear the burden of its own folly in not being prepared.

Men who held the Givenchy, Festubert, or Ferme de Bois sectors of our line during the months of June and July of 1916, and survived, will recall the extraordinary circumstances under which we lived. Except for the hill at Givenchy, we had no trenches on the battle-front. Germans and British held lines of sand-bag forts, which stood out white and glaring in contrast with the bright green of the high grass covering the dead level plain. If either side had so desired these forts could have been obliterated by artillery fire in a few minutes, but what one side could do, so could the other. Therefore both British and German guns left the forts alone. If they wished to shoot, both shot at Givenchy, where we had dug-outs, and the Boche had tunnelled into the great brick stacks for protection. Four or five hundred yards behind the German front line, the ground rose to a height of some twenty feet above the level of the plain, thus screening his movements. Six to eight hundred yards behind the British forts, scattered bushes and trees concealed our movements, and masked a number of farmhouses nestling in orchards and

3-2

clumps of poplars and willows. This formed our second, or Village, line. Here British troops and Belgian peasants lived less than a mile from the German front line. It was an extraordinary position. Civilian and soldier moving about the homesteads reminded me of an 'off' day during manœuvres in England. An occasional strafing of our battery positions by the Boche artillery recalled to mind the fact that we were at war and death lurked about us.

Three days in the forts and three in the Village line was the programme. When in the former, German snipers took their toll, and we retaliated. When in the latter position we rested during the day, or trained our officers and men under the cover of the trees. At dusk I took the Battalion into the fields to practise the attack, for it was no secret that a great allied offensive was looming on the horizon. At that time of day the hostile aircraft could not see what we were doing.

I welcomed those days in the Village line. The whole spirit, military knowledge, and bodily and mental condition of all ranks grew and prospered. In civil life the mentality of man is influenced by his surroundings. If he lives in a dirty room and wears dirty clothes he allows himself to become dirty in mind and body and loses self-respect; and when he loses that he loses all. It is the same with a soldier.

We cleaned our billets, built new latrines and cook-houses, made plunge-baths with the waggon tarpaulins and washing benches, and started a laundry system. The latter was of the utmost importance, for looking for your clothing in the Corps laundry at Gorre was like putting your hand into a bran-tub at a bazaar: you were bound to get something back—but what? I have seen a pair of woollen drawers go in fit for a big man, and come out too small for a dwarf baby. As a nation we are shockingly bad laundrymen, and we kept up that reputation during the war. The Second Army did this work better than any other, but were lacking in humour. Someone had invented a system for killing lice in clothing before it was washed. I was deputed to find a suitable building in the Ypres area, and decided on a disused theatre which I christened 'The Lyceum', but the Quartermaster General's department failed to see the connection and named it 'The Delousing Station'.

The opening of the Somme battle further south necessitated diversions being made on the 39th Divisional front. The Sussex of the 116th Brigade carried out an attack on our immediate right. Although successful in its initial stages, it eventually broke down, and 'B' and 'D' Companies spent many hours in the darkness searching No Man's Land with stretcher-parties and bringing in the wounded.

Our own effort, which was on a minor scale, consisted of a strong fighting patrol under Wood, which attempted to enter the enemy lines north of the La Bassée Canal to obtain identifications. The raid proved unsuccessful owing to uncut wire; the raiding party forced their way right up to the enemy's front trench but were unable to enter. In the bombing battle which ensued Herman and Rawlinson were unfortunately missing, and most of our wounded would have fallen into the enemy's hands but for the gallantry shown by Looker, who was awarded the D.S.O. Fearless and unruffled Looker took up a position within a few feet of the enemy, and held them at bay with his stock of bombs whilst the raiding party carried away their wounded. He had already received several wounds but stood his ground until ordered to withdraw. Wood handled a serious situation with great skill, and his M.C. was a tardy recognition of his powers of leadership.

A Commanding Officer should always have an intelligent orderly to accompany him on his daily rounds in times of war. A few days after I assumed command of the 1st Battalion The Cambridgeshire Regiment I was listening to comments on the units dispositions as voiced by a shrewd-looking, small, but powerfully built private soldier. He was looking across the plain stretching from the Village line to the forts whilst he discoursed to his three companions. As he picked out one object after another, I marvelled at the abnormal strength of his eyesight, noted the concentration of purpose written on his face, and wondered what he had been in civil life. Then he spoke: 'See them canvas sheets? That's the cleverest thing I've seen in the war'.

He was calling his companions' attention to the sheets of canvas about seven feet high which took the place of communication trenches where the ground was too swampy to dig. Behind the cover of these sheets men could move to and from the front line unobserved. At intervals the canvas was lined with sandbags to stop bullets. Where the ground was dry enough, a trench had been dug. In other places there was nothing but the canvas.

'I can't see any bloody sense in it, Nighty. It's just a target for the Boche. Any bloke behind the canvas could be shot through it', said one of the men.

'Yes, but hows the Boche to know he's behind the canvas an' not behind the bloody sandbags', was 'Nighty's' remark. 'Fritz would have to shoot along the whole line if he wanted to get one man, an' that's an 'ard job with a canvas trench zigzagging all over the field.'

I came out of my place of concealment and spoke to 'Nighty'. His real name was Nightingale. That is how I made the acquaintance of one of the bravest men I ever knew, and one of the most observant soldiers. He was always alert, never tired, always washed and shaved, always with something wrong about his uniform, always there when wanted, clean of speech (except for an occasional 'bloody'). The colloquial language of the soldier, regular or territorial, especially in times of stress and danger, has no relation to what he might use in civil life, and in what I say of Nightingale and others I speak of them as they appeared to me seventeen or eighteen years ago. Nightingale, like many others, including some of the undergraduates from the

C.U.O.T.C., adopted the colloquial language common to the army. He sometimes asked for a commission, pointing out that he had a mother at home who was dependent on him. I think he made the request several times, until one day, after a pause in conversation while we picked our way in the uncertain light of the coming dawn, he said slowly:

'About that commission, sir; I don't think I'll bother.'

While with me he was a lance-corporal and was awarded the M.M. for his work at St Julien. From that day in June, 1916, to September, 1917, he was my constant companion when the Cambridgeshires were in the line. When I left the regiment I lost Nightingale. Later he was promoted corporal and acting-sergeant.

The days of little fighting and quiet sectors soon ended, for August found us tramping our way south by easy stages to the Somme shambles.

This march towards the great battlefield was, to me, the best part of the war. Every day I saw my Battalion growing fitter and more efficient; every day I learned more about my officers and men, watching their improvement as a trainer watches a much prized racehorse.

At one place we halted for a night; at another for sometimes three or four days. At Moule, in delightful weather, we held a water carnival. Every imaginable kind of boat was requisitioned for the Battalion sculling championship. Sergt. Cooper, our H.Q. cook, and formerly the chef at one of the Cambridge colleges, won this event. In later days he was to prove himself as good a soldier as he was a cook. It was a happy day and everybody got wet, washed, and weary. The men were in good billets, and were well cared for by their officers and N.C.O.'s. There was no crime or sign of dissatisfaction. True comradeship, coupled with a rapidly increasing pride in their regiment, was more and more evident as the days went by.

If officers or men had been addicted to drink, or the women

living in the villages where we were billeted had been immoral, the fact must have come to my knowledge. I discovered every other fault. Why should I fail to discover these, if they existed? I knew every officer and N.C.O. and nearly every man. And I was not alone. The two padres (R.C. and C. of E.) were very zealous and popular; surely they must have known. The more I think of the unadulterated rubbish written on this subject by a number of 'war novelists', the more I marvel at the credulity of the section of the British public that is stupid enough to swallow this fiction.

At public subscription balls in England, during the past year, I have seen more (alleged) gentlemen the worse for drink than I saw officers in a similar condition during the whole war in the battle areas of France or Flanders.

Judging by the moral standard of the units I served with, I am convinced that the fighting soldier was not addicted to sexual immorality. Occasionally cases came to my notice, but less frequently than when serving in times of peace. The fact that there are a number of children in France to-day whose male parent served in the British army, is proof of the natural call of man to woman but not of flagrant immorality. A Scots soldier mated to a pretty French peasant girl in Bailleul, married her a few days before their son was born. On enquiring after the health of the child some weeks later, a British padre was surprised at the grandmother's remarks:

'Oh, we love the little fellow so much. The worst of it is that we won't understand a word he says.'

Chapter VIII

DOWN TO THE SOMME

August—September 1916

E. R.

'They shall grow not old, as we that are left grow old:
Age shall not weary them, nor the years condemn.
At the going down of the sun and in the morning
We will remember them.'

TO me, it has always been a matter of great wonder how the war-time infantryman managed to carry his kit, arms, ammunition and equipment. Within a margin of two or three pounds, every man carried the same weight, were he five or six feet in height. No company of civilians taken at random from any of our rural towns in England to-day could carry a similar load along our roads for more than an hour. Yet one saw tens of thousands of men, perhaps hundreds of thousands, marching south along those unyielding sun-scorched *pavé* roads that led to the great slaughter-house, the Somme Area.

With half a hundredweight slung round him—tramp, tramp, tramp, feet, feet, feet—his shoulders hunched, sweat coming through his thick clothing, under the armpits, through the back where the heavy pack touched, and down his cheeks from under his cap or steel helmet, marched that miraculous being, the infantryman. And why? Because he was out to lick the Boche; because he didn't like to get beaten himself; because he had lately developed the idea that it was rather a fine thing to be a British subject; because he did not like to let his pals down; and finally, because he wanted to go Home, and knew that he must first win the war. And of these four reasons I think the penultimate one carried most weight.

Yet half the present day war-novelists want the present and coming generation to believe that our soldiers in France undermined their strength by excesses with drink and women! The average athlete knows from experience that he cannot keep fit unless he gives drink and women the 'go-by'. Either would have undermined the physique of the infantry officer or man.

Leading an infantry battalion on a long march is like nursing the endurance of a horse in a race. To take it out of its pace or beyond its distance is fatal. Those four days' marching in the sweltering heat of August, 1916, when we averaged fourteen miles a day, bore testimony to the value of the preceding training.

During the first and second days of our march no man fell out of the ranks. On the third day the sun blazed down on us. We had arranged to cover thirteen miles, but, when within a mile of our destination, news reached me that the water-supply at our intended billets had failed, and we must push on for an additional three miles. When you are near the end of your tether any additional burden leads to a breakdown.

I have always held that it is sound policy to tell the soldier what you expect of him; for, if he is any good, and has any pride in his regiment, he'll do his best. We halted for an hour, during which time the officers explained the situation. When we moved off again the men sang:

'Over the hills to Mary,
My Mary.
Over the hills to Mary mine,'

as we breasted the rise for the last stage of our journey.

Everybody stuck it out. With only one mile to go, I walked first with one Company and then with another, calling their attention to the group of houses ahead of us nestling in the cool shadows of the trees, which was our destination. Scarcely anyone answered me, but they knew why I spoke to them, they knew what their comradeship meant to me, and they

knew the deep affection and pride in which I held them,
stinking with sweat though they were. This affection was
born of a knowledge of their loyalty and grit, and deepened
by the anticipation of the human sacrifices to come in the
very near future.

A last great effort to pull themselves together before the
eyes of the villagers was too much for half-a-dozen.

'March to attention', shouted the young corporal at my
side. Then, spinning round, he crashed to the ground within
ten yards of his billet door. He had fainted.

The next day (26 August) we went up through Auchonvillers to the sector of the line just north of Hamel, with our
H.Q. in Knightsbridge and a long journey down to the front
line by Gabion Avenue.

The trenches (cut through red clay) showed little improvement on those around Festubert when it rained heavily (as it
did on the 31st), though there was high ground affording very
good observation of the country behind the German lines far
beyond Serre, Miraumont and Grandcourt.

A thousand yards to the south lay the ruins of Hamel,
perched on the hill a hundred feet above the wooded and
marshy valley of the Ancre, in whose clear waters lurked big
trout, recalling to the mind of the dry-fly fishermen happier
days spent on Itchen or Test. Beyond the Ancre the ground
rose in a uniform slope for some four or five hundred yards,
to the great German fortress known as the Schwaben Redoubt,
beyond which lay what had been the village of Thiepval.
Away to the south again the British line extended down to
the river Somme, where it joined hands with the French.

North of the Fifth Army (General Gough), to which we
were now attached, came the Third Army (General Allenby),
the Fourth Army (General Rawlinson) continuing the line
to the south.

On 2 September the Cambridgeshires came out of the line
to occupy some trenches about a mile back in close reserve,

whilst our former trenches were taken over by the 17th
K.R.R., Sherwood Foresters, and the 4/5th Black Watch
(Colonel Sceales), who were to attack eastward towards
Beaucourt on the morrow.

From our position, the frowning face of a shell-scarred hill
masked our view. To this hill I sent Eric Wood with a platoon
of 'B' Company and half-a-dozen signallers with flags and
telephone to keep me informed of the progress of the battle.
My Brigade Commander (Finch-Hatton) was with the Divisional Commander (General Cuthbert) a mile-and-a-half
back, with whom I was supposed to keep in touch by means
of two overland field-telephone lines (to which I added a
third).

To the south-east, through the trees, on the other side of
the Ancre, we could see some of the British trenches, from
which other troops were to advance on Thiepval at dawn.

Just before daylight on 3 September the roar of British
artillery from the field-guns between us and Hamel and along
the Hamel–Mesnil road deafened our ears and drowned the
sound of the guns we knew to be firing to the north, south,
and east.

Right to the end of my time in France I never ceased to
experience a strange feeling of indescribable elation and
excitement when our guns opened a bombardment heralding
the attack. In the creeping dawn, like ten thousand drums,
the guns rolled their deafening challenge, whilst tongues of
fire darted and flashed in the valley below us, in front, to our
right, left, behind us.

Young Adam, one of my Company Commanders, turning
his bespectacled eyes towards me, shouted above the din:

'Nothing on earth can withstand that. Will this mean the
end of the war?'

Twenty seconds later other flashes and explosions from the
direction of our batteries showed us that the Boche heavies
were hammering our batteries, and I rejoiced that the light

was not good enough for my men to see; for it was their first experience of a great artillery duel.

As the light improved, Wood telephoned:

'The Black Watch have crossed No Man's Land and are in the German trenches. They are still advancing splendidly in spite of very heavy losses....'

Then the telephone line went. Two minutes later all my wires back to Brigade were cut by artillery fire.

The sun came out, and Wood's 'flag-waggers' told me that our troops were three hundred yards into the enemy lines and still advancing rapidly. Away to the south, across the valley of the Ancre, we had failed: our men were coming back. Through my strong field-glasses I could make out the running, stumbling, bent-up figures of men; now clearly visible, now lost in fountains of earth thrown up by bursting shells, but always going back—those who had not fallen.

The failure of our right wing allowed the German machine-gunners from the Schwaben Redoubt and its neighbourhood to turn their attention to our Division across the river. They enfiladed our newly captured trenches, which now afforded little cover to our men owing to the devastating effect of our preliminary bombardment.

Reports from Wood became less reassuring. Our men were making no progress, and were suffering heavy losses.

The artillery on both sides still crashed and thundered, completely deadening all other sounds.

Then the signallers' flags told me that the German counter-attack had begun. They could be seen coming up from Beaucourt and Miraumont in shirt sleeves. I sent the remainder of Wood's Company to him, and decided to advance to meet the Boche counter-attack.

Down the hill into the valley went the Cambridgeshires. Slowly wending our way through the gaps between the batteries, we climbed the hill in the wake of Wood's men, keeping out of the communication trenches which were now full of stretcher-bearers with their ghastly burdens on their way to the dressing-stations.

I was in front now to show the line of advance. On my left, as we climbed the steep hill, there ran a deep communication trench down which two men were carrying a Black Watch subaltern, whose legs from the thigh downwards were nothing but a pulp of bleeding flesh and clothing. This hero saluted, smiled, and then shouted:

'Get into the trench, sir; our shells are only just clearing the crest of the hill, and will kill your fellows if you cross the top in the open.'

He was a man and a soldier, thinking of his comrades in what was probably his last hour in the world.

I do not know if it was admiration for the dying man or the soldier that was in him that made me stand still and salute. As I write of it, that action seems so theatrical, but I fancy I must have been influenced by the knowledge that here was a far better soldier and man than I.

As we pushed and scrambled along the battered communication trench to the crest of the hill, I got a glimpse of No Man's Land. A few khaki-clad figures were walking from the German lines towards our trenches, a few were still using their rifles and Lewis guns in the enemy trenches, holding up the advance of the shirt-sleeved Germans. Six or seven hundred yards back in the German lines, our shells were throwing up clouds of dust, clods of earth, pieces of timber and corrugated iron—and men.

Two of our Companies ('B' and 'C') advanced through the German shell fire to occupy the old British front line, from which the attack had been launched some two or three hours earlier. On reaching their positions, these two Companies just had time to clean their rifles and Lewis guns, when the leading men of the German counter-attack advanced into No Man's Land.

From where we were on the high ground we could see everything that took place within a mile of us. We saw the little drama, little only in comparison with the whole. We saw the Germans advance a few yards. Above the din of guns we heard the tac-tac-tac of our Lewis guns and the rattle of rifle-fire. We saw the Germans fall dead or wounded and their few survivors run back to their trenches.

The infantry battle was over, for neither side made any further advance. The artillery duel gradually died down to a desultory fire.

Our attack had failed, but the Cambridgeshires had held up the German counter-stroke.

Leaving my position, I made my way down the hill through the almost unrecognizable network of trenches. On arrival at what had been the assembly position for the support Companies for the attack at dawn, I saw the work of the German artillery and machine-guns. Officers and men lay dead so thickly that it was with difficulty that I picked my way without treading on the bodies. I think most of these men had been killed by machine-gun fire or shrapnel, for so many of them looked as if they were asleep; it was only when their staring dull eyes were visible that Nightingale and I knew that they were dead.

In contrast with the silence of the place I had left, I found the front-line trench occupied by live men elated at the success of their efforts to repel the German counter-attack; laughing, smoking, eating, and talking about the prospects of getting tea sent up to them.

Finding all well with the leading Companies, I retraced my steps.

As dusk crept over all the firing gradually died away. Then all was still. And the cowards (for there are some in every army) crept from the dug-outs and slunk away. We did not attempt to stop them. There were only a few. They were no good. They did not matter.

We were relieved—by the Hertfordshires, I think—and went back to some dug-outs and trenches over the hill in the deep, narrow valley, above which Wood's signallers had taken up their position in the morning.

All available stretcher-bearers had gone into No Man's Land on their errand of mercy. With them, unknown to me, went the two padres, Northcote the R.C., and Popham the C. of E.

These two men, holding very different religious views, were of one mind in their care for the spiritual and bodily welfare of all soldiers. In estimating the military value of men, I placed them higher up the list than many others who bore arms. The Cambridgeshires called them 'the Terriers' for they always worked in couples. Their work that night was beyond all praise.

Shortly after dark, whilst the work of the Good Samaritans was in progress, the Germans swept No Man's Land with machine-gun and rifle-fire, fearing, I presume, a renewal of our offensive. Many of those who were endeavouring to save the wounded were, in their turn, killed or wounded; but the two padres stayed to the end, ministering to the dying and wounded according to the rites of their Churches.

In many 'war-books' the chaplain has been pictured as the black-coated clown in the circus of our youthful days: a man who looked very busy, did no good, got in everybody's way, and was completely out of place. With this picture I am most emphatically in disagreement. There were good and bad chaplains, but the good far outnumbered the bad. As a body I have no hesitation in saying that their unit was the best in France, and very highly valued by all commanding officers who knew how to make use of their services. The more manly they were the better they were, for a soldier must be a MAN.

From 11 p.m. until dawn the German artillery saturated the valley in which the Cambridgeshires were with gas shells.

Those who have worn the old grey flannel gas-mask for five or six hours continuously will know what that means. All night the fluttering sound of those shells as they fell amongst us made rest impossible. Those who removed their masks were immediately incapacitated.

I continuously begged our guns to retaliate, and received definite assurance that they would open fire, but no guns spoke. Later it transpired that it had been found impossible to bring ammunition forward to our batteries. Had the Germans only known our plight—blinded, coughing, exhausted infantry, and ammunitionless guns!!

When dawn came I took Bradford with me to find out if the gas was on the face of the steep hill above us or only in the valley; for we knew that the gas, being heavier than air, would hang in the valley and, perhaps, not on the hill, unless the enemy had succeeded in dropping his shells on the steep face of the slope.

After we had climbed some seventy or eighty feet, according to my rough calculations, I told Bradford that I was going to take off my mask in order to test the air. He was to convey the result of my experiment to the Battalion. Then we waited for two or three minutes to breathe. Climbing a hill in a pig-nosed gas-mask would try the respiratory organs of a native deep-sea pearl diver.

I took off the mask. Merciful Heavens! I breathed pure, fresh air. Throwing back my head, I swallowed, and filled my lungs again and again with such ecstasy that I was only recalled to things earthly by Bradford's muffled enquiry:

'Are you ill, sir? For God's sake put on your mask.'

'Take off yours. It's glorious', I shouted. 'Go down and bring up the whole Battalion.' He turned back; and, exhausted, I threw myself on the ground and—went to sleep.

I awakened to hear two men laughing uproariously at my side. I had gone to sleep with my arm about an old ration rum jar.

Chapter IX

THE SOMME

6–16 *September* 1916

E. R.

TWO days' rest in tents under the trees of Mailly Wood, although not quite far enough away from the enemy's guns, soon dispelled all signs of war-weariness. The men caught lice in their clothing, and washed themselves and their undergarments, read letters and wrote home, cleaned rifles and Lewis guns, and slept. In times of stress and trial, complete rest is the best salve for mind and body.

Then followed the usual spell of carrying war material to the forward zone, and repairing damage done by shell-fire. No wonder we were known as the P.B.I. (Poor Bloody Infantry). In modern warfare horse-drawn vehicles can convey stores along roads to within a few miles of the front line; beyond that distance the burden falls on the shoulders of the P.B.I.

Guns, machine-guns, aircraft, cavalry, and mines kill men, obtain information, or destroy fortifications; but nine out of ten strongholds are captured or held by the P.B.I. In spite of modern weapons, war is still prehistoric in its conduct. As primeval man fought, so we fight to-day. The human element, mental and physical, is still paramount in war.

We moved into the Hamel sector of the line on 12 September and remained there until 3 October. I doubt if any other battalion held a sector of the front for so long a period during the battle of the Somme. An average of seventy-four shells a day fell in our battalion lines during that time, and no day passed without some human casualties, or destruction of material.

In days of peace Hamel must have been a delightfully picturesque little village, with its houses clinging to the western face and crest of a very steep hill, some hundred feet above the thickly-wooded valley of the river Ancre. Our Battalion H.Q. were in dug-outs burrowed out of the hill-side, and screened by a number of anaemic-looking apple-trees. The ruins of the ten or twelve houses, that had constituted the village, surrounded us; but they had been so much battered that an argument between two of the signallers on their architectural beginnings and endings led to a pugilistic combat of considerable merit, without solving the problem.

In order to improve our observation of enemy movements and British operations south of the Ancre, we constructed a hidden passage-way above H.Q., leading us into the remains of a house on the top of the hill overlooking the river. It was here that I spent much time examining the country through my telescope, hatching out schemes of a defensive and offensive nature which future events proved to be of incalculable value to us and, perhaps, the whole British army. Below me, three hundred yards away, lay Hamel Mill (held by us as a detached post), in front of which I could, with difficulty, pick out a German strong-point known as the 'Summer House', almost hidden by trees and thick under-growth. Further south-east, on high ground, was the labyrinth of trenches, concrete emplacements and deep dug-outs, forming the famous German earthwork, the Schwaben Redoubt. Looking a mile north-east I could see St Pierre-Division, with Beaucourt-sur-Ancre, Grandcourt and Miraumont beyond. At the latter place (distant about three miles) the Germans had a dressing-station where ambulances were constantly coming and going. In a clear light I could see nearly all movement behind the German lines for five miles

4-2

in a north-easterly and easterly direction, except in the
Y Ravine, where we knew that many hostile batteries were
hidden.

To prevent the movement of German troops from quieter
parts of the line in order to concentrate at points where pressure was being brought to bear, the higher authorities decreed
that raids should be made. The more an officer knew about
his profession the less he liked these isolated attacks on points
well defended by artillery and machine-guns. Although there
was never any lack of volunteers for these dangerous exploits,
very few battalion commanders, or generals, sought for permission to attempt them. It is one thing to essay the dangerous, and another to ask, or order, any other man to do it.
But in war tactical and strategical reasons outweigh all
others; thus it was that the Cambridgeshires raided the
German lines on 16 and 23 September.

The Allied intelligence-agents working in and behind the
German lines managed, as a rule, to keep our General Staff
well informed of the movements of the enemy's corps and
divisions; but there were occasions when we were compelled
to resort to raiding, in order to capture prisoners for the
purpose of identifying the Division holding the line in front
of us. The General Staff did not know which division was
against us, so I was ordered to get an 'identification'.

After the battle of 3 September, the Germans had unfortunately had plenty of time to thicken the barbed-wire
entanglements covering their trenches to such an extent that
we had to resort to wire-cutting tactics by our artillery and
trench mortars. I disliked this plan from the first, as it made
our intentions obvious and eliminated the chance of surprise.
Nevertheless, the Germans must have been in doubt as to
the details of our scheme, for we shelled their wire in many
places.

'C' Company, under the command of its captain (Marr),
were lined up in the trench when I visited them just before

dusk. Marr was superintending the issue of a ration of rum to his men. Now, if we were to believe the testimony of the writers of recent 'best-seller' war-books, everybody in Marr's Company would have greedily grasped this golden opportunity of swallowing drink. I watched the men file past. Less than one-third took the rum.

Corfield, Nightingale, and I stood near the trench-mortars in a deep trench a hundred yards behind our front line, from which Marr's Company were to launch their raid. I had selected this place for a double reason. From it I could direct the fire of the trench-mortars and look down the valley to the south, where an attempt was to be made to capture the garrison of the 'Summer House', by a small party under Shaw, who was now holding Hamel Mill.

A father awaiting the signal for his sons to undertake some hazardous exploit, trembles for their safety, and, though longing for the thing to commence, dreads its coming. One moment he is thrilled with the hope of their success, whilst in another he fears failure and its consequences. It was thus with me. I had lived with these men for three months, worked for their welfare, trained them, grown confident in their ability as soldiers, and developed an affection for them akin to that of a parent. Moreover, I realized the dawn of their confidence in me, and trembled at the possibility of its loss. Success would seal that confidence; but failure might disperse it beyond retrieve.

I did not like the plan for Marr's raid, but felt very confident about the affair at the 'Summer House'.

The raid began. At one moment all was quiet. The next, trench-mortars fired, and shells from our artillery swished over our heads to the German wire and trenches, while machine-guns rattled.

As I expected, the enemy was prepared. His shells crashed into the ground about us and tore up our communication trenches in his first fear of an attack in force.

We three stood very close together, each knowing what was in the other's mind. A blinding flash, and a shell burst a few feet above us. We all went down; then scrambled to our feet and looked at one another.

'That boot never let water in before, and now it's got a hole in it. Curse them bloody Germans!' said Nightingale in an aggrieved voice. Then, looking round, added, 'Anybody 'urt, sir?'

I had a feeling as if someone had hit the top of my steel helmet with a hammer: subsequent investigation disclosed two deep cracks in it, and a little blood on my head. Corfield was examining his torn haversack, through which a piece of shell had passed.

It was a heroic affair, as indeed all these raids were; but it failed. Young Allpress forced his way into the German wire with unrivalled bravery, only to be killed. The splendid efforts of his men to recover his body being of no avail, the Company returned to our lines with eight of their number wounded.

Meanwhile misfortune had befallen the little party at the 'Summer House'.

Shaw, with eight or ten men carrying a portable bridge to span the Ancre, succeeded in crossing that stream unobserved, and they were in the act of approaching their objective when they were seen and fired on. A lively exchange of bombs and rifle-fire followed, disclosing the unexpected strength of the enemy. All hope of effecting a surprise being at an end, Shaw ordered the retirement of his men. This was accomplished with great skill, only one man being wounded. Adam, who commanded the Company from which the raiders had been drawn, thinking probably that his presence on our side of the portable bridge would have been of assistance, had accompanied Shaw as far as the crossing-place over the stream. Under the scheme for the attack Shaw was to be the only officer with the party; but they were all mere lads, and who

could blame one so young and fearless for desiring to be with
those he commanded in their hour of danger? He had worked
for his men day in and day out, and loved them all. As a
soldier he was wrong, but as a man he felt that he could not
leave them. Knowing the man, I am convinced that it was
loyalty to, and anxiety for, his men that influenced his
actions.

Upon the party's reapproaching the mill whence they had
set out, it was discovered that the wounded man was missing.
Adam and Shaw returned to look for him. Sir Guy Butlin,
my adjutant, who was supervising the operation, finding that
the party had returned without its officers, crawled out
through the undergrowth with Bradford (the machine-gun
officer), an orderly, and a stretcher-bearer. He found the
officers lying wounded near the bridge. Sending Bradford
back to the mill for assistance, Butlin attended to the injuries
sustained by Shaw, who was more seriously wounded than
Adam. Whilst ministering to the needs of the sufferers, Butlin
and the stretcher-bearer were hit by snipers. Then the only
survivor, the adjutant's orderly, was ordered to go back for
help.

At this juncture I arrived at the mill. Daylight was breaking, and any attempt to reach the wounded by the track
along the river-bank was to court almost certain death. The
ground between our lines and the river was flooded to a
depth varying between six inches and, perhaps, six feet of
water, except where the road ran to the mill and along the
river-bank. Trees and bushes rose out of the water, and reeds
from the shallower places. A mist hung over all. No sound
broke the silence save the call of a water-hen wending her
way through the vegetation.

Bradford, confident of success, offered again to try to
rescue his brother-officers by way of the river-track. I could
not give my consent to such a forlorn hope. Instead, I
suggested an approach from our lines through the flooded

area by way of the shallow stretches. Nightingale having
offered to accompany Bradford, both men, armed with
revolvers and carrying bandages in their pockets, crawled
into the water and disappeared from view amidst the reeds
and bushes. They had agreed to raise their heads in the
branches of a leafy bush on the edge of thicker undergrowth,
fifty yards beyond which they hoped to find the victims of the
ill-fated raid. This was to show us where to direct our fire if
action on our part became necessary.

Minutes passed by as we prayed that the sun would not
break its way through the mist and disperse its protective
covering. Anxiously we watched through our field-glasses for
the appearance of the two heads that were to show us the
rescuers' whereabouts. Both showed for a second. I signalled
with my helmet and they disappeared.

For fully ten minutes we waited before we saw Bradford
run down the Mill Road to the western end of our trench. He
told us he had reached a point from which the bridge was
visible, but had found no trace of the wounded officers.
Where was Nightingale? He did not know. He had lost him
in the thick bushes.

I knew that every eye at the machine-gun post twenty feet
above us, at the Lewis guns by my side, and at the mill were
straining for any movement in the reeds or undergrowth,
which might indicate the position of my orderly. No one
spoke. No breath of wind stirred the air. We all waited.
There was nothing else to do.

To our left front, some sixty yards away, lay a German
advanced post hidden from view by stunted willows. A water-
hen was swimming towards it. Suddenly she turned and
made off into the reeds. Something must have frightened her
at the advanced post! The Germans were occupying it!

'There, sir', whispered one of the Lewis-gunners, pointing
to the high reeds in front of us. Looking in the direction he
indicated, I saw Nightingale. He was crawling towards the

German post. He had lost his direction. If we shouted we would draw the enemy's attention to him. If he went on in the direction he was going he would be shot by the Germans. If wounded he would be drowned in the water.

More than half-way between us and the advanced post stood a thick bush. Slipping over the parapet, I crawled on hands and knees to this bush, for I must head off Nightingale. I was a good revolver shot, and could take care of myself; Nightingale would not have hit Westminster Abbey with his revolver.

I reached the bush. Nightingale saw me and stopped. His face was running with sweat and literally black with midges. His drenched clothes were covered with water-weeds. Raising my hand, I signalled to him to retire. In his eyes I could see the look which I can only liken to that of a faithful dog. He turned back towards the mill.

It was all over, this deplorable adventure. Nothing could be done until friendly night came with her dark shadows to help us.

We had lost four brave officers and two gallant men, and gained nothing.

Bradford, Nightingale and I returned to Battalion H.Q. in silence.

When night came, a patrol visited the bridge. All traces of the wounded officers and stretcher-bearer had disappeared.

Are we to chronicle all the human failings of such men whilst forgetting their heroic sacrifices? If we believe in Divine Charity and Justice, we can rest assured that God will not forget the great good that was in them.

'Greater love hath no man than this, that a man lay down his life for his friends.'

Chapter X

THIEPVAL

16 September—10 October 1916

E. R.

THE activities of the Cambridgeshires on 16 September, and subsequent days, led to a feeling of insecurity and sensitiveness in the enemy lines. He strengthened his front, and subjected our positions to heavy bombardments.

From my concealed observation-post I could see all movement up the valley of the river Ancre, and away to the south as far as Thiepval.

With great difficulty, under the cover of darkness, an 18-pounder gun had been placed in a cellar near my outlook. In case of necessity, this gun could enfilade the German trenches which led to the Schwaben Redoubt a thousand yards away. It was to play an important part in the attack on that famous stronghold.

On the 26th Thiepval fell to the attack of the 18th Division.

On the 28th the same Division captured half of the Schwaben. We co-operated, with rifle, Lewis gun and machine-gun, killing many Germans. During the following day the enemy retook some of their lost ground. On the morning of the 30th the East Surreys took the northern face of the redoubt, but in spite of courageous fighting were driven back again to the southern face. Later in the day another German counter-attack gained some ground. The first of October saw the Buffs recapture a corner of this heap of earth, timber, iron, concrete, and—men's bodies. In the afternoon the Germans again advanced to the attack from the direction of St Pierre-Divion. Our 18-pounder, Lewis and machine-guns cut them down until their communication trenches, pounded almost out of recognition, were heaped with dead and dying men. From my observation-post I could see every German soldier as he advanced up the sloping ground. With our 18-pounder the gunners were firing over open sights and could not miss. It was a bloody slaughter.

Few, Corfield, Nightingale and I watched a German officer lead his company up a communication trench from St Pierre-Divion towards the Schwaben until he came under the fire of our guns. His men hesitated, wavered, and then bolted. Running after them he rallied his command, and led them back again. Our guns and machine-guns reopened fire. His men fell dead or wounded behind him, but, nothing daunted, on he pressed. He seemed to have a charmed life in the midst of death. Again and again he brought his fast-dwindling company to the attack. The slanting rays of an afternoon sun showed the actors in that drama in clear relief, and we of the audience, concealed by a curtain of shattered brickwork and bushes, gazed across the amphitheatre through our telescopes —not all of us, for Nightingale's eyes were abnormally keen —and followed the movements of the human ants as they walked, ran, climbed or fell, whilst our forces pelted the dry crumbling earth with shell and bullet.

I ordered Few to ask the guns to fire shrapnel.

Once more that German hero, advancing with a handful of men, appeared through the cloud of dust and smoke. We saw a shell burst over his head. We saw him fall. A deep-drawn breath from Corfield:

'My God!'

Nightingale, looking at the little speck of field-grey that had been a gallant enemy, ejaculated:

''Ard cheese. Another good chap gorn.'

I did not quite trust myself to speak. I don't think Corfield did.

Another good man gone. And thousands, hundreds of

thousands more would go. Perhaps we should be among those to go. When?....The less we thought about it the better.

Great happenings often hinge on trivialities. The loss of one brave man was of little importance in the world-wide war, but the death of this particular officer appeared to kill the German offensive spirit for the time being. Soon all firing ceased. All was quiet again.

We three, remaining at our observation-post, continued to look across the battlefield; Nightingale, because he had to go where I went, and stay where I stayed; Corfield, because I told him to memorize the battle as he had seen it, and to make notes on many points to which I had called his attention; I, to think how I would attack the Schwaben should that formidable task come my way.

The setting sun, bathing the valley of the Ancre and the hill-crest to the south-east, favoured our vision. We could see the white covered ambulances coming and going along the road between Grandcourt and Miraumont, and the wounded being carried to the first-aid post near Beaucourt. There was always a cruel yet understandable satisfaction to be got out of seeing a lot of wounded Germans. The enemy's losses showed us that our forces were not the only ones to pay the penalty of war.

In front of Grandcourt a munition waggon was dumping shells for a heavy battery which had been in action throughout the day, unmolested, as far as I could see, by our artillery.

Having made notes of these, and many other things, I returned to Battalion H.Q. to think out the solution of the problem which the much-desired capture of the Schwaben Redoubt presented.

.   .   .   .   .

Our time in the Hamel sector drew to a close on 3 October. What a delight it must have been for my officers and men to get away from it! There could have been no regrets at

Imperial War Museum photo.

Stretcher-bearers carrying a wounded man at Thiepval,
near the Schwaben Redoubt (September)

Cambridge Chronicle photo.

Lord French, Hon. Colonel of the Regiment, inspecting
recruits at Cambridge (June)

THE SOMME, 1916

parting with those lice-infested 'Kentish Caves' which had sheltered one or other of my Companies for three weeks; those swarms of rats which gave me such excellent revolver practice; the Mill Road along which all repairing materials, trench-mortar shells, and half our rations must needs be carried in face of a nightly barrage. How it is that more men are not killed in modern war will remain a mystery to me: they seem to fit between the shells and bullets in a miraculous way. I often visited these carrying parties at the resting-place, which I had established in a big cellar at the eastern end of the road, and talked to the men while they drank hot soup or tea. Many of the survivors must turn uneasily in their beds when they think of their nocturnal journey along Mill Road.

It was all over for the moment. We were back in tents in Aveloy Wood, full of hope that we were to be withdrawn from the line. Like many another good hope, it 'went west'. Twenty-four hours later we crossed the Ancre to join Jacob's Corps facing the Schwaben Redoubt, the key of which still remained in German hands.

We were accommodated in dug-outs on the North and South Bluffs near Authuile, our work being the supply of war-material for the 117th Brigade, now preparing for another attack on the Schwaben.

I spent the major part of the following three days in examining the lines of approach to the great stronghold. The days lived in the Hamel sector had prepared me for a shambles. Had I not seen men in thousands killed in a score of attempts to capture or recapture this all-important hill-top, which dominated the field of battle for many miles in every direction? During my previous experience of trench warfare, I had found little difficulty in burying the dead even in our front-line trenches; but here was something I had not visualized. A communication trench, known as Martin's Lane, ran up the southern slope of the hill which stretched from the river Ancre to the redoubt. I was on my way to visit Herbert-

Stepney, commanding the 16th Sherwood Foresters (Notts. and Derby), who was to make the next attack. Five hundred yards from the river I came on the first human wreck; it was covered with flies and had been dead for some days. Climbing and tramping on I passed more bodies, until I reached a point which my map told me must be within a hundred yards of Herbert-Stepney's H.Q. Here the trench, or what had been a trench, was literally paved with dead in every conceivable state of decomposition. The bodies had been trampled into the earth, their close proximity rendering it impossible for me to advance without walking on them. The stench was nauseating.

Looking to my left, I noticed that the ground sloped to a slight depression before rising again to the west. There was no trench in this depression, but the fold of the ground at once struck me as being likely to afford cover from view to troops advancing towards the redoubt. I could not see any bodies lying out there, and determined to explore this line of approach at dusk. Anything would be better than Martin's Lane.

I found Herbert-Stepney in a most inadequate dug-out. He told me his men were to 'go over the top' on the morrow, and gave me a guide to take me to his front line.

A quarter of an hour's crawl took me to the first British post. I found a group of men eating a meal by the side of a dead soldier belonging to a regiment which had held the line some days previously. They did not seem to notice the presence of their dead companion. What did one extra body matter where there were so many?

Dead men everywhere!! In the trench, behind it, and across the front towards the Boche lines! How many German and British regiments were represented by those twisted heaps of flesh and clothing that had once been men? God knows—yes, He knows—and, perhaps, our historians; but I doubt it.

Why had these bodies been left to rot? Because a dead soldier is just as heavy to carry as a wounded soldier, and, whilst we honour our dead, we must save our wounded. With the shades of night, those amazing people, the stretcher-bearers, would be there exercising their corporal works of mercy. Then, if a lull came in the fighting, burying parties would come up and silently shovel a little earth over the dead —silently, for fear the Boche machine-guns would open on them and cut down another harvest of men.

I returned to Herbert-Stepney's dug-out. We discussed the possibility of burying the dead in the trenches. Eventually it was decided that his men could not do it; they were to attack on the morrow and must have rest. There was no sign of rain; the ground was dry, and they might sleep. It was left to the Cambridgeshires to undertake the ghastly task. They managed to bury fifty bodies in one section of the trench alone.

It transpired that our troops held the southern side of the Schwaben Redoubt only. They were two hundred yards from the crest of the hill along which ran Splutter trench, that network of machine-gun posts. Previous attacks had captured a lot of ground, but at the beginning of the second week of October we had but a slender grip on the main defences.

Under the cover of dusk, accompanied by Nightingale, I reconnoitred the miniature valley to the west of Martin's Lane, leading from the river Ancre to the Schwaben. This slight depression was concealed from the vigilant eyes of the enemy and offered an excellent line of approach. It must have been overlooked by others for there were no signs of its use, save one. A solitary body of a soldier lay in the grass. Grasped in his hand was a scrap of paper on which was written a message signed by an officer of the 4th Battalion Lancashire Fusiliers. To a suggestion that stretcher-bearers should not use Martin's Lane, was added a request that the bearer might not be called upon to return with an answer, as he had already frequently risked his life that day. The irony of Fate!

I spent the evening writing my scheme for an attack on the Schwaben, for I put no trust in the plan and instructions given to Herbert-Stepney.

The Sherwood Foresters failed in their attempt to dislodge the enemy. Later, when I visited their H.Q., Stepney said:

'They went over the top—and disappeared. I think they were all lost.' He paused and added:

'I suppose you haven't got a cigarette to spare?'

I gave him the contents of my case and a small flask of brandy, for he was obviously very near the end of his tether. Then I left him.

Chapter XI

PREPARING THE SCHEME

11–13 *October* 1916

E. R.

BRIGADE summoned me to attend at H.Q. early on the morning of 11 October. No stretch of imagination was required to anticipate the reason for this 'urgent priority' call.

I set out with my Schwaben Redoubt scheme in my pocket.

Finch-Hatton, the Brigadier, took me into his room, shut the door, and said:

'You've got to take on the next attack with your battalion on the 13th. I want you to discuss plans with me now.'

I handed to him my written scheme, telling him when, and how, I had conceived it. The Brigadier read the first few lines, looked at me as if to be sure of my sanity, and ejaculated:

'Good Heavens, man, I told you that your battalion had to take on this job; and you ask for two-and-a-half battalions, the guns of three divisions, and half the Corps Artillery!'

Five minutes later Finch-Hatton was talking over the telephone to Gerald Cuthbert who commanded the 39th Division.

'The General's coming here to see us', was his next remark.

'All right, Riddell; I'll go to General Jacob at once, and put your plan before him. I know he'll do all in his power to help us', was Cuthbert's remark after half-an-hour's conversation.

We saw the small, cool, cheery, and immaculately dressed Divisional Commander to his car, and watched it bump its way along the rough road towards Corps H.Q.

My plan was to attack the Schwaben from the south,

between 2 p.m. and 3 p.m. with two battalions, whilst two Companies of infantry held the enemy on the left. The Corps' 'heavies' were to engage the hostile artillery in the Y Ravine and the neighbourhood of Miraumont; and the guns of three Divisions were to provide a dense creeping barrage over the whole area to be covered by our infantry, and then engage all lines of approach to the Schwaben from the north and north-west. The troops on our right and left, especially those holding the Hamel sector, were to plaster the Germans when retiring or attempting a counter-attack. It was the latter I feared most of all, for during our sojourn at Hamel we had seen our troops overrun the enemy's defences only to be driven back by counter-attacks.

I had decided on this midday assault because of the almost mechanical regularity with which Germans and British alike attacked at dawn or dusk. Moreover, when no action was in progress, the hours between noon and 3 p.m. were generally quiet. The opposing forces were sleeping after their midday meal, and the sentries less alert. Habit is a god, worshipped by all men; it controls our lives and destiny.

For many weeks we had enjoyed complete command in the air. Our planes flew over the enemy lines unchallenged. I had noticed that, whenever our observation machines flew over the Schwaben, the hostile batteries ceased fire. Consequently, I requested that one plane should hover over our assembly position between 2 p.m. and 3 p.m.

Hitherto, all assaulting troops had been content to occupy the northern face of the redoubt (if they ever got so far). The German artillery knew the exact limits of that face, and could turn their guns on to it and shoot by the map, even if the smoke-clouds obscured the vision of their observation officers. I, therefore, asked that our infantry might be allowed to overrun the redoubt, and, under cover of the bursts of our high explosive shells throwing up clouds of dust and earth, dig a trench one hundred yards north of the Schwaben.

It was over an hour since the Divisional Commander had left to interview General Jacob. Diggles, the Brigade major, came in with the news:

'Corps wants to speak to you on the telephone, sir.'

Finch-Hatton took the instrument: 'Yes, sir,......Yes, sir,......Everything......Very good, sir,......At 2 p.m. here......Good-bye, sir'.

Turning to me he said:

'The Corps Commander says that, as you have to do the job, he'll do everything he can to help you. All the C.R.A.'s will come here at 2 o'clock and you can tell them your plan.'

Then he turned to Diggles, but that worthy was already getting through to the Black Watch and Cheshires to warn their C.O.'s to come to Brigade H.Q.

All went well at the conference, except that one C.R.A. (I think it was the 29th Division) did not like the idea of putting down the creeping barrage only fifty yards in front of our infantry. He said that his guns were worn, and that he might kill some of our men as they advanced. My contention was that we would all prefer to risk a few lives from our own guns than be shot for a certainty by the Boche machine-guns. It was agreed that two Divisions should fire the creeping barrage and the 29th fire on the redoubt. The Corps' heavies would look after the hostile batteries. It was suggested that we should complete the assembly of our battalions on the 'jumping-off' place one hour before zero. I did not want to get there more than fifteen minutes before zero, for the longer we remained at the 'jumping-off' place, the more time the Boche observers would have to find us. Eventually Finch-Hatton decided that we must complete our assembly thirty minutes before zero. My protest being of no avail, it was left at that. How often, in this world, do great things hinge on a few minutes of time!

Early the next morning, Knyvett, the C. of E. padre, walked with me across the Leipzig Redoubt to look at our objective from another angle. It was his first experience of a battlefield, and that which had become to me, by familiarity, a matter of little concern, was to him a horrible revelation. After passing through an indescribable scene of smashed-up rifles, machine-guns, barbed wire, ammunition boxes, beams of wood, corrugated iron, soldiers' equipment and clothing, etc., etc., we were drawing near our desired point of vantage, when Knyvett exclaimed in horrified tones: 'There is a dead German'. It would have been a strange thing for anyone to walk abroad in that area and not find something dead, so I passed on without a remark.

On our return by the same route Knyvett asked if our orderlies might be allowed to bury the German. Naturally I consented, apologizing for my apparent callousness, and pleading weighty matters on my mind.

Spades by dozens were to be found within easy reach, so the work was not long in the doing.

'I wonder if he was a Protestant or a Catholic', said Knyvett.

He stood with bared head and prayed. The orderlies, unaccustomed to such a sight, watched him, then took off their steel helmets. When it was over, three of us turned and walked towards Battalion H.Q. Looking back I saw the padre's orderly bending over the grave, planting a rifle in the ground, butt uppermost, with a bayonet crosswise through the trigger-guard. My thoughts went back nearly two thousand years— to another Cross.

.   .   .   .   .

By noon on 12 October all the Company and platoon commanders joined me at Paisley Dump on the banks of the Ancre. We had selected this place as a base for our reconnaissance of the Battalion's line of advance on the morrow for two reasons. Under the cover of the remains of the trees of Thiepval Wood we could not be seen by German airmen in the unlikely event of a hostile plane venturing over our lines, and from this position we could see the whole of the ground to be traversed by Companies on their way to the position of assembly. The man who takes unnecessary risks in war is a fool; only those who attend to details, anticipate possible happenings, and look at tactical situations from the enemy's as well as their own point of view, can hope to succeed.

We were to avoid the main communication trenches—Martin's Lane, and that which ran east of Thiepval Wood—owing to the enemy's conservative habit of shelling them whenever he had nothing better to do. Our route lay up the little valley reconnoitred by me and Nightingale after my visit to Herbert-Stepney. This dip in the ground afforded shelter from view right up to our jumping-off place.

The four Company commanders, Formby, Wood, Marr and Strickland, with their platoon leaders, moved off along the exact line they were to take on the following day. It was 1 p.m.

When they had finished their examination of the ground, all the captains of Companies were to meet me at the point selected for my abode during the battle. Three captains arrived, but there was no sign of Formby and his 'A' Company platoon leaders. I decided to send the others away, and, with Nightingale, to await the arrival of Formby.

Two shells had burst away to our right, but nobody took much notice of an odd shell or two in those days, so we sat down and waited.

A quarter of an hour passed.

'I'd better see if Captain Formby's abart anywhere', said Nightingale.

I consented, and he departed towards the right.

It was a lonely wait. I wondered if I should be alive by that time to-morrow, and how many of the men, so deep in my affection, would survive the next forty-eight hours. That we should succeed in capturing and holding the position

I never doubted for one moment. My confidence in the Cambridgeshires was too strong to admit of any thought of failure.

Not a breath of wind stirred the air. Apart from the droning of two British planes above my head there was no sign of life. I remember thinking that the ground about me looked as if a thousand giants, with a thousand spades, had ruthlessly rooted up the ground and strewn it with broken baulks of timber, twisted corrugated iron sheeting, bits of military equipment, ammunition boxes, and all the flotsam of a battlefield; whilst many pygmies had burrowed out aimless tracks in every direction from their hiding-holes, the dug-outs.

Nightingale came back.

'I found one of them, sir, but 'e's orf 'is 'ed—couple of 'undred yards away—quite balmy', he said.

We went to the poor fellow, who was crouching against a section of unbroken parapet. All he could say was:

'They—are—all dead—all of them—dead.'

I examined him, but could not find any wound.

'Shell shock—and pretty bad too', said Nightingale.

The unfortunate officer began to mutter and point to the right, shuddering as if he were cold. Then he said:

'Over there—all dead—don't touch me—don't touch me.'

Time pressed. I told Nightingale to go in the direction indicated. He returned ten minutes later, after finding three bodies.

'He's right, sir', indicating the shell-shocked officer. 'Must have been one of them two shells we saw han hour ergo'; then, after a pause, 'they looked that peaceful an' quiet-like, jest as if they was asleep; strange ain't it?'

Two shells, only two, which might have burst anywhere! It was a fluke, of course, for the Boche could not see that part of the ground. The fortune of war! Only the day before one of my officers had found the body of Howell, Brigadier-

General of the IInd Corps Staff, killed by a stray shell when returning from a visit to the front-line trenches.

Had those men died in battle, leading their men, glory, posthumous Victoria Crosses, perhaps, might have been theirs. Who knows? To me their glory was none the less great.

The half-demented officer by my side was muttering incoherently. He fought against us, as men often do when shell-shocked. He was strong and begged us to leave him. We, too, were strong. Overpowering him, we dragged him down to the valley. Eventually, whimpering like a child, he walked beside us to the first-aid post. He, whom I knew to be a very brave man, was now a physical wreck. Three months later he did heroic work as a patrol leader, earning the highest praise from his C.O.

I had lost all the officers of my right Company, and must needs take four more to reconnoitre the ground.

The attack was postponed for twenty-four hours.

After a reshuffling of platoon leaders, I took four more officers to examine the approaches to the Schwaben. This time we were fortunate.

The following evening I set out, with my faithful orderly, to inspect the laying out, by a sapper officer, of brown-coloured tapes which were to indicate the line of advance of our men in the attack. I met him returning from his task. It must have been my Guardian Angel who prompted me to turn back with him to make sure that all was well. I tested the magnetic bearing with my compass, and found that the tapes were seventeen degrees out of the true. Merciful Heavens! We should have missed half the redoubt, for our objective was two hundred and fifty yards from our assembly position. The sapper's compass was faulty.

I corrected the error as far as my own Battalion was concerned, finishing the work in the dark, but could not undertake the Black Watch sector.

On my way back I called on Sceales of the Black Watch and told him about the tapes. He said he thought his officers would be able to see the objective as soon as they jumped up to advance. I hoped he was right. Anyhow nothing could be done now as the Boche machine-guns were always active after dark. Very weary, I went back to issue my final written instructions and fell asleep while dictating them.

Waking up with a start, I found my orderly-room clerk (Fenton) sitting beside me.

'How long have I been asleep?' I asked.

'About three hours, sir', he replied. 'I thought you wanted a rest.'

He knew that a clear brain was needed for the task in hand.

The orders finished I went to bed, but Fenton sat up through the night making copies to be issued in the morning. He was not one of those fools who disturb soldiers when sleep may mean the difference between victory and failure.

Chapter XII

THE SCHWABEN

14–15 *October* 1916

E. R.

A HEALTHY body and mind, however tired, is always refreshed by sleep.

I spent a dreamless, contented night, and by 9 a.m. on 14 October met Bowes-Lyon of the Black Watch at South Bluff. I wanted to see the camouflage erected by the engineers across the road along which our men were to march to Paisley Dump. There had been a point in that road visible from the German lines at Beaumont-Hamel—only a few yards, it is true; but I knew that every yard of road behind the Germans was watched by our Intelligence Staff, so I gave credit to the enemy for the same vigilance. The work had been well done. At four hundred yards it was difficult to distinguish it from the brown-and-green-leafed branches of the trees. The enemy observation-post was six thousand yards away, so we felt safe. Nothing must be left to chance.

I went on to Paisley Dump, where Dunlop of the Cambridgeshires was arranging the bombs, Verey lights, rockets, and two days' rations for issue to the Companies on their arrival at 12.30 p.m.

All was prepared for the advance up the valley. The men had been given a canteen of tea and a light meal.

I had stated, in my orders, that the Battalion canteen would open at 3.30 p.m. at point 19.d.47 (a dug-out then in German hands). Diggle, the very worthy but rather red-tape-bound Brigade major, objected to this on the ground that frivolity, under the circumstances, was 'contrary to the custom of the service'. My reply was that it is the duty of a commander to inspire his men with confidence. So the order remained.

It was nearly time to move off. I walked forward with two men carrying a stretcher laden with cigarettes, chocolates, matches, and biscuits, and bearing a large notice:

'CAMBS' CANTEEN.'

A suppressed murmur of applause greeted its arrival. The broad grins on the faces of all gave the final touch of confidence which heralds success.

I heard a voice saying, 'He's sure'.

The observation-plane droned overhead in the clear blue sky.

The R.C. chaplain, just arrived from England, remarked: 'I understand that this will be a very simple affair. May I come with you?'

'Your place is at the dressing-station', I replied. 'There will be plenty of work for you in a couple of hours' time.' Then I explained. I left him, standing with bared head, giving the passing men the Benediction.

I had disobeyed orders. I had deliberately timed my advance so that the men would reach the 'jumping-off' place ten minutes instead of thirty minutes before zero hour. It was the first time I had strayed from the path of military obedience.

'B', 'C' and 'D' Companies went straight to their appointed places, but 'A' Company lost its way in the maze of battered trenches. Nightingale and I ran to head them off. Gasping for breath we reached the head of the Company just in time to lead Strickland to the tapes. It was a near thing. We had four minutes to spare before zero hour.

Going back towards our H.Q., at Point 91, was difficult for the first hundred yards. We had to crawl on hands and knees. When in dead-ground, we ran. We had still fifty yards to go when the storm broke.

Shells sizzled overhead like rain. A second later they burst on the rising ground two hundred yards to the north, throwing up fountains of earth mingled with the debris of a battlefield; and although we could not discriminate between one clod of something in the air and another, we knew that men, too, were being blown to pieces. Silhouetted against this cloud of spurting earth and smoke were my Cambridgeshires advancing to victory.

The drumming of the gunfire, the explosion of the shells, and the continuous rattle of machine-guns and rifles, are beyond the descriptive powers of literature. No pen could picture that weird, deafening, terrifying, yet, in some indescribable way, elating din. Painters and the film have done something towards the instruction of the uninitiated, but they fall far short of reality.

I stood up in the open, spell-bound with admiration for the men who were steadily advancing into that upheaval of earth, with the sunlight gleaming on their bayonets.

Then came the German reply. All round me the ground was thrown into the air by shells bursting everywhere, but no bullets came my way. Why no bullets? The answer was before me. I could see my men jumping into something. It was the north face of the Schwaben. I could see them thrusting with their bayonets and then disappearing into the German trenches. The second wave of men, swinging on, were over the first line of resistance. Then they disappeared from view as they swept unhesitatingly down the reverse slope of the hill. They were there. They had won.

One glance to the right, and my heart stood still. The Black Watch had not reached their objectives. They were being mown down by machine-guns as a reaper cuts corn. I knew the battalion to be one of the finest fighting-units in France. Had the Boche seen them assembling before the attack? If they had, the absence of machine-gun bullets was explained: all the machine-guns had been turned on to the unfortunate Black Watch.

It was horrible to look at; but how glorious! The surviving Jocks were pushing on in spite of appalling losses. Isolated figures pressed forward, threw themselves down to fire, or—died. Never in the history of that famous regiment have its officers and men behaved with greater gallantry.

The observation-plane overhead dipped in salute. I knew our first objectives had been occupied.

It takes time to record these happenings. In reality the fight had lasted six minutes.

I tumbled down the stairway to my dug-out, with Nightingale at my heels. We found Corfield talking to Brigade over the telephone, Rostron of the Cheshires in one corner, and the artillery liaison officer in another. My intelligence officer, Bradford, was there also.

Brigade rang up. It was Diggle. 'Plane just dropped a message. Can you hear? Damn this line. Plane just dropped a message. Cambridgeshires going over as if on parade. Congratulations. Any news, sir?'

I had got half-way through my message in reply when the line went.

'Get me through to Brigade on another line', I shouted to the signallers.

'All four lines have gone dished, sir', came the reply.

We were cut off!!

'Get the linesmen out at once', I ordered.

Shells were bursting all round the dug-out entrance. Up the steps went the linesmen and disappeared into the inferno raging without.

No sooner had they taken their departure than a messenger ran down the stairway and sank to the ground. He was a Cheshire runner. His written message was to the effect that the Company of his regiment on our left had captured its objective and thirty prisoners.

It was about 3.30 p.m. when a voice came over the wire:

'Aeroplane reports all your objectives taken. Splendid! Any news of the Black Watch?'

There never is much news on these occasions. There was the Cheshire report, of course, and, no doubt, somebody was trying to send me information from our new front by runner, if anybody had time to write a message.

What wonderful men those runners were! Carrying a message along a good trench under fire was no holiday; but scrambling over ground which was being incessantly blown up by high explosive shells, whilst shrapnel burst overhead, was to pass through Hell; if they did pass through.

The lines to Brigade were again broken by shell-fire.

'Blarst yer. Get inside. Prod 'im, Bill!...Who the bloody Hell d'yer think yer are? Ther Crown Prince?...Get 'im in, Bill', was the running commentary reaching our ears as three men came stumbling down the stairway.

For a few seconds they stood blinking at the unaccustomed light from the two candles on my rough table, the flames of which jumped as shells struck the ground without. Breathing in gasps, two soldiers crouched ready to drive their bayonets into a small, thick-set, figure in field-grey uniform, bearing the badges of a German non-commissioned officer.

The prisoner stood at attention. The escort gradually relaxed their tense positions. At last one man spoke.

'Captain Marr (a gasp for breath) sent us down with this chap. ...We got thousands of 'em, sir...hundreds of dead. They're comin' in droves—'eaps of 'em, sir—prisoners Oi mean, sir.'

A shell struck the head of the stairway, filling the dug-out with a cloud of earth-dust, and the candles went out. Instantly, someone flashed on an electric torch. Its beam of light rested on the prisoner. He still stood at attention looking steadily at me.

I told the two soldiers who had escorted the German to sit down clear of the entrance, and turned my attention to the prisoner.

He was a fair-haired, blue-eyed Bavarian, about thirty years of age. There was not the slightest sign of fear on his good-looking face. An almost imperceptible twitching of the fingers of the left hand was the sole indication of mental and physical strain.

I studied this remarkable man for a few moments before asking the number of his regiment and division, if his unit had expected our attack, if their casualties had been heavy, how long they had been in the line, etc., to all of which questions he replied politely and without hesitation. It was only when I asked him where the reserves to his regiment were, and from which direction their counter-attack would come, that he made no reply.

The shells crashed outside. I waited.

'What is your answer?' I asked.

No reply was forthcoming. The candle flames flickered and jumped as the shells fell—thud—crash—thud—crash—thud —crash.

'What is your answer?'

Standing motionless, my prisoner replied:

'Sir, it is a very fine day.'

A brave answer from a very brave man.

'A cup of tea, sir', said Sergeant Cooper, placing a tin mug by my side.

The German remained motionless, his eyes, respectful, but unflinching, on mine.

I spoke:

'Bring another cup of tea, sergeant, if you please.'

I offered my tin mug to the prisoner, saying:

'You are a brave man—may I offer you some tea?'

He did not move or reply. I drank some of the contents of the mug, and again held it out saying:

'You see it is not drugged; a British officer knows how to treat a brave opponent.'

Sergeant Cooper arrived with another mug, and we toasted each other, the prisoner and I, in silence.

I liked that German. He was a sportsman.

'You will rest here for a while; perhaps your friends may stop shooting. In half-an-hour you will be escorted to the prisoners' cage', I said.

Many messages now came from the Company commanders. We had been successful everywhere. All our objectives had been taken. After passing on the good tidings to Brigade, I set out with two runners as guides to reconnoitre the position.

The hostile shell-fire had slackened, but ours drummed away merrily.

Germans, with their hands above their heads, were walking or running back to the lines held by the K.R.R. Every few yards, as shells burst amongst them, they threw themselves to the ground, jumped up again, and hurried on. It is not a pleasant sight to see soldiers, whether they be Germans or British, running to surrender. I have seen both. These men looked ridiculous with their arms stretched high in the air, their heads, with frightened eyes, turning first one way and then another.

'Kamerad! Kamerad!'

Most of them were crossing the open, but, turning a bend in a length of trench, which had miraculously survived the bombardment, we came on a group cowering on the ground. Screaming for mercy they held out their arms towards us, with terror written on their faces. My guides, laughing, pushed past. What a world of difference there is in battle between being the victor or the vanquished!

We had reached a point from which I could see beyond the Schwaben. The military value of this shell-blasted mound was more conspicuous than ever. Below stretched the valley of the Ancre, naked and exposed; a friendly swirl of wind had given me a brief glimpse of it through the clouds of dust kicked up by our standing barrage. In a second it was gone; but, were I to be killed then, I had seen the promised land— and my men had taken it, and held it.

Could they hold it? Yes, if any troops could, the Cambridgeshires could—and would.

The crash of bombs bursting, and the rattle of rifle-fire was coming from the right. We hurried on over the dead bodies of many Germans and a few Cambridgeshires to where I found one of my platoons consolidating a strong-point. The men were talking and shouting, and some of them laughing and eating. The British soldier always eats.

I organized an attack. Creeping down a length of trench we took the resisting Germans in flank, and drove them back, captured them, or killed them. Then I remembered. This was not my job. My work was at Battalion H.Q. The back of my neck was hot, and felt wet. I put my hand to it. My hand was covered with blood.

On reaching my dug-out I found reports from all Companies telling me of complete success everywhere, and asking for wire to entangle the new front against the certain coming of a German counter-stroke.

Corfield, the adjutant, had dealt with urgent matters in my absence, but our path was not smooth. The dumps of wire, water-cans and ammunition had been blown to pieces. The telephone wires were cut to ribbons, and nearly all the linesmen killed or wounded whilst endeavouring to repair them.

The hostile shell-fire suddenly increased in violence. It thundered and crashed above us.

We had brought carrier-pigeons with us. Where were they? The answer to that question came unexpectedly. To give the birds air, a signaller had put the basket on the steps of the dug-out. A high-explosive shell struck the entrance, smashing half of it down and hurling the broken basket down the stairway. The pigeons were dead. Another line of communication had 'gone west'.

Shortly after 5 p.m. we got news from the 17th K.R.R., who were in reserve. They had received orders from Division that two Companies were to advance across the Black Watch front and bomb down the northern face of the redoubt, whilst the Cambridgeshires worked eastward to meet them. And so the fight went on.

From written messages (it would be gross exaggeration to name them reports) scribbled by men with death around them; from the wounded in the dug-out adjoining mine—that ever-increasing crowd of patient, blood-stained men; and from the verbal descriptions of runners given to me as they drank tea and munched biscuits on the floor of my H.Q., I gathered the story of the fight.

Our men had reached the German front line without loss. There the infantryman's battle began. It was grim work. The Germans had contested every foot of their ground. With bayonet and bomb the opposing sides had fought to a finish, as one pack of wolves fights another. In the daylight of the trenches, and the dark of the dug-outs, the battle raged. Hot blood, the lust of war, and fear, allowed of no quarter being given or asked for. Those who wished to live must first kill.

A bayonet-fighting instructor, turning the corner of a deep trench, encountered a group of Boches. The men behind the instructor were in file, and were, therefore, unable to use their rifles. The Boches were in a similar position in regard to their leading man. Normally, the instructor was an amiable, peaceful countryman, who in civil life would not have hurt a fly. Now he was fighting for his life. At first it was to save his own life that he killed: then blind madness took him. Thrusting, parrying, shouting, he beat down all opposition until every German was dead: eight men dead! Then the horror of it struck him. They took him away, lest he might go mad.

Whilst the first wave of the Cambridgeshires were at their grim work in the labyrinths of the north face of the Schwaben, the second and third waves swept on to complete the victory, and to construct a new line of defence a hundred yards deeper into the German lines.

The struggle on the Cambridgeshire front lasted for two hours. Then our men turned their attention to the right, where the Germans had held back our friends, the Black Watch. There the struggle for supremacy went on far into the night. Being short of bombs and ammunition, our men used those of the enemy until, about 10 o'clock, they, with the 17th K.R.R. and Black Watch, were in possession of the whole of the Schwaben Redoubt. From now onwards, the work of consolidating the captured positions was pushed forward with all speed, the 234th Field Company R.E. and two Companies of the Gloucesters assisting.

Towards midnight the hostile shelling slackened; then died away.

I went out into the still, starlit night. By the entrance to my dug-out lay the body of my brave intelligence officer, Bradford. Fearless in life, he had done his work nobly. I am afraid I sobbed like a child; but I was not ashamed of this breakdown. The stretcher-bearers were carrying their burdens past the now overcrowded first-aid-post on their way to the dressing-station in the valley below.

Rowe, my signalling officer, with his few remaining linesmen, had mended the wires to Brigade and put our signal lamp in position. Wire, screw pickets, water, rations, ammunition, machine-guns, and trench mortars were being carried forward. Marr, and the few surviving officers, had reorganized their Companies and were hard at work wiring our new front-line trench. Soon all would be ready for the Germans when they came, as come they most certainly would, for the Schwaben was the key to the valley of the Ancre.

It was about 4 o'clock in the morning when the storm broke out afresh.

Few, my second-in-command, had arrived from Brigade,

and taken over command of the front line. Rostron, Corfield, and the gunner were asleep on their wire bunks.

Suddenly the Boche barrage fell on us. A concentration of heavy shells shook the ground about us. Earth and timber crashed into the dug-out. The lights went out. Something struck me across the back. For a moment I was stunned. Scrambling to my feet, staggering, I groped for the table, found a candle and lit it. The dug-out was full of smoke and dust. The noise outside was deafening. Dazed, I reeled to Rostron's bunk and tried to wake him.

'Get up, man', I shouted. He muttered something about it being 'All right...all right, sir. I'm coming'. Then he fell back.

The gunner and Corfield were just the same—all knocked out.

I was alone.

'Signals', I shouted, 'get through to the guns.'

'I'm through, sir, and guns are firing', came the answer from the operator. 'I saw the S.O.S. signal go up from the front line, sir, just when the big 'un knocked you out.'

How long had I been knocked out? I don't know.

Again I tried to rouse Rostron and the others. They all talked rot. They were shell-shocked.

Later, news came by runner from Marr. The Germans had advanced on the redoubt from the north. Evidently they knew nothing of our new trench in front of the northern face, for they had moved up to it in close formation, only to be mown down by our men at point-blank range when they reached our wire. We had lost very few men, owing to the enemy's shell-fire being directed onto the Schwaben a hundred yards behind Marr's men. If we had been in the Schwaben instead of in front of it, how different the future might have been!!

How my head ached! I sat down to write a report for the information of Brigade, all my wires being again cut and my lamp blown goodness knows where. I had nearly finished my message when I fainted.

'Fan 'im, Sergeant, he's comin' rand', came a voice from far—so far—away.

'Fan, yer ——, fan.'

For a moment I saw Nightingale and Sergeant Cooper waving something white, and felt the cool air on my face. Then it was dark again.

I came to. They got me to my feet and up the dug-out stairs. Somebody brought a chair for me to sit on.

How delightful it was out there in the sunlight!

'Now, don't worry, sir. Everything is all right. I've been all along the line and everybody is merry and bright.' It was Few leaning over me with Sergeant Cooper by his side.

'I wish you'd get inside the dug-out, sir. It really isn't safe here', said Cooper, but his voice was far away. I knew no more.

Something hit my forehead. A steel helmet fell off my chest. Where was I? I was on my back. I was being carried. Yes, that was a shell bursting. It didn't matter....Nothing mattered...I was so tired, so very tired.

'There yer are, yer bloody fool, yer've bust 'is bloody konk', came the familiar voice of Nightingale from beyond my feet.

'I ducked from that shell and dropped my tin hat on him', said someone I could not see behind me. I looked up and saw Sergeant Cooper's tall frame above me.

These two were carrying me on a stretcher. We were in the valley near Paisley Dump. Two men, so different in outlook of life, demeanour and stature, but identical in two respects, bravery and fidelity, had brought me to a place that seemed to be Paradise.

I tried to explain the military situation to a group of Generals and Staff officers. Looking very grave, they saw me safely into an ambulance and told me not to worry, because they knew all that was required.

How did they know?

Few had collapsed when I fainted, the other officers at H.Q. were suffering from shell-shock. Sergeant Cooper took command. Finding my book which contained duplicates of all my messages and reports, he had sent it to Brigade by two trusted runners.

That's how Brigade knew.

Chapter XIII

ST PIERRE-DIVION

15 *October*—11 *November* 1916

M. C. C.

THE casualties to Battalion H.Q. during the attack and subsequent holding of the Schwaben Redoubt left Marr in command. In addition to the counter-attack on the morning of 15 October a further one developed at 9 p.m., but like the first it was beaten off.

But what made the strain so severe was the constant pounding of the redoubt by the enemy's guns. The loss of this commanding position, which had held out for months, was a severe blow, and if the German infantry could not re-enter it, it was up to the German gunners to make life there unendurable, if not impossible.

The recent tenants of the redoubt knew the exact position of every dug-out and piece of trench. The fact that any of our men were still alive was due to Riddell's prescience in constructing and occupying a line in front of the redoubt and not in the battered maze itself.

Wrixon reported that 'the men in the front line were astonishingly cheerful and very pleased with what they had accomplished. Later, the strain and the want of proper food began to tell. . . . The real business was to get in and get out; luckily most of the wounded had been evacuated before the Germans really began to open up'.

Relief came on the night of the 15th when the Cambridge-shires and Black Watch spent the night at Wood Post, moving the next day to Senlis. The losses had been heavy: Bradford, Reed, Vine and Bowyer being killed, whilst Eric Wood and eight others were wounded. The casualties amongst the men were exactly 200.

But whilst the losses were deplored, the Battalion was intensely proud of its achievement. Congratulatory messages flowed in, including one from Haig himself. The latter sent an A.D.C. with a consignment of fruit as a practical appreciation of the effort made by the Cambridgeshires and Black Watch.

Corfield and Marr set to work to reorganize the Battalion; two Companies had two officers, and the others one each. Equally serious, Battalion H.Q., the nerve-centre, had lost Bradford, whilst Sergt. Piggins and many of the communication section had been killed. Corfield wrote to me: 'We have taken the strongest position on the Western Front. The Battalion is all to pieces; in your next draft include all possible signallers, Lewis gunners and N.C.O.'s'. The Reserve Battalion did its best; we sent 110 picked men, many of them volunteering for the draft. It was probably the best draft we ever sent; I saw it as far as Étaples. The authorities promptly split it up amongst strange battalions, and transferred from the Bedfords to the Cambridgeshires a batch of raw, inexperienced men.

On 23 October the Cambridgeshires moved back to the old German dug-outs at Thiepval. Wrixon states that 'these were the best accommodation to be had in the area. They went underground about twenty feet, and three or four of them easily took in the Battalion at its present strength. It rained all day and every day; great trouble moving the wounded—six men to a stretcher to get them through the appalling mud'.

Fatigue parties and constant moves were the order of the day; the officers were occupied with preparations for the next attack. Murray of the Black Watch took over temporary command. The assembly position for the attack would be on the west face of the Schwaben. Wrixon with four scouts spent days taking observations in readiness; the success of the assembly was largely due to his painstaking work carried out in this shell-swept area.

The attack was fixed for 13 November; whilst the 63rd Division were to advance from Hamel on Beaumont-Hamel, the 118th Brigade with the Sherwoods were to descend from the Schwaben to St Pierre-Divion and the south side of the Ancre.

The shelling on the 12th was heavy during the early part of the evening, then it died down. A fog came up from the Ancre and, thanks to the work carried out by Wrixon and a sapper officer, the assembly was completed without a casualty. The barrage fell at 5.45 a.m.; the enemy (barraged twice daily for some time) was taken by surprise and found mostly in his dug-outs. When the first advance of two hundred and fifty yards had been carried out, the Battalion had to wheel to the left and advance six hundred yards on Serb Road. This difficult manœuvre was hindered by the fog, two Companies losing direction, but on the whole the fog helped by screening the advance to the river. Short of officers and N.C.O.'s, the Companies worked their way forward through the fog, rushed the machine-gun posts and gained touch with the 63rd Division on the final objective.

The converging nature of the attack and the successes gained by the troops on both flanks pinched out the Cambridgeshires' front and the Battalion was withdrawn. Casualties had been slight, thanks to the fog, and the men were cheerful over this fresh success.

Murray returned to the Black Watch, Major J. A. Methuen, D.S.O., of the 17th K.R.R., took over command, and the Cambridgeshires, together with the rest of the 39th Division, was at last withdrawn from the Somme battle.

No mention of the Somme battles would be complete without a word of praise for the way in which the transport and Q.M. stores carried out their work. Their nightly journeys to and from the line were arduous and dangerous, but they never failed their comrades in the line.

A three days' march to Doullens and a train thence brought the Division to Poperinghe, and a nine days' rest at Herzeele; it had been earned.

Chapter XIV

YPRES 1917

January and February 1917

M. C. C.

I HAD left the 1/1 Cambridgeshires at Ypres in 1915. I rejoined them at Ypres early in January, 1917, after duty for over a year as Adjutant of the 3/1 Battalion in England. I did so with considerable trepidation. I had had nearly 150 officers and 2,000 men through my hands during that period; the majority of the Battalion I was rejoining had had to endure my efforts to fit them to take their place, and now I myself would have to put my theories into practice under their watchful eyes.

Two old stagers in Platt-Higgins and Pooley greeted me at Poperinghe; the first to meet me on the Ypres Canal Bank was Bowes, followed by a hail from Corfield on the opposite bank. I went into H.Q. and met Methuen, the temporary C.O. A mining engineer from South Africa, Methuen was a fighting soldier pure and simple. He was in his element as a leader of a desperate enterprise, his greatest assets were his quickness at making decisions and his sense of humour.

The Battalion was working alternately with the Hertfordshires in holding the line at Wieltje, five days in the line and then five days in support at the Canal Bank. When in the line Battalion H.Q. were at St Jean; the front trenches were good, with long communication trenches.

Battalion H.Q., communication trenches and certain parts of the front line were shelled several times daily; fortunately the times never varied by a minute. One could be tolerably certain that 5·9's would descend on H.Q. at 7.5 a.m., 1.30 p.m. and 5.10 p.m., just as one knew that it was unwise

to be in the left communication trench at 12.25 p.m. and
3.20 p.m. Once the details of the time-table had been
grasped, life was quite bearable; occasionally, however, one
or other side would carry out a raid, and the time-table
would take several days to readjust itself.

The Hertfordshires came up to conduct a raid whilst we
held the line. I was extremely interested in the details,
which included a shoot by the Corps Heavy Artillery and
the Division's own guns. The raid was successful and two
prisoners were extracted from the enemy's line.

The next night 'C' Company, with the aid of two Verey
lights, caught a prisoner who had lost his way on a patrol. This
was too good an opportunity for Methuen to miss. He gravely
wrote to the Brigade, pointing out that the cost per prisoner
of the Hertfordshires' raid, allowing for the several thousand
shells fired, worked out at £x000, whereas the cost of the
Cambridgeshires' method was 4¾d., the cost of two Verey
lights.

The men were experiencing a lot of trouble from 'trench
feet', due to the wet and cold. The compulsory oiling of feet
with whale oil became the order of the day, and each officer
had to render a daily certificate to the effect that he had inspected his men's feet, and woe betide anyone who had a case
of trench foot in his platoon.

The cold grew more intense; the parapets became frozen
rocks, whilst the flooded trenches became dangerous through
snipers, because one had to walk on the ice several inches
above the normal (mud) level. I was amazed to see men
sleeping peacefully on a floor of ice in the front line.

Back at the Canal Bank we played football on the ice,
whilst Charles Tebbutt routed out an ancient pair of skates
and skated down from 116th Brigade H.Q., where he was
acting as intelligence officer. We awoke in the morning to find
our blankets coated with ice where our breath had condensed
during the night. Geoffrey Barker wore 'ttt...two cccc...c.

cardigans', and the men's comments in their letters on the cold were unprintable. Shells had an added terror; they burst immediately on contact instead of first ploughing into the ground, whilst machine-gun bullets ricocheted at all angles.

Our great fear was that the thaw would come whilst we were in the line; fortunately we were relieved the night previous. The incoming troops found their parapets melting and slipping into the trench, and for a day or two there was an unofficial truce whilst both sides 'baled' themselves in again.

The next time we entered the line was at Observatory Ridge in front of Sanctuary Wood. In April, 1915, as Company Commander, I had supervised the digging of the greater part of this line, now I was commanding the Battalion as Methuen was away. Apart from shelling and an unsuccessful enemy raid, my four days in command were uneventful. On relief I went down to second-in-command, as Riddell had returned to take over from Methuen, and the following day a step further down, as Saint rejoined as second-in-command and I was posted as O.C. 'B' Company. My tenure of this post was, however, brief, as Riddell appointed me Adjutant in place of Corfield, who had gone sick.

Whilst the period under notice was uneventful from the purely infantry point of view, it was overshadowed by the reverses suffered by the Royal Flying Corps. For some reason (alleged to be a strike) the delivery of the 'new spring models' had been delayed. As a result, our squadrons for several weeks were opposed by enemy squadrons using infinitely faster and handier machines. Every day over the Salient it was the same; our fighting planes were intercepted and outmanœuvred, and on some days as many as six of our machines were sent down in flames. Day after day we watched the combats with fear in our hearts, but our squadrons never flinched from carrying out their duty of guarding the observation-planes, without which our guns would have been blind.

At last the day arrived when a British Squadron circled into the sky equipped with new machines. A great cheer went round the Salient when it was seen that at long last the tables had been turned; but the infantry had learned the meaning of 'Per Ardua ad Astra'.

Chapter XV

THE CANAL BANK

February—June 1917

E. R.

IN February, 1917, I rejoined the Cambridgeshires near Poperinghe.

Winter had called a halt in major operations on the Western Front, but the dull routine of trench life still went on. Three days in the trenches; three days in huts or tents behind the lines (beyond the range of field-guns, but well within reach of the Boche 'heavies'), and then three days in the dug-outs on the banks of the Ypres canal.

The opposing forces were being fattened-up in anticipation of the coming Spring. Then the real business would start again. No attempt was made to conceal the intentions of our Higher Command. New roads, leading to the Ypres Salient, were in course of construction, and a network of railway lines, like a spider's web, stretched across the dead-level country. The infantry of Divisions which were at 'rest' laboured on these transport highways, and, I think, on the whole enjoyed the change from the accustomed rôle of the soldier.

The pre-war Regular Army officer and N.C.O. were taught to allot definite tasks to working-parties of soldiers. They were practised in methods for the mathematical calculation of the exact number of men required to accomplish an engineering task in a given time, and demonstrations were given to prove the value of these methods. Now Canadian engineers had been charged with the construction of that part of the railway-line on which the Cambridgeshires were working. They were accustomed to call upon the Battalion to parade one Company at one place and another Company or platoon at another. As the whole army had been encouraged to foster *esprit de corps* within the smaller units, this system would have worked very well, but there was a snag in it. Owing to the wastage of war, Companies and platoons were never of the same strength. Consequently, one unit frequently had too much work, and another too little. The result was general dissatisfaction amongst the officers and men. As usual, the poor old General Staff got the blame, though it was not the fault of that department of the army. After a lengthy discussion with the Canadian colonel, we arranged for the tasks to be allotted to us on the evening previous to the day on which our Companies were to work. By this means we were enabled to subdivide sections of the proposed line according to the strength of our Companies. The result of this plan was that the best Company always finished for the day long before the worst Company. This led to a keen and healthy rivalry.

I mention this incident as an illustration of the too frequent blaming of Higher Commands when regimental or departmental officers were at fault. The amateur-soldier literary critic of to-day often lays the blame at the wrong door. I have no desire to throw mud at him on account of his ignorance of the truth, but I wish to expose these frequently undeserved condemnations. The Staff, regimental officer, and soldier made many mistakes. It would be futile to deny this fact, for nothing is gained, though much may be lost, by overstating one's case; but, though the amateur soldier of a few months' experience may be a good novelist, he remains an amateur military critic until he has completed an apprenticeship of many years' duration. If an attempt is to be made to criticize or praise the conduct of the Great War, let us leave it to those who, by knowledge, ability, fairness, and experience are best fitted to undertake such a stupendous task. I do not aspire to such heights. I merely wish to see justice done to all, irrespective of rank or appointment.

Every C.O. worthy of his position sought to turn the thoughts of his men, in their leisure hours, along some channel calculated to make them forget the war. When in one of the camps to the south-west of Ypres, we decided to make a vegetable garden. The first thing to do was to find a head-gardener. Of course, Nightingale said he knew all about it. I did not believe him, but soon found I was wrong. A barbed wire fence round a piece of ground, which had been, in happier times, under cultivation, was an easy matter. An enterprising subaltern obtained a day's leave, and, by judicious 'lorry-jumping', disappeared into the back areas, from which he emerged with a few hundreds of young cabbages. These were planted, some seeds were sown, and a number of ration potatoes were duly interred, under the supervision of Nightingale. The potatoes were, I regret to say, subsequently exhumed by an over-zealous Company cook of another regiment many weeks before they had produced a family, but the cabbages survived until the advent of a Welsh battalion.

Those soldiers who lived on the Canal Bank (Ypres) will remember a Battalion H.Q. known as 'The Pike and Eel'. A wooden rustic fence enclosed some twenty-five yards of ground between the entrance of the dug-out and the water's edge. We converted this plot of land into a garden. A few rose-bushes, discovered in the derelict flower-beds of a neighbouring château, were transferred to 'The Pike and Eel', and plots were sown with mustard and cress and lettuce. A notice, dealing with the care and culture of our allotment, was pasted on the interior wall of H.Q.

A successful raid on the German trenches opposite the Hill Top sector had produced a prisoner who, in due course, arrived at 'The Pike and Eel' for interrogation. A search of his pockets revealed the presence of a dozen fish-hooks. Since these would be of little use to a prisoner of war, they were passed on to Jonas and Spicer of 'C' Company, who happened to have a number of keen anglers in their command.

When life is short and no man knows what the morrow may bring, it is sound policy to be up and doing. The supple branch of a willow tree, some string, or half-a-dozen boot-laces, with a couple of yards of stout thread, and one of the German's fish-hooks, combined to make an angler's equipment unlike anything produced by Messrs Hardy of Alnwick, but it served the purpose of Messrs T. Atkins of 'The Pike and Eel', and late of the Isle of Ely.

A correct atmosphere does much to ensure the pleasure to be derived from any pastime. This axiom led one of Izaak Walton's disciples to stage his piscatorial efforts in surroundings reminiscent of a backwater of the river Cam. On the evening of the day following the raid, a burst of cheering and loud laughter greeted my ears on returning from a visit to the Brigade. As I stepped onto the wooden footbridge spanning the canal, an unaccustomed scene lay before me. The bank was thronged with soldiers, shouting gibes and words of ironical encouragement. Looking up the canal I saw a member of 'C' Company seated in a packing-case which floated on the untroubled waters, his fishing-rod in his hand, and a slice of bread, a tin of bully-beef and a large bottle by his side. He was a picture of placid contentment.

But the spoils do not always fall to the scientifically equipped angler. The business of a cook is to get food. He does not mind how he gets it. A big pike, lurking in the shadow of the footbridge, had defied all attempts made to lure him out of the water. A Company-cook had reason to cross the bridge. He saw the pike lying very close to the surface. He retraced his steps, and, coming back with a piece of railway metal about two feet long, deftly dropped it on top of the pike. I was offered a slice for dinner, but pike live on strange things, and no doubt there were strange things in that canal, so I declined with thanks. A too active imagination is not always a pleasant possession.

I record these apparently trivial happenings because of their real effect on the mentality of the soldier. Men like Sir Ivor Maxse, who had commanded our Corps, and Kentish,

who ran the 3rd Army School, and a thousand others, realized their importance. Would that many more had done so!
'All work and no play makes Jack a sad lad.' The occasional
diversion of thoughts from the work in hand gives rest to the
mind and the body. Whenever opportunities occurred, I encouraged officers and men to go to Poperinghe, where the
former could dine at Skindle's and visit the club or attend
the performances at the theatre, and the latter had a choice
of Divisional Concert Parties, many of which reached a high
standard of excellence. Moreover, all ranks were sure of a
welcome at any hour, day or night, at Talbot House (Toc H,
a name now known all the world over). Regimental officers
were, however, always faced with the difficulty of getting the
rank and file transported from the camps to the town. In this
respect, I think our Staff was lacking in sympathy and enterprise. The strain of war was infinitely greater on the fighting
branches of the army than on departmental corps living in
back areas, consequently greater facilities should have been
afforded them for transport. I know that there were many
obstacles in the way, but they should, and could, have been
overcome.

It was during this period of semi-inactivity that I must have
seen the resultant effects of excessive alcoholism or immorality had such excess been prevalent. I studied the 'sick-
reports' and 'crimes sheets' and consulted the medical officer.
My eyes were always open for all that was good and bad in
my own officers and men, and those of neighbouring units
when they came my way. The military police were very
active, never hesitating to report misconduct. The few cases
of venereal disease which came to my notice were traceable
to the 'base' or England. Even when we were working on
the railways, and, later, training for ten days in a district
populated by civilians, I saw no signs of moral deterioration.

Chapter XVI

ST JULIEN

31 *July*—1 *August* 1917

E. R.

IT had been common property for some time that a British offensive on a huge scale was intended in the Ypres Salient. The highly successful attack on Messines Ridge, a masterpiece of Staff work and of military mining, was now history. A vast concentration of artillery, tanks and military stores was in progress. The new railways and roads, often empty by day, were humming under the cloak of night. New camps and hutments were springing up in the heavily-wooded areas. There was every indication that the curtain would soon ring up in the Salient theatre.

Ivor Maxse was one of those officers who believed in taking the soldier into his confidence as much as possible. Accordingly, he summoned all unit commanders to Corps H.Q. to listen to the plans for the coming attack by General Gough's army. Then, being fully conversant with the details of the whole scheme, I returned to my Battalion. The whole of the second week in July was taken up, by my officers and N.C.O.'s, in observation of the line to be traversed by the Cambridge-shires. We made 'look-outs' from which we could see the country with the naked eye, for telescopes or field-glasses, excellent though they are for picking out details, do not give a sufficiently wide field-vision to enable the observer to make a comprehensive mind-picture.

From our observation-post we could see for a distance of about two thousand yards to the east and north. Beyond that our vision was blocked by Kitchener's Wood and the ridge running east and west across the front. A thousand yards

beyond that ridge lay the village of St Julien, with the rising
ground, on its eastern outskirts, known to us as Hill 19. This
was really only an apology for a hill—nothing more than a
piece of ground, four hundred yards in length, rising some
fifteen feet on the northern bank of the Hanebeek, a little
stream a man could jump across. Hill 19 was the objective
of the Cambridgeshire regiment. Although we could not see
it, or St Julien, we knew exactly where they were, for the maps
provided by the Corps' topographical section were excellent.

Our look-outs, on high ground, enabled us to imagine the
earlier stages of the advance as far as Canteen Trench, the
strongly fortified German line along the ridge east of Kitchener's Wood. There, in front of us, half-way to the ridge,
lay Mouse Trap Farm with its ponds and a few decapitated
trees. Two hundred yards to the right of the farm the line of
the road leading from Wieltje to St Julien was discernible to
the practised eye—at present. But how much of these landmarks would be left after the guns had been given their own
sweet way?

'I expect them ponds 'ul be there, sir. They'll take a bit o'
shiftin', said Nightingale. As it happened, he was right; but
there were hundreds of other ponds by the time we eventually
reached Mouse Trap Farm.

On 16 July the Cambridgeshires entrained at 'Pop' *en route*
for Houlle, where the whole of the 39th Division was under-
going training for the offensive. This place had been selected
as the formation of the ground in the vicinity closely resembled that over which we should soon be called upon to
advance. Here, a replica of the German defence-system, in-
corporating all the features, had been dug, planted, or built,
under the direction of the Staff. The whole was a life-sized
model in which every detail was easily recognisable, a remarkable piece of work. A careful reconnaissance revealed
a laborious study of detail by those responsible for the setting
of this stage. All known concrete machine-gun emplace-

ments were represented in canvas. Trees, fifteen to twenty
feet in height, represented Kitchener's Wood. There was
the tree-bordered road between Wieltje and St Julien, Mouse
Trap Farm with its ponds, and all the trenches.

Equipped exactly as it would be on the day of the attack,
the 39th Division rehearsed the advance on St Julien and
beyond. Thus every officer and man knew exactly what was
expected of him. It was all very real, except for the absence
of shells and bullets—and of the dead and wounded. That
these rehearsals were of incalculable value no soldier would
deny, but in war the thunder of the guns, the bursting of
shells, the 'zip' of the bullets, and the rattle of rifle- and
machine-gun fire dulls the bravest man's sense of direction,
for then fear, and perhaps elation, comes to all of us.

The Third Battle of Ypres was to commence at 3.30 a.m.
on 31 July. Rain had fallen heavily throughout the whole of
29 July and the early morning of 30 July. Our camp at
Brandhoek was a sea of mud on the morning of the 30th,
when the Brigadier (Bellingham) informed me that, unless
the rain ceased, the attack would be postponed. It ceased
about noon. A bright sun, and a slight wind began to dry the
surface of the ground. After 'dinners' the whole camp was
ordered to rest. With a knowledge that all had been done that
could be done, I went to sleep.

We paraded at 9.30 p.m. for our four-mile march to the
Canal Bank. The bagpipes were playing the Black Watch out
of the camp. As we turned onto the log road through the
trees, Major Murray, of that regiment, saw us coming. He
shouted, 'Here come the Cambridgeshires; play up the
pipes', and we marched past, followed by many shouts of
'Good luck!' I said 'Good-bye' to Clayton, my second-in-
command, and went through the fast-gathering darkness to
the head of my beloved Cambridgeshires. The sound of the
pipes became fainter, still fainter, then died away.

The scene around us was weird and fantastic as we stumbled

along through the now pitch-dark night. At one moment all
was black about us, the next moment the flash of one of our
heavy guns lit up the trees for a second, and then left us in
darkness. Occasionally a great flare would light up the
country to our right or left, giving a momentary glimpse of
the figures and faces of the men marching behind me. This
was when a Boche shell had hit one of our 'dumps' of
munitions. Our guns quickened their rate of fire until the
darkness about us was pierced by their flashes as far as the
eye could see. Then the rate of fire dropped again, rumbled
slowly on, and finally died away. We were back again at
'The Pike and Eel'.

The plan for the attack was that our Corps (Maxse) was
to advance on a front of one mile for a distance of three miles
into the German trench-system. Maxse divided his front,
giving the right half to our Division (the 39th) and the left
half to the 51st Division. The XIXth Corps was on our right,
and the XIVth Corps and other troops away to the left of the
51st Division.

There were five main objectives on our Corps' front, each
one of which contained features of tactical importance. Each
objective was given a name and allotted to a brigade for
capture. The first of these objectives was the German front-
line system, including (on our front) Mouse Trap Farm. This
was called the Blue Line. The second was Kitchener's Wood
and the ridge to the east of it, including Canteen Trench,
which cut the Wieltje–St Julien road, five hundred yards
south of St Julien at Corner Cot. This was the Black Line.
Two hundred yards northwards was the Black Dotted Line,
whence the ground sloped to the Steenbeek, which flowed
through St Julien. At the eastern end of the village the Steenbeek was joined by the Hanebeek (East), and from the south
by another brook which the Corps had, unfortunately, named
Hanebeek (South). Two hundred yards beyond the Steenbeek the Green Dotted Line ran from north-west to south-

east, and looped round the St Julien outskirts eastward across Hill 19 and over the Hanebeek (East) to the little knoll on which stood Border House. The final objective for the day was the Green Line on the hill-crest a thousand yards north-east of St Julien. This was the goal of the 118th Brigade represented by the Cheshires and Hertfordshires, supported by the Black Watch and Cambridgeshires if necessary. The general scheme was for the 116th and 117th Brigades to capture positions up to and including the Green Dotted Line, and for the 118th Brigade to 'leap-frog' that line and pass on to the final objective.

With the assistance of ear-defenders which had been issued to all ranks, we managed to get some sleep in spite of the noise of our 18-pounders.

At 3.45 a.m. Hollis and I with the faithful Nightingale climbed to the top of the Canal Bank to watch the opening of the bombardment. It was very dark and still. We waited. Zero hour was 3.50 a.m.

'Now', I said, 'it's coming.'

A roar like thunder broke the stillness and thousands of flashes pierced the darkness. The air seemed filled with the hissing sound of shells passing overhead towards the enemy's lines. We shouted to one another, but the crash of the 18-pounders, standing almost wheel to wheel close by, made our voices inaudible. The flashes from our guns and their reflection in the sky lit up the surrounding scenery in a way I had not thought possible.

We turned our eyes towards the north-east. In the sky above the German lines our shrapnel was bursting like innumerable rockets. Or was it the German shrapnel over our lines? It was impossible to say. Hundreds of coloured balls of light were rising and slowly falling as far over the enemy's trenches as we could see. It was an amazing spectacle, the like of which I had never seen. We were watching the most intense bombardment the world had ever known.

After the first three minutes our artillery slowed down, making it possible to distinguish the fire of one gun from another. Occasionally I saw the burst of a heavy German shell where it had fallen near our batteries, but these bursts were few and far between. Our 'heavies' had done their work well.

At 4.45 a.m. we all had breakfast undisturbed by hostile artillery.

It was nearing the time for us to start. Officers were leading their men up the steep banks of the Canal to the appointed place for parade, their figures looking ghost-like in the morning mist. Looking towards Ypres I saw some of our artillery crossing the bridges over the Canal at a trot, a good sign. We must have captured the Blue Line.

I climbed onto the top of the Canal Bank, with Nightingale at my heels, and looking towards the north saw the Cambridgeshires drawn up in artillery formation (platoons in column, with fifty yards interval between platoons and two hundred yards between Companies from front to rear). 'D' Company (Raven) was on the right, 'A' Company (Dunlop) on the left, and behind these two came 'C' Company (Jonas) and 'B' Company (Fison). Tebbutt, my intelligence officer, who was to guide our advance, was standing in front of 'D' Company taking a compass-bearing, with his scouts by his side. To the right of the Cambridgeshires about twenty 4.5 howitzers suddenly opened fire, almost drowning Nightingale's shouted remark: 'That's er tidy bunch o' Fritzes, sir.... Look at 'em.... They're carryin' our chaps.' Through the mist I could just distinguish a long line of German prisoners carrying wounded on stretchers towards one of the Canal bridges.

'Come on, Nightingale.... It's time', and I walked to the head of the Battalion.

We had about two miles to march over the open before reaching the British front line of the morning. Tebbutt moved off through the tall thistles and long grass, now very wet from the dew, and we all followed.

All went well for the first mile. To the left, near Hammond's Corner, several groups of German prisoners were coming back under escort and one of our tanks was making the best of its way forward over the soft ground.

Up till now no shells had fallen near us. I was congratulating myself on our good fortune when a bunch of a dozen threw up fountains of earth a hundred yards in front of us, directly in our path. We halted for a couple of minutes, then moved on into the area which had been shelled, for I guessed the Boche was starting an 'area shoot'. He would not shoot at the same place twice. Therefore, the best thing to do was to march straight towards the place where shells were bursting, wait until the shoot stopped, and then move across the shell-holes.

I suppose it was during these zigzag movements that Tebbutt lost touch with us, for on rising to move forward after one of our halts I could see nothing of him or his scouts. We had been lucky so far in guessing where the Boche would not shoot. After all, he could not see the ground over which we were crossing. He, too, was guessing. It was a toss-up who won, with a shade of odds on us, but for once our fortune was out. We walked right into it. Nightingale stepped in front of me and marched as policemen march when going on duty, the leading man almost touching the man behind him. I was the man behind....A flash and crash, and we were smothered with mud and earth....We pushed on, but not before I had seen Nightingale stagger and put his hand to his face. He was advancing again when, taking him by the shoulder, I tried to turn his face towards mine, but he averted it.

'Are you hit?'

'No, sir', he answered, still pushing on. He knew my orders, that all men wounded in the advance as far as the

Blue Line were to report to an officer and be sent back to the nearest Aid Post.

'Yer carn't get on wivout me....It's 'ardly er scratch.... Oi did it puttin' on me equipment afor' we started....Give us a charnse, sir....Give us a charnse.' Blood was slowly trickling down his face from a slight wound in his nose. I ordered him to go back with the other wounded; there were seven of them. Only two men had been killed. We had been lucky.

Just before we crossed our old front line, a battery of 18-pounders galloped past us bumping over the gaps cut for them by the engineers. The gunners shouted, 'Good old foot-sloggers....See yer in Berlin'. Some wag replied, 'Keep a bottle of lager for us, mate. We'll be a bit thirsty before we get to Fritz-town'.

The men were as steady as rocks and full of cheer. When the news reached us that our tanks were in Kitchener's Wood, 'D' Company sang, 'Oh! Oh! Oh! It's a loverly war'.

We stopped for another breakfast in what had been No Man's Land before the advance. Here, as I had anticipated, the Boche gunners left us in peace. They continued to shell everything else. Thank God, they were always conservative in their shooting whatever they may have become since in their politics. Knowing that they would expect us, like good soldiers, to halt in the trenches, I, like the general in *The Green Curve*, did the unexpected and halted in the open. The men rested for an hour in peace and comparative comfort, if not in quiet, while the officers accompanied me on a tour of reconnaissance as far as Mouse Trap Farm.

Tebbutt and his scouts rejoined us. He had been like the little boy at the fair, he had 'seen so many other funny things around him that he lost father'. We saw only two dead Englishmen and about twenty dead Germans.

The Battalion 'fell in', and we continued our advance in accordance with the Brigade time-table.

Things were different now. As we picked our way through the shell-torn ground to the east of Mouse Trap Farm the hostile fire increased in density. Fritz was hammering the Wieltje–St Julien road on our right with his 'heavies'. Many wounded of both sides and a number of prisoners were moving down it. Poor devils! It was all very horrible. I waved my map to signal to the leading Companies to incline to their left in order to keep clear of the road. I might have given the signal on a barrack square in good old peaceful England. The whole Battalion inclined to the left with the precision of a drill movement.

Away behind us, on Hill Top (so I heard afterwards), two brigadiers were watching the progress of the battle.

'Isn't it splendid!' ejaculated Bellingham.

'Splendid?...It's magnificent!' said Hornby. 'My God! Bellingham, my God!...Look, man, look at your Cambridge-shires! It's glorious! It's glorious!'

They had seen the Battalion approaching the Black Line—and the Boche had seen us also. We were getting it hot and strong, guns and machine-guns. But the men never wavered. The officers led on. A signal, and the platoons split up into sections in file and headed on for St Julien, now lost in the smoke of the shell-burst, now coming in view again; shaken for the moment as shells exploded amongst them, then re-forming, but ever advancing steadily and slowly as if nothing unusual had happened. From our position in the Black Line, two hundred yards in front, Tebbutt and I watched them coming, the German trench affording us unexpectedly good cover. This mere lad, fascinated by what were, to him, novel surroundings, kept calling my attention to dead Germans, bundles of brand new steel body-armour, the almost con-tinuous concrete machine-gun emplacements, loaves of bread, and abandoned rifles in the trench.

Five hundred yards to the north-east, below us, on the banks of the Steenbeek, stood the ruins of St Julien. Over the

tops of the nearest houses I could see the bush-covered banks
of the Hanebeek (East), from which rose the mound known
to us as Hill 19. To our right the Hanebeek (South) oozed its
way through the bog-land to meet the Hanebeek (East) at
the eastern end of St Julien. To the east of this bog-land the
ground rose to a height a little above that on which we now
were, but I could distinguish the ruins of Fortuin, and further
north, Border House.

Our shells were bursting in a line running east and west
beyond St Julien. Could that feeble fire be our artillery
barrage that was to creep to the final objective and cover the
Cheshires, Hertfordshires and the Black Watch in their
advance? The mist was thickening, and I could not be sure
if I saw troops moving near the line where our shells were
bursting, but I knew from my watch that all the other battalions of my brigade must be well over the Steenbeek and
Hanebeek (East). On my right our machine-guns were
firing from Canteen Trench. One of their officers put my
mind at rest when he said that the Cheshires, Hertfordshires,
and the Black Watch were approaching the hamlets, Winnipeg and Springfield, seven or eight hundred yards north-east
of St Julien.

Swinging the Cambridgeshires to the right, so as not to
interfere with the fire of our machine-guns, we entered the
Black Line on the eastern side of the Steenbeek. Here we had
to halt, for Stanway's reserve company of the Cheshires was
preparing to move forward in support of the rest of his
battalion.

My Battalion, still retaining its formation, took cover in
Canvas Trench and shell-holes. My God! how proud I was
of those men! They had been under fire, increasing in density,
for four-and-a-half hours with no cover save a slight mist, and
now a few battered trenches and hundreds of muddy shell-
holes. Bullets and shells were taking their toll. Fison, of 'B'
Company, was wounded and his place taken by that 'Cœur

Half-submerged tank near St Julien

General Riddell inspecting ex-service men before unveiling the
War Memorial at St Mark's Church, Cambridge, Oct. 1920

THE YPRES SALIENT, 1917—AND AFTER

de Lion', 'Jerry' Walker. When passing a shell-hole I spoke a few words of congratulation to Awberry, who drew my attention to the fact that bullets were coming from our right where the 55th Division should have been level with us.

'Awberry, send a platoon up there so that it can see Fortuin village', I said, pointing in the direction he had indicated. But as I turned towards his shell-hole I saw that he was dead, shot through the head. It was Awberry who had led the raid from Hill Top which resulted in the capture of the German with the fish-hooks. Poor Awberry, how he had hated it all! Two subalterns (Ritchie and Rash) were wounded, and 35 N.C.O.'s and men killed or wounded, and we had not fired a single shot! Yet everybody was cool and collected. Wonderful fellows!

A patrol, sent into St Julien, found two 5·9 German guns with a lot of ammunition. They might be of use to us, so a runner was despatched with a message to the nearest artillery observation-officer giving an exact description of their whereabouts.

The hour for our advance to Hill 19 having arrived, 'A' and 'D' Companies moved forward. 'Jock' Dunlop, commanding 'A', smiled, saluted me, led on, and disappeared in a cloud of mud, earth and smoke. On my right I had glimpses of two platoons of 'C' Company, under Spicer, running eastward on the crest of the rising ground. What could have happened to the 55th Division? Had it failed? If it had, the position of my right flank and that of the whole of the 39th Division was getting more precarious every yard we advanced to the north-east. Fortunately, Canvas and Capital Trenches had been dug by the Boches against an attack from the east (i.e. the direction of Fortuin). I sent Jonas with his remaining two platoons of 'C' Company to occupy Border House and hold it at all costs. Nothing was to tempt him from his position save a written order from me or my successor.

That was the last I saw of the gallant Jonas. His Company still contained many of the original N.C.O.'s and men recruited from around Wisbech and Whittlesey. They were destined to play the rôle of a breakwater against successive waves of the German counter-attacks. This they carried out to the uttermost, but at the cost of their own annihilation. As is told later, Private Muffett's party withdrew in the evening on the receipt of the written order; repatriated prisoners have also told how two parties of 'C' Company held on to two advanced concrete dug-outs. These were full of wounded, but they held out for two days, hoping against hope that further British attacks would carry the line forward again. Eventually shortage of ammunition and the septic condition of the wounded, several of whom were delirious, forced them to bow to the inevitable.

Jonas and the majority of his men have no known resting-place; their names are graven on the Memorials to the Missing and their deeds on our hearts.

In times of stress it is remarkable how trivial things attract a man's attention from great matters. Prisoners had been drifting through our lines, some terrified, with but one desire, to reach a place of safety, and others defiant. I was speaking to an officer of another regiment when, pointing to an approaching figure, he shouted:

'Lor', blimy! Here comes Prince Ruprecht himself.'

The man walking towards us was a German officer immaculately dressed, wearing white kid gloves and carrying a black ebony cane with a silver knob. Addressing my companion, he said in excellent English:

'I am a German officer, and demand an officer escort to take me to a place of safety.'

'Half a mo', Cocky, you won't want these', casually remarked England's representative as he relieved the prisoner of his automatic pistol, field-glasses and cane, and dropped them into a sand-bag held open by an orderly. Then running his hands over the German's pockets he extracted a watch and note-case, adding, 'Nor these'.

Here I intervened. The watch and money must be returned. 'Here you!' said my companion, addressing a diminutive Cheshire private who, with the aid of his rifle as a walking-stick, was limping back towards the place whence he had set out at dawn. 'Take this back with you, and see that he doesn't dirty his gloves.'

A runner brought me news that 'A' and 'D' had reached Hill 19 and that 'C' Company had occupied Border House, killing or capturing its garrison. The German officer was forgotten, and I moved forward to a concrete gun-pit, where Baynes Smith, my acting adjutant, had established Battalion H.Q. about two hundred yards short of Border House. When I got there the first man I met was Nightingale, a patch of field-dressing and plaster across his nose. He was much engaged with the task of forcing upwards of a dozen prisoners to leave the shelter of the gun-pit for the less salubrious road leading to the prisoners' cage.

For a few brief moments the mist lifted. On the crest of the hill, a mile to our front, we saw German artillery and infantry retiring in disorder, and, north of Winnipeg, a crowd of two or three hundred Germans that had surrendered to the Cheshires, whilst the Hertfordshires looked to be fighting around Springfield, but the trees and hedgerows interfered with our view. Not a single man of the 55th Division could be seen north of the Hanebeek (East). Then the fog fell like a curtain and all was mystery again. It was 11 a.m.

A ghost-like figure loomed through the mist. It was a runner from Canvas Trench where Spicer was watching our right rear. His written message conveyed the disturbing information that fifty men of the Liverpool Scottish and one officer had been seen on the banks of the Hanebeek (South) where that stream was cut by the Black Line. These troops were moving westward instead of north-eastward! They had mistaken the Hanebeek (South) for the Hanebeek (East). Had we been able to teach all our officers and non-commissioned officers the proper use of the compass this mistake would have been averted. Battles are lost by mistakes, just as they are won by their avoidance. In war there is no time for training. It is in the days of peace that a soldier is made. We had so few soldiers in peace-time that we were compelled to attempt to train an army in war-time. Will England ever learn?

The Liverpool Scots were collected by Spicer and put to swell the garrison of Canvas Trench, where they did noble work and got into touch with some troops of the 55th Division holding Fortuin farm, three hundred yards south of Border House. It was now clear that the whole of the right flank of the Cheshires and Cambridgeshires was 'in the air'. A report on the situation was sent to advanced Brigade H.Q. at Corner Cot.

The question was, 'What does "A" do now?' I thought of my pipe (like Mr Baldwin). I put my hand into my haversack and drew it out. A bullet had passed through the bowl, but, thank goodness, it had not split the wood. Some clay to plug the two holes, and a couple of inches of plaster from my field-dressing case, remedied the disaster, and Mr Dunhill's creation was smoking soothingly. As I puffed my pipe in the shelter of the gun-pit my mind ran through all that we had done and what we ought to do. The Black Watch, I knew, had gained most of their objectives, the Cambridgeshires were well advanced in their work of consolidating their positions, but had lost a number of officers and men, how many I could not be sure. The feeble fire of the artillery covering the early stages of the advance of the Black Watch, Hertfordshires and Cheshires, had been explained by an Intelligence Officer, who said that he had seen many of our guns stuck in the mud. But why had the 55th Division failed to reach the Hanebeek east of Border House? Well, it was no good worrying about the why and the wherefore of it; the fact remained—they had failed. That was all about it. No doubt they would push on as soon as possible. I was just about to send a suggestion to the nearest brigade commander of the 55th that, as our brigade had advanced right up to the Green Line, he should bring his reserves into the 39th Division area and attack the Boche in flank from Border House and Canvas Trench, when an unexpected change altered everything. Suddenly the German gun-fire increased. Shells crashed around us. News of a disconcerting nature reached me from my forward Companies. They could see the Hertfordshires and Cheshires retiring.

It was all so confusing. Droves of Germans, their hands above their heads, crying 'Kamerad, Kamerad', were running past my gun-pit. They said they had been captured near Winnipeg, and they had but one thought, to get to the prisoners' cage. I wondered how many would get there through that barrage of shells and bullets.

It was 11.30 a.m. The mist was clearing away. Long lines of Germans could be seen crossing the Winnipeg–Spring-field road, and one battalion was advancing on Border House and Hill 19 from the east. If nothing was done to help them, the Black Watch would be cut off and the Cheshires and Hertfordshires wiped out. The Brigade signallers had failed to get a telephone-line through to me. (They had about as much chance of doing that as of finding a snowball in Hell.) Therefore, it would have to be an infantryman's battle, for I could not warn our artillery in time. There was just a hope that the 'gunner' officer at our advanced Brigade H.Q. at Corner Cot would see the Germans and get through to his guns. Anyway, with luck, my runners would reach him, sooner or later.

Walker with 'B' Company was in St Julien. I told him to move across the Steenbeek west of that village and to attack the right of the advancing Boches; at the same time assuring him that Spicer and the remaining two platoons of 'C' Company were moving forward to help him. The crews of two derelict tanks, with half-a-dozen Lewis guns, were willing and anxious to fight anybody. They took Spicer's place in guarding our right flank.

Our gun-pit, with roof and sides of concrete, was open at each end. To protect us from the German side we had piled up a mound of earth, leaving the British, or south, end open. Over the concrete roof, and for five or six yards beyond the concrete sides, the Germans had heaped earth, which was now overgrown with grass. It was not a residence calculated to command a high rent in times of peace, but at that hour many a soldier would have given all he possessed to be allowed to stay beneath its shelter. The floor of the gun-pit was roughly ten feet square. Besides Baynes Smith and Sergt.-Major Pull I had 'Baby Smith' the signalling officer, some runners, and Nightingale, so we had a 'full house'.

As I sat at the southern entrance, anxiously waiting for any sign of life from the telephone, a dismal picture presented itself. Thirty yards away a very gallant officer had, for the last hour, made frantic efforts to extract his tank from a net-work of barbed wire and a sea of mud. During a momentary lift of the mist the Boche gunners had spotted him and had never ceased to pelt him with high explosive shells. He had sent his crew away to help guard our right flank, but, like a good sea-captain, had stuck to his ship—alone. (After he was killed we took the remaining Lewis guns from his tank and mounted them on our gun-pit.) A wounded German boy, with a bayonet wound in the abdomen, had been slowly dying in the mud outside the gun-pit. We could not help him; Hunter, our doctor, was killed. Each one of us would have wished to put a bullet through the poor boy's head to end his agony, but no one had the courage or the right to do it. His pleading eyes fascinated us until, his head falling back into the mud, they stared fixedly at the sky.

Although messages had been received from my Companies, they grew less frequent as time went on. Often, under such circumstances, no news was good news: sometimes it is different, for there may not be anyone left to send news.

It will be remembered that Tebbutt, my very youthful Intelligence Officer, had been with me when we crossed the Black Line. He, with his scouts, had pushed on through St Julien and eventually to Hill 19. There he had done excellent work in supplying the Company officers with such information of the general situation as he had gathered in his wanderings. He mounted a 'salved' German machine-gun and got it manned and in action. His narrative is so well and simply told that I give it in his own words, from the time when the Hertfordshires and Cheshires were being driven back. He writes of the situation on Hill 19:

'Seeing that there were only two subalterns left in charge who, though very cool, had very little military imagination or idea what special measures were needed to meet the contingency, I thought I had better take over the command of the front line. The situation was rather obscure. There appeared to be no one on our right or left. It seemed certain that there must be some Cheshires and Hertfordshires in front, but I did not know if they were merely stragglers or a formed body. It was, therefore, difficult to know if it was advisable to have a barrage put down by our guns in front of us. I could see troops some five hundred yards in front of us, but could not determine who they were. It seemed the best thing to find the Colonel, report the situation, and get his orders.... During the last half-hour I had been watching the men rather carefully, as I was not sure how the fact of other men retiring through them would affect them. They were very quiet, and hardly talked at all, but were very steady and obeyed orders promptly. They had dug a good trench. ...Telling Corporal Tabor I was going back to find the Colonel, and my servant to go on digging a trench for me (as

he had hurt himself going over some barbed wire), I went
back over the Hanebeek (East) alone. A little way on I saw
Twelvetrees going back, wounded in the jaw. He could not
speak much, but he did not seem badly hurt although bleeding quite a lot. He went on while I was having a look round.
A few minutes later, when walking back, I was aware of a
shell bursting close behind me and of a burning sensation in
my left hand, and of the fact that I was sitting on the ground.
I picked myself up and, on looking at my hand, found that it
was mostly gone, and there was a fountain of blood spurting
up from the middle of the back of it. Though a bit dazed, I
had enough sense to realize that I must stop this, so I grabbed
the wrist with my other hand and was relieved to find that
the violent spurts stopped. I started walking back, as I could
not take my hand away to get out my shell-dressing, hoping
to find someone in the Black Line who could do it up. After
walking for a few minutes, getting rather alarmed by the fact
that there seemed to be no one about, I heard a shout from
behind me and, turning, found the Colonel, Adjutant, Spicer
and the Sergeant-Major standing at the entrance of a gun-
position some fifty yards behind me. I went back to them.
Sergeant-Major Pull started to do up my wound. I remember
the Colonel telling him to do something, and him saying that
he thought that would hurt me, and the Colonel saying not
to take any notice of that, and of saying myself that it was not
likely to hurt any more than it was doing at present. The
gun-pit was a concrete affair open at both ends, and sunk
about two feet below the level of the ground. The Colonel,
Baynes Smith, "Baby" Smith, Spicer and Pull were there.
Sitting down by the side were Twelvetrees and a Cheshire
sergeant. Spicer gave me some brandy and I sat down. I felt
very faint and the Colonel gave me some more. I told them
all I could about the situation. I remember Smith sending
off a runner rather sharply. Then Spicer was told to go to
St Julien to make sure who was in it, with a crowd of Cheshires

and Hertfordshires who had been collected there. I thought what a rotten job it would be. The Colonel also told Smith to clear the place out, as it was getting too crowded. I also asked where the doctor was, and heard he was killed. After a bit, a runner came in with a message, and the Colonel said that the Brigadier had gone out and he must go across to Brigade to take over. He told Baynes Smith to take command of the Battalion, and asked him if he was quite sure he understood the situation. His orderly took away the pack I was sitting against, and they both went out. After that Walker came in and talked to Baynes Smith. I thought he seemed a bit shaky (as he has since told me he was). His orderly had been shot by a sniper, going across the open, and he asked for another man to go back with him. He showed Baynes Smith where he thought the sniper was operating from. It was gradually dawning on me that there was little chance of getting any stretcher-bearers to take me down, and Baynes Smith also told me that, if I thought I could manage it, he thought it would be best to try and walk down; so, at last, I determined to have a shot at it. I borrowed a stick from Spicer and took my brandy flask in my hand, so that I could take a sip at it when I felt faint, and started off. Once on my feet I did not feel so bad. There were odd shells dropping about pretty continuously. Before reaching the Black Line, I saw Hill in a shell-hole with Twelvetrees looking after him. Twelvetrees said he was pretty bad, and he looked it. His orderly was dead in the same hole. Passing the Black Line, the signalling officer of the Cheshires shouted out something about a blighty one which annoyed me. I did not cross the Hanebeek (South) at once as I wanted to avoid the Vanheule Farm, which was being shelled. Just in front of me, as I crossed, was a Tommy, and as a shell burst close to us I gave vent to my feelings by saying that I thought it the limit being shelled after being hit. I passed him, and walked up the edge of the wire of the Black Line. I only saw one dead Sussex in it on a stretch of about three hundred yards. I got on to the road just in front of Vanheule Farm. In front of me was another officer whom I caught up and found to be Fison. He was hit in the side and arm and looked very white. I could walk faster than he, but had to lie down every now and again, which he could not do, so we kept passing and repassing each other. We passed some German dead, and I discarded my steel hat for a German one which I thought would make a good souvenir. Later on we passed some pioneers, who were making up the road, who asked us if there was anything they could do for us. I was only anxious to get somewhere where I should be attended to, and get an ambulance. After passing them, my memory fails me till I arrived at Hammond's Corner. I must have been very faint and know I went off quite once. Here there was a sort of aid-post, and several doctors, but they were very busy. I lay down and a padre gave me some more brandy. I gathered from him that there was no chance of getting a lift there. This, followed by a "5·9", which burst about ten yards away and covered me with dirt, decided me to go on to the Canal Bank. The road from there on was pretty crowded. There was a six-inch battery coming up, and lots of limbers about. At last I got down to the Canal Bank, crossed it by Bridge 4 and walked into the First Aid Station. There I was promptly very faint, and had some more brandy. I hardly remember having my wound dressed, only asking the doctor if he thought my hand would have to come off, and he said he thought it would. He said that I should be a stretcher-case and, almost at once, I was put on an ambulance and sent off to the Corps' Dressing-Station.'

It was noon when a battalion of the enemy attacked 'D' and 'A' Companies. Thanks to stout hearts, well-sited trenches, and the number of Lewis and machine-guns salved from tanks, the hostile assaulting troops were almost decimated, save at the northern end of Hill 19, where the Winnipeg

-St Julien road ran through a shallow cutting situated fifty yards in front of our trench. The Germans had got into the cutting but they could not get out, for elements of the Sussex, Hertfordshires and Cheshires, still in the north-east end of St Julien, were able to shoot any men attempting to leave the west end of the cutting, and 'D' Company covered the other end. The Boche was a good fighter, and did a brave thing— he attacked, and was wiped out by the Cambridgeshires, who added two Boche machine-guns to their armament store. It was during the progress of this attack that Tebbutt came to Battalion H.Q.

Although repulsed on its left wing, the hostile attack was nearing the north-east end of St Julien. Walker had crossed the Steenbeek, and, keeping under cover of the trees and houses, presently appeared at the north end of the village; catching the Germans' right in enfilade, he inflicted heavy losses, and, for the moment, drove it back. The Cambridge-shires, and mixed troops of other units, together with the Black Watch, were putting up a good fight unaided by our own artillery.

The mist which had left us in doubt as to what was hap-pening now lifted.

Down came the German artillery and machine-gun barrage, crashing, thundering, and whistling on our front line, where we were, and back beyond Vanheule Farm, where we had located advanced Brigade H.Q. Across the whole of our Corps' front and that of the Corps on our right the Boche was advancing in force. He reached the outskirts of St Julien. A runner from 'D' Company brought the news that there were only three officers alive between 'A' and 'D' Companies, one of whom was wounded, and none in 'C' Company at Border House. They were all running short of ammunition, to replenish which volunteers had been called for to attempt to salve cartridges from the derelict tanks. This perilous work was successfully accomplished.

As our wire to the Brigade was again cut, and every man
with a rifle needed, Nightingale and I set off to run the seven
hundred yards to Vanheule Farm to get the assistance of our
artillery. As may be readily imagined I did not loiter by the
way to admire the view. Probably the men I passed thought
I was running away. I think they did, for in reply to some
shouted remarks I have a recollection of Nightingale bawling
back:

'Cowards? Bloody liars! I'll punch yer bloody 'eds when
Oi come back.'

We got to Vanheule Farm. When I had recovered my
breath I set the machine-guns at work from the Black Line
to fire on the line Winnipeg Cemetery–Northern Houses of
St Julien. Then I got through to the Brigadier and asked for
our artillery to fire on the same line. He told me that most
of our guns had been stuck in the mud when the Cheshires
and Hertfordshires had advanced against the Green Line.
That would have accounted for the feeble creeping barrage.
He assured me that the 55th Division had reported the arrival
of its leading battalions at the Hanebeek (East), whereas
I knew they had lost their direction and, in the mist, had
mistaken the Hanebeek (South) for the Hanebeek (East).
One of the Companies of the Liverpool Scots had, in fact,
attacked our advanced Brigade H.Q. while the Hertfordshires and Cheshires were approaching Winnipeg and Springfield. I presume it was these contradictory reports that led
the Division and Corps to hold back their artillery fire and
leave us to fight our battles without the support of our guns.
The great advance, which had progressed so much in favour
of the British forces in the early morning, was now degenerat-
ing into a disjointed fight. I begged the Brigadier to come to
his advanced Brigade H.Q. and conduct the battle, and urged
that the 116th Brigade be ordered to advance up the line of
the Hanebeek (East) to relieve the pressure on my right and
the left of the 55th Division. I do not know who, or what

circumstances, prevented this plan being put into operation, but I am convinced it would have succeeded. On looking through my diary, I find that I despatched two runners to Brigade with this scheme in writing as early as 11.10 a.m., but they must have been killed or wounded, for Bellingham did not receive it—the fortune of war.

With the Brigadier's promise to turn our artillery on to assist us in the defence of Hill 19 and St Julien I left Vanheule Farm for my journey back to the gun-pit.

It was half-an-hour before our artillery opened fire. I have no idea what caused this delay. The result was immediate. The enemy fell back everywhere between Winnipeg and St Julien. As the Boches left the cover of hedgerows, ditches and trenches, they were cut down by our machine-guns, Lewis guns and rifles. After this, except for desultory fire by snipers, and occasional shells, comparative quiet reigned for an hour. More ammunition and Lewis guns were collected from the tanks for the garrison of St Julien, Hill 19, and Border House. The gun-pit was cleared of all wounded and reconstructed for defence with four Lewis guns on its roof. The Liverpool Scots and Stanway's Cheshires were ready for all comers in Canvas and Capital Trenches. West of St Julien, Walker with the survivors of his own Company, and a few of the Hertfordshires and Sussex, were awaiting developments.

The light had improved so much as to enable us to see the whole length of the ridge which runs east of Winnipeg–Springfield road. Baynes Smith and I were looking at Wurst Farm (five hundred yards east of Winnipeg), where we noticed some movement, when the German artillery opened out in real earnest across the front of the Corps on our right. From Fortuin to the south-west nothing could be seen save smoke, spurts of rising or falling earth, and the white 'woolly-bears' of the bursting shrapnel. Wave upon wave of advancing German infantry were passing to the right of Hill 19, our shells bursting amongst them, whilst the Cambridgeshires, on

Hill 19 and Border House, enfiladed them with Lewis guns. Suddenly the position of my Battalion was blotted out of view by an intense bombardment from hostile guns.

By this time I knew that all the officers of 'C' and 'D' Companies were either killed or wounded, and that Sergt.-Major Burbridge had taken command.

The rattle of rifle-fire from Border House and Capital Trench told me that the Germans were across the Hanebeek. The Sussex were falling back through St Julien, but Walker and the Black Watch still held both banks of the Steenbeek west of St Julien. Fearing a complete envelopment of my forward position, I withdrew 'A' and 'D' Companies to the line Border House–St Julien. This was the position when, at 5.45 p.m., I heard that the Germans were at Fortuin and still attacking. The bombardment of our position increased in density. The climax came half-an-hour later, when our own guns opened on our position. Battalion H.Q. came in for rather more than its share. We were being shot at from north, south and east. My telephone-wire was cut. Outside the shelter of the gun-pit the German machine-gun bullets whipped flicks of mud into the air, or zipped by to find a billet about the Black Line. All my runners were dead, wounded or exhausted. I had begun to write a message when one of our shrapnel shells burst overhead, killing Company Sergt.-Major Pull and blowing the writing-pad out of my hand. Having told Baynes Smith to withdraw the Cambridgeshires, except 'B' Company, to the Black Line, I shouted to Nightingale that I was going to Brigade and started to run for it. The first three hundred yards was the worst part of that race against shells, bullets, and time. We ran, threw ourselves into shell-holes to get our breath, and then ran on again. Every time we got up to run the Boche machine-gun bullets zipped past us. Automatically we took to diving from one shell-hole to another. A wounded Liverpool Scot raised his head and begged us to carry him to safety. But it was not one life we had set out to save; it was, possibly, three hundred. Poor devil, we had to leave him. Another rush and I dived into a wet hole. I had lost Nightingale!

'Beg pardin, sir', came a familiar voice from behind me on my right. I turned my head, very slightly, for I was terribly afraid. My heart was thumping as if it would burst. I shouted, 'Are you hurt?'

Two fierce brown eyes looked at me out of a white face beneath a steel helmet.

'Oh! no, sir; but I was jest thinkin', we ain't both goin' to get to Brigade—leastways not likely—Oi was jest thinkin'. . . .' Then he disappeared in a cloud of mud as a shell burst between us. 'As I was sayin', sir, 'adn't you best tell me wot you was goin' ter sy to the Brigade?—Jest in case, yer know.'

I told him. Then we did the run-and-tumble turn until we reached Canteen Trench, from whence we ran, or walked, to Vanheule Farm. Fortunately, the telephone to the Brigadier was through. Thus it came about that our guns were told that we did not want them to shoot at us as we did not like it.

Some food, and two bottles of German soda-water, consumed under the thick stone roof of what had probably been Vanheule Mill, revived us. After a pipe and a talk with Brown, Nightingale and I started back for the gun-pit. The hostile shelling was not so severe. Our guns had found some other target and the mist was again thickening. We passed the Liverpool Scot. He was dead.

When we reached the gun-pit 'A' and 'D' Companies were falling back towards the Black Line. Baynes Smith and two men were lying on the roof firing Lewis guns. Taking his pipe from his mouth, 'Baynes' turned half round and said:

'There's no sign of anybody coming back from Border House, although Burbridge says he sent an orderly through with a verbal message for "C" Company to retire.'

All the wounded had been sent back to Canteen Trench. And although we waited for a quarter-of-an-hour, no one came from Border House.

'Did "C" Company ever get that message to withdraw?' I asked 'Baynes'.

'I expect so, sir', replied the imperturbable adjutant, and continued shooting.

Then a runner, with a bandaged head, came over from Canvas Trench. He brought a written message out of his pocket, handed it to me, and collapsed to the ground.

'There's firing at Border House', said 'Baynes'.

I read the message:

'I received a message, by orderly, to retire, but as Captain Jonas, before he was killed, said we were not to retire without written orders from the C.O., I am holding Border House. There are only three of us left alive, and two of those chaps is wounded. I am holding Border House until I get written order to retire. (signed) Private Muffett. 7.30 p.m.'

I asked for volunteers to carry a written message to the gallant defender of Border House ordering his retirement. Spicer and the wounded orderly crept back to Canvas Trench, and after many hairbreadth escapes delivered my order to withdraw.

Throughout the day Muffett had held the advance post with his Lewis gun. Every time he ran short of ammunition he made a trip across the open to an abandoned tank and replenished his store of drums. Targets at long range did not interest him, he 'preferred to wait and make sure'. He was one of the two men I recommended during the war for the V.C. (he was awarded the D.C.M.). A fine Lewis gunner and a natural soldier, Muffett was prominent again during the Somme battle in March, 1918. Clayton, for whom he worked in peace time, persuaded him after the war to try to enlist in the Regular Army. He possessed the strength of a horse and abnormal powers of endurance, but the recruiting authorities rejected him as being 'under the required standard of physique'.

It was nearly 8.30 p.m. when Baynes Smith fired the last drum of cartridges and slid off the roof of the gun-pit. We threw the Lewis guns into a water-logged shell-hole, and those of us who had not been hit—'Baynes', Nightingale and I—each helping a wounded man, set out for Corner Cot.

It took me nearly an hour to get my man in safety to Canteen Trench. The poor fellow had lost a lot of blood, and had to rest every hundred yards. I remember that he never said a single word until we reached the trench. Then he just took my hand and, grasping it, whispered, 'Thanks!'

I found Baynes Smith talking to the adjutant of the 13th Sussex—an able and stout-hearted officer who was full of information and sound ideas. By the time we had got the units composing the Cambridgeshires, Cheshires, Hertfordshires, Sussex and Liverpool Scottish sorted out and distributed along Canteen and Canvas Trenches, and had linked up with the 55th Division at Wine House, it was dark. Firing had ceased and all was quiet.

We all wanted sleep more than anything else, but there was to be no rest for me that night. The adjutant of the Sussex confided to me the disturbing news that his C.O. had sent a report to his Brigadier to say that the Germans held St Julien. It was then 1.30 a.m. on 1 August. The Sussex commanding officer, like many others in a similar position, was prostrate from exhaustion, and could give me no clear information. I at once informed my Brigadier that Walker (with 'B' Company and part of 'C' Company) was still holding the whole of St Julien, in the centre of which a medical officer had an aid-post, in a cellar, full of wounded men. We collected a party of Sussex and Cambridgeshires and set to work to carry the wounded out of St Julien, and to drag two captured German guns out of the village. Whilst this work was in progress, a message from the Division reached us.

St Julien would be subjected to an intense bombardment by our artillery at dawn! It was the fog of war again. Of the lot of us, the Sussex adjutant was the only one to keep his head.

He said, 'We must get your men out, sir, and the wounded, and leave the guns'.

This brought me to my senses. It was pouring with rain. Walker and his men, together with the Sussex, brought all the wounded back, and the village, for the retention of which we had fought all day, was abandoned.

The G.H.Q. official communiqué stated 'that the Germans had recaptured St Julien'!

It was still raining heavily when, about noon, I received orders to withdraw the 118th Brigade from the line, leaving the position in charge of the 116th Brigade.

Of the 19 officers and 451 other ranks of the Cambridge-shires who took part in the battle, 16 officers and 286 other ranks were killed or wounded.

Chapter XVII

RAIN AND MUD

1-4 August 1917

E. R.

NIGHTINGALE and I saw the last man leave the Black Line before, turning our backs on St Julien, we slithered across the mud and dragged our weary way over the maze of water-logged trenches. We saw no living creature. Save for the steady downpour of rain all was still. No guns fired. The loneliness began to play on our strained nerves. It was as if we were struggling to pass through a land which had been smitten by a plague. There were only the dead to remind us of our troops' all-conquering advance of the day before. It was only when we struck the old No Man's Land that Nightingale began to place any reliance on my compass. We tarried a few minutes in the late German front line to examine the trench from which poor Awberry's men had captured the German with the fish-hooks. Then we passed on.

I have a dim recollection of seeing the Cambridge-blue silk handkerchief hanging, wet and limp, outside the entrance to a dug-out in Coney Street Trench, near La Belle Alliance. Some days before the battle, some heraldic student had stitched a vertical black band in the centre of the Battalion flag out of compliment to the Rifleman commanding officer. Clayton, my second-in-command—a Cambridgeshire to the tips of his fingers—called it a bar-sinister, but even that did not shake our great friendship. The little blue flag was a very welcome sight.

That veritable conjurer, Sergt. Cooper, produced hot soup from nowhere. I sat in my wet and now steaming clothing,

and ate an excellent repast, whilst Clayton, who had arrived
from 'Battle Surplus', told me of his arrangements for the
comfort of the men.

Throughout the remainder of the day and the following
night rain fell unceasingly.

About two o'clock on the next day I was returning from
a visit to the Black Line when I saw the Cambridgeshires
in artillery formation crossing No Man's Land to the old
German front line. Clayton told me of an expected enemy
counter-attack. It was still raining. After nightfall we were
ordered to move forward to Mouse Trap Farm, and to 'dig
in'. Some genius found the place in the inky darkness, and
the skeleton of the Battalion, now numbering about two
hundred of all ranks, slithered away into the rain, led by the
four remaining officers.

An hour passed, two hours, and no news reached me. I
left my shelter to find out what had happened.

It was not a pleasant walk, if taking a step forward, falling
face downwards over some barbed wire, and then stumbling
into a shell-hole half full of water, can be called a walk. I
really had not the foggiest idea where I had got to and was
feeling very miserable and wet when, from a few feet away,
I heard a melodious voice cheerily singing, 'When yer've
come to the end of a perfct day, and yer sit alone at yer ease'.

I stepped forward and promptly fell into two feet of water.
The singer stopped and, out of the darkness at my elbow,
there came the remark, ''Allo, mate! Comin' bathin'?'

I asked my neighbour if there was an officer anywhere near.

'Beg pardon, sir', he replied, 'I didn't know it wus you.
There's no officer about 'ere.'

'Is there any N.C.O. in charge of this canal?' I asked.

'Well, sir, as there wus no officer and no "nom-com", I
thought I'd better take charge. So I got the chaps lined in
this 'ere trench, and I wus givin' 'em a bit of a song, to while
away the time like.'

To my question, 'What is your rank?' he answered, 'Private Burrows, sir'.

He was the type of man who is worth his weight in gold when things go wrong.

'You're Corporal Burrows now', I told him.

The enemy did not counter-attack, so at dawn we dropped back to the concrete shelters in the old German front line and there spent the day trying to dry our clothes. It had, at last, stopped raining.

In war, fine weather generally leads to a lot of ill-feeling. Consequently, the atmospheric conditions having improved, the temper of the 'gunners', on both sides, deteriorated. The Black Line, to the east of Kitchener's Wood, received much attention throughout the 3rd and 4th of August from the Boche 'heavies'. On the evening of 4 August we received orders to relieve the 17th Sherwood Foresters in the front line.

The light was failing when Clayton, Nightingale and I reached the Sherwood's H.Q. in the Black Line at the south-east corner of Kitchener's Wood. Had it been possible for me to visit the outgoing Battalion earlier in the day a better position for our H.Q. could have been found, but in the rapidly growing darkness a search for 'a better 'ole' might have had disappointing results. This section of the Black Line had been the target of our heavy artillery for many days previous to the great advance. It was battered almost out of recognition, except where strongly built reinforced concrete shelters had withstood our shells. One of these was to be our home for the night. Its double entrance faced the north-east, and was thus open to receive anything the Boche liked to hurl at us, from a bullet, which would have hit anybody seated opposite the entrance, to a shell, which would have killed all the occupants of the shelter. On the roof the Germans had mounted a new pattern anti-tank gun. Perhaps it was with a view to the destruction of this novel weapon that they shelled us every ten minutes throughout the night. I imagine that the Sherwoods' Colonel and staff were very glad to clear out and make room for us.

After the late occupants had taken their departure, we had a chance of examining our house. It consisted of two rooms, each about seven feet square and little more than seven feet in height. The concrete floor, two feet below the level of the trench, was covered with water to a depth of six inches. Facing towards the entrance, on the left of each room, there were two wire beds, one above the other, the upper bed being barely two feet six inches from the roof, and the lower one eighteen inches from the floor. The entrances, opening into the trench, were about two feet six inches in width. There were no doors. The parados (or back of the German trench) was, of course, now the front of our trench. Half of it had been blown away by shell-fire, thus allowing for the free passage of bullets through the upper part of the entrances to the shelter. The only bright spot about our residence was the roof of reinforced concrete, which was strong enough to protect us from anything except very heavy artillery.

A theatrical manager would have been delighted, for we were certainly a 'full house'. I had with me Clayton, the doctor, the signalling officer, Baynes Smith, and Murray (of the Black Watch). Three of us sat on the lower bed, with our feet on Boche ammunition boxes to keep them out of the water. The remaining three sat on a row of ammunition boxes standing on end, with another row, lengthways in the water, on which to rest their feet. We took the canvas which covered the wire beds and fixed it over the entrances to screen the light of our candle. This last precaution savoured of shutting the stable-door after the horse had gone, for as our predecessors had evidently neglected to take similar steps the Boche was sure to know our whereabouts. On the other hand, not seeing a light, he might think we had come to the conclusion that the drains were bad, or the rent too high, and had changed our country-seat. The other compartment was a replica of that already described. It accommodated three signallers, Nightingale, and two runners, and, we expected, Sergt. Cooper, but search where we might we could not find the burly mess-cook. For the first time in my knowledge Cooper was 'absent without leave'. The prospect of a night without food, other than the block of chocolate and ration-biscuit which always resided in my haversack, did not add to the hilarity of the evening. Moreover, Cooper was a comrade for whom we had an affection born of something far deeper than a liking for his cooking. The idea that he had deliberately failed us never entered into our minds. When a good soldier was lost on the way to the front line, we feared the worst.

It was raining heavily when Clayton went out to visit the nearest Company at 10 o'clock. Returning an hour later, he reported that Cooper had been seen near the old German front line, just before the Battalion advanced, and that he was then carrying a large sack of provisions in addition to his rifle and pack. Where he was now nobody knew.

The show started at 11.20 p.m. That was the time at which I made an entry in my diary of the arrival of the first shell. It hit the trench three or four yards to the right of our shelter. Long experience had enabled us to recognize the explosion of the German 5·9 shell. We knew, too well, the accuracy of the gun from which it was fired, and waited in silence for the coming of the next shell. A rushing sound, followed almost simultaneously by a thud and another explosion, told us that the second shell had struck the ground somewhere behind us, probably fifty yards away. Someone said, 'Where did that one go to, Herbert?' But no one laughed. We were waiting for the third shot to show us the 'bracket'. No one spoke. Two minutes later a flash and a roar, followed by the fall of earth into the trench at the entrance to the shelter, told us that our position was the target. We might have left the shelter, but if a soldier has to die he prefers to die in the most com-

fortable place available, and the trench outside, in the dark
and rain, was not a place in which a man would wish to meet
his end. It was so cold and slimy. The candle on the wall-
bracket, shaded by a piece of tin, had almost passed its span
of life. Presently its wick toppled over into the little pool of
wax, spluttered, and went out. It was like the passing of
another life; we waited then till the shells came again. One,
two, three, and all had passed over us and burst behind us.
I thought that, after all, the guns might be directing their
attention to Juliet Farm. I produced another candle from
my haversack and lit it. Murray held the inverted bowl of
his pipe in the flame till the tobacco began to glow. On his
strong, rugged face there were no signs of fear. I blew out
the candle lest anyone should notice mine, for it is not wise
for a commanding officer to let those under his leadership
know that he is afraid. Another wait of five minutes followed.
Then there came a crash. Pieces of earth splashed into the
water at our feet. A cry came from the adjoining compartment. What a relief that cry for help was! Anything was
better than that awful inactivity, that waiting for death, or
was it that hoping for life? I dashed out into the trench and
turned into the next compartment. One of the signallers
thought he had been hit by a piece of shell, but my electric
torch showed nothing more serious than a clod of mud sticking over his right eye. Evidently we were all getting a bit
jumpy. Then number two shell came and burst beyond us.
A minute later number three came, and that also passed over
us. I went back to join the other officers. The excitement,
care for the signaller, and the administration of a sound cursing
for making a fuss about nothing, had done me good. I was
no longer afraid of myself. The next 'bracket' of shells was
similar to the others. Somebody lit the candle, I got my pipe
going, and Murray performed the acrobatic feat of hoisting
his fifteen stone of forty-five-year-old brawn and bone into
the upper bed, remarking that he preferred to die in comfort,

and hoped that, sooner or later, somebody would produce some food. The noise made by the next 'bracket' of shells was modified by Murray's snores.

Gradually fatigue overcame the hypnotic effect of waiting for the next shell to come, and, sitting back against the wall, I fell asleep.

The pale soft light of dawn was creeping through the improvised curtain hanging over the entrance to our shelter when someone told me that the Boche guns had ceased to shoot. I went out into the thick mist hanging like a veil about us. In contrast with the horror of the night the day was weirdly awe-inspiring. That uncanny stillness, and that effort to make one's eyes pierce the grey mist of a newly born day, are things still fresh in the memory of all infantrymen who served in the Great War. It is the hour at which the vitality of man is at its lowest. It is the hour at which all troops in the forward areas 'stand to arms'.

A giant frame carrying a sack on his broad shoulders towered above me for a moment, then dropped into the trench. It was Sergt. Cooper. He had been searching for us throughout the night.

Another early arrival was Clayton. At 11 p.m. the previous night he had sallied forth to visit the Companies. Soon after he left, a thick blanket of fog blotted out every feature of the battlefield. He had contrived to leave his compass behind in the dug-out. He wandered throughout the night, his only guide being the bursting of shells. This was of little help as these were being fired from three points of the compass.

For some time he tried to identify his position from the shoulder-badges of the dead: but this did not prove an infallible guide as some of the supporting Companies in the attack had not kept to the exact battalion limits.

At last, after he and his runner had wandered all night without meeting a living soul, he spotted in the half light a man of the Sherwoods sitting on a bank against a tree, holding the leading-rein of a dead pack-mule. He pressed forward only to find that the Sherwood was dead, killed by the concussion of the shell that had killed the mule.

The presence of the Sherwood was, however, a clue that Clayton was in the vicinity of Kitchener's Wood, and shortly afterwards he slithered into H.Q. vowing that never again would he go out without a compass.

Everybody, except the signaller on duty at the telephone and the orderly acting as sentry, set to work to repair the damage done to the trench by the night's bombardment. The growing light revealed a heap of earth, wooden posts, smashed anti-tank gun shell-boxes and broken wattle-hurdles, together with mud and puddles of water. The anti-tank gun on the roof of the shelter was intact. Whilst I was trying to swing it round on its revolving base, the first shell of the day burst overhead and I fell into the trench. On rising I saw that a piece of metal had cut a hole in my leg about two inches long and an inch deep. The doctor was binding up my wound when a voice said, 'Your breakfast, sir'. By my side, with a fizzling plate of eggs and bacon in one hand and a steaming cup of tea in the other, stood the never-failing Cooper.

Chapter XVIII

CORPS HEADQUARTERS

6 *August* 1917

E. R.

URING the following night we came out of the line and moved into a camp near Vlamertinghe.

There was always much for the officer to do after five days under fire. Care and comfort of the men was the first thing to be thought of. Much of this duty was taken from my shoulders by that worthy quartermaster, Pooley, ably backed by Platt-Higgins, the best of transport officers. Pooley had hoarded quantities of food and produced all available clean underclothing. The sun shone on a peaceful scene of men cleaning themselves, their rifles, and their equipment. I limped through the groups of tired, contented men, happy in the knowledge that we were to entrain that night for some distant rest-camp. Where it was I did not care. There is something intensely comforting in the friendly glance of a soldier. I felt as if I would like to stop and talk to every man, to tell him how proud I was to be permitted to be his associate, and to thank him. In all probability I should have made a fool of myself, so I went to my tent. I had work to do.

In the Great War a man's life was short. No one could foresee the happenings of the morrow. With this knowledge I set myself the pleasant task of making out a list of recommendations for 'immediate awards' for distinguished conduct during the five days that had passed. Looking up from my bed, on which I was resting my injured leg, I saw the neatly-clad figure of a junior Staff officer. At that period of the war nearly all Staff officers wore a decoration of some sort. This one bore no such distinction.

He said, 'Good morning, sir. The Corps Commander's compliments and he wishes to see you at once at Corps H.Q.'

That meant one of three things—that you were to be 'sacked', complimented, or have your brains picked.

'Which is it?' I asked.

He laughed and answered, 'I don't know, sir, but the Chief said you were not to delay'.

Fifteen minutes later, heedless of the jolting of a comfortable motor-car as it bumped its way along the *pavé* road, I was sound asleep.

The car stopped. I woke up. An officer stood at the now open door.

'Will you come with me, sir?' Then, as we arrived at one of the huts, he added, 'There is a hot bath ready for you. After which, the Corps Commander wishes you to go to sleep in that bed. You will be called when you are required. He wants to consult you on some tactical matters. I'll leave you now'. He turned, stepped out of the hut, and closed the door.

A steaming bath was on the clean canvas-covered floor, with a large bath-towel on a chair beside it. On the spotless sheeted bed lay a suit of pyjamas. The delight of that bath is still very fresh in my memory. I do not know what time it was. I remember the soothing feeling of that comfortable bed and then—oblivion.

Somebody was speaking to me. 'Tea will be ready in a quarter-of-an-hour, sir. Your clothes are ready for you on the chair.' An orderly stood by my bed.

Clean and rested in body, and refreshed in mind, I appeared before that much discussed soldier, Ivor Maxse. He was one of those men you definitely disliked, or liked. If you did your work well, Maxse liked you, and stood by you through thick and thin. He knew his work and yours. Behind the character of a hard taskmaster lay a deep admiration for the fighting soldier. He looked upon the Staffs of Higher Commands as the machinery which must devote its whole energy towards assisting the smaller units. He judged a commanding officer by the standard of well-being and efficiency of the privates serving under him. Few officers liked him. Some succeeded in bluffing him, but much that is good in the methods of military education in the Army is due to his energy and ability. He had sent for me in order that he might pick my brains (such as they were) concerning the next tactical move. As was his wont, he went straight to the point.

'I have brought you here to tell me, and three Divisional Commanders, how we are to take the Green Line. You have had an opportunity (denied to us) of seeing the ground, at close quarters, over which we must advance.'

He handed me a map, and added, 'We will meet you here in half-an-hour'.

I give this as an illustration of how some of our generals recognized the value of first-hand information from the man in the front row. It is not a sign of weakness for those in high places to use the knowledge possessed by their subordinates. It is only a great mind that will condescend to search for learning in the brains of the lowly: a weak intellect would fear exposure.

The junior ranks of the Army seldom saw the Generals or Staff, and, knowing nothing of the duties performed by the Higher Command, abused it when things went wrong, and seldom allowed its existence to enter into their thoughts when things went right. I do not blame our fighting men for that: the uninitiated are always the most critical. Every general in the British army realized that ultimate success depended on the maintenance of a high standard of morale in the forefront of the battle. To effect this he had the assistance of an improvised and partially trained staff. Maxse overcame some of his difficulties by the establishment of schools and training camps near Corps H.Q., where he could come in closer contact with the junior ranks of the Army.

I have but one great criticism of our generals. They allowed the Staff to receive more decorations (in proportion to its strength) than the fighting branches of our troops. After a heavy leakage at Army and Corps H.Q., a very few foreign decorations filtered through to Divisions. By the time this process of elimination had had its way, the fighting man, like Mother Hubbard's poor dog, had none. The Military Cross was introduced for junior officers or warrant officers as a reward for conspicuous bravery, yet a cook at Rouen got it, and nine-tenths of the A.D.C.'s wore the ribbon. Commanders in the fighting units had to spin amazing yarns before awards reached their gallant officers or men. Maxse held strong views on this point. When I dined with him after my meeting with the three Divisional Commanders, he remarked that my men had done splendidly at St Julien. 'You must send in a long list of recommendations for awards', he said. Then, pointing to his two A.D.C.'s, he added, 'Those fellows would like some decorations, but I tell them that comfortable beds and good food are sufficient rewards for A.D.C.'s. If they want more, they can go and fight for them'.

In consequence of the wholesale 'dumping' of decorations on the Staff, a breast-full of ribbons cuts no ice with the ex-service man. To him it is merely an indication that the wearer spent more of his time out of the line than in it. In the army which came from the British Isles there are two decorations that carry weight—a 'bar', and, thank God, the V.C.

Chapter XIX

TOWER HAMLETS

August and September 1917

E. R.

DRAFTS of officers and men came to fill up the depleted ranks of the Cambridgeshires.

Ten days' rest in comparatively comfortable billets had restored our strength. It was a fine Battalion that took over the line east of Hill 60. There were no trenches here, only a maze of shell-holes converted into little forts. Each of these miniature strongholds gave inadequate cover to a corporal and five men. The garrison crouched on the ground by day, for it was a suicidal act to show your head. As dusk was changing into night the relieving sections crept out for their twenty-four hours of duty. It was during one of these reliefs that we found clear proof of the shortage of food in Germany.

From the cover of a shelter, dug out of the face of the hill, the leader of the outgoing section kept his eyes fixed on the nearest end of the strand of wire that was to guide him to his position. The mist was slowly thickening. Soon it would be dense enough to prevent the Boche from seeing him and his men as they moved forward to the end of the wire.

'Go out, and good luck to you', whispered the platoon commander.

The little force moved out in Indian file, carrying their rifles, bombs, and rations for twenty-four hours. Like ghosts they gradually faded away into the grey-black damp mist, and all was again still.

Muffled sounds of a struggle came to the ears of the platoon commander, then silence. The men at the shelter could not fire for fear of hitting their comrades. The situation must be left in the hands of those who were out there in the mist.

A quarter of an hour passed. Men were approaching along the strand of wire. Surely they were our men, for they were in Indian file.

'Beg pardon, sir, there are eight of them', whispered the platoon sergeant. 'There ought to be six. Shall we shoot?'

The word was passed down the line, 'Bayonets only'. The dim outline of the approaching figures grew more distinct. From the night came the word 'Ely'. It was the password.

'Just as well we didn't shoot' muttered someone as our men and two prisoners reached the shelter.

Two German orderlies, carrying the outgoing mail from the front line, had lost their way in the dark and instead of walking eastward had gone westward and run into our garrisoned shell-hole. Nearly all the letters contained messages of condolence with the civil population of the Fatherland on its lack of proper nourishment. Many of the Boche soldiers were sending home slices of bread, biscuits, tinned-meat and cigars. Our naval blockade was, evidently, more successful than the average soldier realized. We took care that our men understood its importance.

The great battle which had begun on 31 July continued to rage along the whole front of the Ypres Salient. Fresh Divisions went 'over the top', fell back to rest, received drafts of recruits or patched-up old soldiers, returned to the line, and then they went 'over the top' again. The Cambridge-shires' turn to attack came on 26 September.

Before Europe went mad, a traveller, wending his way from Ypres to Gheluvelt, would pass through the sylvan lands bordering the banks of the Bassevillebeek. From the high ground, a thousand yards north-west of Gheluvelt, he would drop down to the valley, cross the stream, and climb the gentle gradient to the village. On the morning of 22 September, 1917, when young Quin, Nightingale and I looked across that valley, all its beauty had gone. The cultivated fields between the woodlands had given place to land bereft of vegetation. As far as the eye could see the ground looked as if a hundred thousand primeval monsters had burrowed in it, thrown it about, trampled on it, killed it, and, having satisfied their lust for destruction, left it. A few poor shell-stunted trees spread their maimed limbs as if appealing to Heaven for mercy. Below us a boggy swamp, devoid of any indication of human, animal or vegetable life, showed the course of the Bassevillebeek.

A few days before, the 41st Division had attacked Tower Hamlets Ridge which lay on the other side of the valley. It had succeeded in crossing the stream, but had been held up by the enemy fire from the strong network of trenches and concrete 'pill-boxes' lining the ridge between it and Ghelu-velt. The survivors of the attacking units were somewhere down there in the mud. It was our duty to relieve them.

We crawled forward to where the guides, who were to lead us to Battalion H.Q., were hidden in a hole. One of these weary and nerve-racked men indicated the place we wished to reach. It lay two hundred yards to our left front. We could see the top of its concrete roof. The intervening ground was level and, except for shell-holes, devoid of cover. Looking over the lip of our hole I saw the German trenches six hundred yards away, and, on the crest of the ridge immediately behind them, the white southern wall of a large concrete block-house gleaming in the sunlight. This fort was to be the left of the Cambridgeshires' objective. On the direct line between my position and the Battalion H.Q. the bodies of four dead soldiers lay at intervals along the track made by the frequent passage of runners. Our way to H.Q. was by that track.

'When were those men killed?' I asked the guides.

'They're runners, sir; there are more over the hill; the last one was killed two hours ago."

Another guide interrupted, 'He means half-an-hour ago'.

'Well, it doesn't matter', said the first guide; 'I've lost time.' Then he moaned, 'What does time matter in this bloody war?'

Nightingale spat on the ground. We sat in silence for quite a minute.

'My map shows an old trench a hundred yards to our left. It leads to your Battalion. Haven't you tried that way?' I asked.

'This is the way we were told to use, sir. Across the flat where those chaps are lyin'. We've been here two days an' haven't found no trench.'

That was not an uncommon thing to happen in those days. Shells had a way of obliterating trenches. There was nothing else for it but to go the way the runners had taken, for our guides would know no other way. I decided to leave Nightingale in the hole. He would come to our assistance if we were wounded. I asked for a volunteer from the guides to show us the best route to take, for the concrete pill-box was some distance over the lip of the hill. Poor fellows, not one of them wanted to go. I explained that I must consult with their C.O. and make arrangements for the relief of their Battalion. They begged me to wait until it was dark. The snipers had shot half the runners already. If three of us went we should only make a better target. I assured them that I was the last man to take any unnecessary risk and that it was absolutely imperative that we should go.

'Come on, sir. We'll go alone', said Quin. 'It'll be a fine sprint.'

'I'm thinkin', sir, I'd better come wid yer. Yer see, wot wiv one thing an' another, them snypers carn't shoot the lot of us, if we deploys like. They'd be arguefyin' as to which of their blokes wus to shoot which of us blokes. Meanwhile, like, we'd get there—leastways—perhaps.' Thus spoke Nightingale.

The idea was quite sound, but there would have been little

difference between three men and four men crossing that open stretch. I felt that I must go now or I should never go. I was becoming afraid. I ordered Nightingale to stay where he was. He sat down on the ground and drew a packet of cigarettes from his pocket.

'Don't smoke, you fool. They'll see the smoke rising and know we're here', I growled at him. He put the cigarette behind his ear.

One of the guides said he would come. I crawled to the left along a length of battered trench with the guide behind me and Quin bringing up the rear. When we had gone about fifty yards I looked backwards. Nightingale was sending columns of smoke from his cigarette into the still air. He had converted himself into a veritable chimney. He knew the Boche would see the smoke—and, perhaps, not see us when we ran. We ran. A hundred yards had been covered before the crack of passing bullets told us we had been seen. Over went my guide into a shell-hole. In battle, when one man throws himself to the ground, the disease is catching. I tumbled into the next shell-hole. Quin went down into another twenty yards to my right.

'Are you hurt?' I called to the guide. I could not see him but his voice came back to me.

'No, sir. Oh God! I cannot go on, I cannot go on.'

A bullet struck my steel helmet with a metallic smack and knocked it sideways. My head was buzzing when I heard Quin shout, 'Well done the tin hat, sir! Are you all right?'

I looked to the left. Forty yards away I saw a line of up-turned earth. It was the trench I had asked the guides about.

I called to Quin, 'I'm going to run for it to that trench on the left. If I get there, follow me'.

A few seconds later I tumbled on top of a wounded Boche lying at the bottom of quite a good trench. He immediately grasped a rifle but I twisted it out of his hand and hit him on the head. I think he must have been a messenger who had lost his way during the previous night, been wounded, and had crept into the trench. To the accompaniment of the 'fut' of three or four bullets I saw Quin jump into the trench twenty yards ahead. I ran on and joined him.

We passed a number of dead and wounded and emerged at the western end of the pill-box which Sceales (of the Black Watch) and I were to make our 'home' during the battle of 26 September.

It was the enemy machine-gun crews firing from this pill-box which had broken up the advance of the 41st Division on 20 September, and there was abundant evidence of the casualties inflicted all round. The dead were lying in little twisted heaps within a large radius, and their number had been added to by the runners and linesmen whose duty it was to cross this open space.

I had no time for reflection; we were to take over the front line that night. This so-called line was clearly visible from the pill-box; in the valley beneath it consisted of a chain of posts, in reality half-flooded shell-holes, held by two or three men with gaps of about thirty-five yards between each post. It was an impossible position in the valley, but on the left our line had swung further forward, and the troops there were fortunate to have reached the drier ground on the slopes of Tower Hamlets Ridge. It was evident that there would be no access to the front line by day, and a further advance to secure the Tower Hamlets Ridge was clearly indicated.

An hour later we retraced our steps past the place where I had left the wounded Boche. He had disappeared. He had supplied one of the mysteries which, in those days, were the wonder of the moment and were dismissed as being too trivial to be of account. Continuing along the trench we came out within a hundred yards of the hole in which we had left Nightingale.

That night the Cambridgeshires relieved the remains of the five disorganized and weary units of the 41st Division, who were holding the line. I spent the day reconnoitring and making plans; the Brigade had informed me that we should be relieved by the Hertfordshires the next night to prepare for an attack on Tower Hamlets Ridge.

Towards evening hostile shelling increased, and at dusk a lance-corporal of 'D' Company, which was holding the high ground on the left, made his way to H.Q. and reported that all his Company officers were casualties. Clayton went up to pull the Company together and conducted the relief. Throughout the night the conduct of this courageous officer was beyond all praise. By the time the relief was completed it was inky darkness, and the Bassevillebeek was not a pleasant place to wander about at any time, especially as we had no exact knowledge of the nearest German posts: in fact, on the way up Clayton had already made the acquaintance of one German post, which he had inadvertently approached through a gap in our line. There were no marked tracks and no landmarks were visible, and before long he realized that losing one's way with a Company within a hundred yards of German posts is rather a trying business. Fortunately he had profited by his experience at Kitchener's Wood and had his compass handy, and he was delighted to find that after an hour's progress through swamps and flooded shell-holes he brought the Company to within fifty yards of Battalion H.Q.

We had a long track back to Ridge Wood, which we reached near the hours of morning. Preparations were made and orders for the attack were issued; and on the evening of 25 September the Cambridgeshires moved into position to take over the line from the Hertfordshires, in readiness for the attack next morning.

At dusk Clayton crossed the Bassevillebeek and laid lines of white tape to guide the Cambridgeshires in their assembly for the attack. Much of our success on the 26th was due to that gallant officer's work.

The attack was carried out with our friends the Black

Watch on our right and the 116th Brigade on our left. In view of communication difficulties I formed a joint Battalion H.Q. at the pill-box with Sceales of the Black Watch. I had Baynes Smith with me as adjutant, and Clayton in the guise of signalling officer ran communications for both the Black Watch and ourselves.

The pill-box as H.Q. had both advantages and disadvantages. The former included the important one of affording us a clear view of the ground over which both the Black Watch and the Cambridgeshires had to attack. Its chief disadvantage was that it was in full view of the enemy, and throughout the period of our occupation was the target of both machine-gun and shell-fire. On two occasions its top received a direct hit, deafening us and extinguishing every candle, and on the second occasion the water on the floor suddenly rose six inches. The joint communication section suffered severely; our lines were continually cut, and they had to resort to lamp-communication with advanced Brigade H.Q. Clayton was getting worried. Six of our best signallers and runners had been killed during the morning; they included men who had given devoted service both at the Schwaben and St Julien. Suddenly there was a shriek of a 5·9 followed by a deafening burst, and a Black Watch signaller with torn kilt hurled himself into the dug-out crying, 'They're a' deid! They're a' deid!'

Clayton grabbed his tin-hat and demanded to know who had been hit.

'They pigeons', replied the shaken signaller. The Boche observers must have wondered what they had hit. A 5·9 shell had scored a direct hit on three crates of carrier-pigeons, and the air for about fifty yards around was full of floating feathers.

The barrage had opened at 5.50 a.m. when 'C', 'D' and 'A' Companies advanced to the attack. The state of the ground had made it very difficult for 'C' and 'D' Companies to keep up to the barrage, and by the time these Companies had cleared the western face of Joist Redoubt 'A' Company under Ford was engaged in a bitter fight for the eastern face of the redoubt. Unfortunately, a gap of three hundred yards had developed between Ford's Company and the Sussex on our left. Machine-gun fire from the left took heavy toll; Ford, Graham and Chaplin (C. W.)* all fell, with many men, and 'A' Company was brought to a standstill in a line of shell-hole posts west of Tower Trench.

Fortunately Walker, on his own initiative, took 'B' Company forward to reinforce 'C' and 'D' at the critical moment, and the growing daylight and clearing of the smoke enabled me to size up the situation.

We had taken all our objectives except the big pill-box on the left of our front. Several attempts were made to oust the garrison. Once, a few men reached it. They got inside but never came out. During the afternoon our 6-inch guns fired on it. Two shells struck the roof. When the smoke had cleared away two large white patches of broken concrete showed where the shells had landed. Walker said he would try to take it during the night.

It was about 1 a.m. on the 28th when a runner from 'B' Company brought the news that Walker's men had crept up to the pill-box and had found that its only occupants were dead men. They must have been killed by concussion when the big shells burst on the roof.

I informed the Brigade by telephone. A few minutes later the Corps commander sent congratulations, and told me that the pill-box had been named 'Riddell's Castle', and the maps altered accordingly.

The dear old gentleman whose battalion was relieving the Cambridgeshires declined to occupy Riddell's Castle because he had not been ordered to do so in his original instructions.

---

* His elder brother Hugh, a pre-war officer and a good soldier, had unfortunately succumbed to wounds four months earlier.

All my persuasive powers failed to alter his insane decision. I tried to ring up Brigade but the wires had been cut. Two hours later I told the Brigadier what had happened. Of course there was 'the devil to pay' about it.

Before dawn the Boche reoccupied Riddell's Castle and held it (I believe) up to the last ten weeks of the war. It was another proof of the folly of going to war with officers who had not been trained in the profession of arms.

When relief was at last carried out the tired Battalion assembled at St Eloi, where buses were waiting to take us back to rest at Westoutre.

I was awakened next morning by Bellingham who, thrusting his head into my tent, said, 'Good morning, General. I've brought you a brass hat and red tabs. You're to leave us to command a brigade. Congratulations'.

I spent the morning in what was to me a labour of love—compiling a long list of officers, non-commissioned officers and men whose conduct during the Tower Hamlets battle called for special mention. I longed to add more and still more names to the roll before me, so that—if I had my way—every member of the Battalion might have the right to wear one of those ribbons which are the outward signs of a nation's gratitude, and mean so much to the soldier, but alas, nowadays, so little to the generation that knows not, or has forgotten, their significance.

After 'dinners' I went to a neighbouring field to say 'Good-bye' to the Battalion. I am sure I made a bad speech, but that did not matter, the officers and men understood. As I turned to leave them, with their cheers ringing in my ears, pride in my heart, and a lump in my throat, the past fifteen months raced before my eyes like a speeded-up film. What memories! What men!

Thus the curtain fell on my last act as the commanding officer of the 1/1st Cambridgeshire Regiment.

.   .   .   .

It was with mingled feelings of pride and fear that I accepted the task of chronicling the actions of the regiment during the time I was privileged to serve with it: pride in the knowledge that I had been selected for this work, and fear—amounting to despair—that I should fail to do justice to the glorious men who had been my companions and ever ready helpmates, come victory or defeat. Is it to be wondered that fear beset me when I knew that no words penned by man could express adequately the admiration I shall always feel for the martial ardour, efficiency, and—perhaps to me, best of all—the friendship of a great battalion?

I have switched off the light; and as I sit in my study gazing into the flames of the fire, the thought comes to me that a rich man without friends is a poor man always, and a poor man with friends is a rich man for ever.

Chapter XX

THE AFTERMATH OF PASSCHENDAELE

1 October—31 December 1917

M. C. C.

RIDDELL'S departure to take up command of a Brigade, though not unexpected, came somewhat as a shock to us. A born leader, fearless to an uncanny extent, he left us at the time when we could ill afford the loss of such an outstanding personality.

The Battalion had already endured ten months' duty in the Salient—months of strain culminating in the great attack. The early promise of this battle had now dwindled to a series of attacks delivered through a sea of mud towards the Passchendaele Ridge.

We were silent on the subject, but in our hearts we began to debate whether the Higher Command who ordered the attacks fully realized the conditions under which the troops lived, fought—and died.

Saint's return to assume command in Riddell's place was a happy coincidence. He would have been the first to admit that he had missed much valuable experience during the past few months, but he had a strong personality, tactical skill to a marked degree, and was fresh and not clogged mentally by the 'sea of mud' in which those of us who had survived had been wallowing for so long.

He took over a battalion well pleased with the result of its own efforts, but worn out by fighting and continuous hardships in the shell-swept swamps of the Ypres Salient.

Little breathing-space was allowed; within three days we were moved to a so-called camp at Kruisstraat. We were employed both by day and night in endeavouring to improve the tracks and communications in the forward area, to help the Anzac Corps in their successive attacks on Passchendaele. Rain fell daily; what little rest was allowed was spent at Kruisstraat, the only cover from the rain being bivouacs made by the men's waterproof-sheets. Their clothes were never really dry, and casualties occurred on most days. The enemy did its best to keep us miserable; the camp was shelled by long-range guns and bombed at night. My efforts to cheer things up by starting a fish-and-chip shop were sadly hampered by the necessity of dousing the fire three and four times a night because of enemy planes.

Things improved during the latter half of the month. We moved into better quarters at Vierstraat, and training took the place of the interminable working-parties. The end of the month saw the Cambridgeshires again in the pestilential Tower Hamlets sector; to quote the Official Diary, 'The relief was carried out successfully on the night of October 31st with only ten casualties'.

The whole of November was spent in holding the flooded line of shell-holes between Tor Top and Polderhoek on either side of the Menin Road, with brief intervals in support at Ridge Wood. But although there was no fighting the shelling never ceased, and during the month Aston and 19 other ranks were killed and 135 wounded. Those who remember the appalling conditions in that sector will realize what this meant to the stretcher-bearers, who had to pick their way round flooded shell-holes back to the dressing-station. Sometimes it took three hours to get a bad stretcher-case down, and the stretcher-bearers were almost invariably wet to the waist before they completed the journey.

I was away on leave during November; but in spite of the awful conditions in which the Cambridgeshires were placed, some kindly souls had gone round collecting to send me a wedding present and a telegram.

When I rejoined at St Jean, daily work-parties were being

supplied for the forward area. Casualties, though few, were a daily occurrence, the weather was frosty, and our tents were bombed nightly. I took up a party of officers to reconnoitre the line to Passchendaele with a view to taking over the front. On the way up I spotted Riddell peering through his glasses at the Ridge; the Staff officer to whom he was talking was a cousin of mine. Riddell's Brigade had taken part in two attacks since he had assumed command. None of us commented on the scene of desolation. Not a tree or a pre-war building was to be seen; nothing but miles of flooded shell-holes, and the inevitable pill-boxes; a few shattered tanks and guns; dead horses and mules by the dozen. Within a hundred yards' radius of the pill-boxes the shell-holes were tenanted by still forms, British and German, which were gradually being swallowed up by the mud. A false step on the edge of a shell-hole might at any time cause nameless horrors to reappear for an instant, before they were sucked down once again in the Flanders slime.

I had several new subalterns with me. It was not a good place for breaking-in purposes, and I was thankful on my return to St Jean to learn that the relief had been cancelled, and shortly afterwards we moved by stages back to Henneveux, near Boulogne.

It was thirteen months since the Cambridgeshires had moved into the Ypres Salient, and now at last we were out of it and the range of its guns, and I devoutly hoped that we might never see Ypres again.

Saint had gone on leave, and my first job was to get the Cambridgeshires cleaned up both in a physical and a military sense. Baths, clean clothing, musketry, bombing and machine-gunning were succeeded by Company training. We scoured the country-side for turkeys and geese, and the cooks accumulated a store of plum-puddings. The officers carved for the Company Christmas dinner, and we all dined together at the Château in the evening. As the gathering broke up heavy snow was falling, and I ordered a Battalion snow-fight for Boxing Day, which proved almost as hazardous as Ypres.

The depth of snow increased daily, and the hard frost made the steep road impossible for transport. When on 29 December we marched to Lottinghem the motor lorries carrying our stores were all snowed up, and we had to return in fatigue dress the next day and man-handle the blankets, etc. to Lottinghem.

Lenninghem was our destination on 31 December; once again our transport had fearful trouble with the frozen roads. Orders had been issued for us to entrain at Wizernes at 6 a.m. on New Year's Day; that meant a ten-mile march and a start at 1 a.m. I turned in early, my thoughts full of the happenings of 1917—those early months holding the line—training for the attack—our high hopes—officers and men, the salt of the earth, who had found their resting-place in the Salient.

Chapter XXI

THE GATHERING STORM

1 *January—March* 1918

M. C. C.

OUR few days out of the line did us a world of good. As we fell in, shortly after midnight, we cheerfully wished one another a Happy New Year, regardless of the fact that we were bound once again for the Salient. I marched at the head of the leading Company. We soon found it impossible to march on the glass-like surface of the frozen road, and made our way through the darkness in file on either side of the road. My brother, who had gone up as Advance Officer, met our train at St Jean, and we were housed in the old Canal Bank dug-outs.

It was bitterly cold. In the afternoon Padre Knyvett and I went for a walk to get warm, and returned in triumph, bearing three small pieces of coal found on the roadside. I doubt whether there was one piece of loose wood to be salvaged within a three miles' radius of Ypres. Few had returned, and Eric Wood was on the way out. The Canal Bank was now a rest area, but large working-parties went forward daily. Riddell sent a note asking me to go to tea; the Corps Command had asked him to suggest a new Commandant of the Corps Infantry School, and with Saint, Few and Wood on the Battalion strength, I need have no qualms about taking the job, especially as it meant promotion. I had, however, already been nominated for the S.O.S. at Aldershot, for which I left the next day.

The Cambridgeshires had only one spell in the front line near Poelcappelle, and on 21 January marched back to Houtekerque. The rumour that they were to leave the Salient, after duty there since 1916, was confirmed. The rolling plains of the Somme country were a pleasant change, and on the last day of the month the Cambridgeshires relieved the South African Brigade in the line at Gouzeaucourt.

Life was comparatively pleasant after Ypres, though casualties were frequent both in and behind the line. A gas shell dropped in the midst of a working-party with fatal results to twelve men; raids to obtain information brought retaliation on our line in the form of heavy shelling. The effects of Ypres, however, were gradually wearing off, but the seriousness of the reinforcement problem was grasped when orders arrived in February for the disbandment of one battalion in each infantry brigade. Henceforth infantry brigades had three instead of four battalions, and our neighbours the Hertfordshires were moved to the 116th Brigade, leaving the Cheshires and the Black Watch with ourselves in the 118th Brigade.

The increase in the number of German Divisions on the Western Front, and the ominous activity behind the German lines, all pointed to an early offensive. As the days passed by the tension increased. Parties out of the line were employed in digging rear lines of defence or training in open warfare or counter-attack.

Troops in the lines watched and waited; the scenes portrayed in *Journey's End* were typical of the atmosphere which was prevailing in the front line in the early days of March 1918. Outgoing troops cheerfully expressed the hope that the storm would break before they returned to the front posts.

We who were on duty in England shared the tension. We knew the storm was gathering: when would it break, and on which part of the line?

Chapter XXII

THE DELUGE

21–30 *March* 1918

M. C. C.

THE morning of 21 March, 1918, found the Cambridgeshires at Moislains, some eight miles behind the lines, the whole of the 39th Division being in the 5th Army Reserve. The enemy bombardment all along the line was the signal for stand-to. Officers and men, shivering in the chilly mist, all thought of the front-line posts; the barrage continued, the mist thickened, the defensive posts would be blinded and their machine-guns useless. The army midday report gave the extent of the front line attacked. As was expected the enemy had overrun our front posts in many places, but the extent of the penetration was not known.

At 5 p.m. orders were received to move forward to Longavesnes to help in the construction of a switch line from Tincourt Wood to Saulcourt. The Cambridgeshires arrived as dark was falling. 'An attack expected during the next morning from the direction of Ronssoy rendered the construction of this work a matter of urgency, the 66th Division on our right flank being withdrawn to the Green Line.' The digging of this switch line was commenced at 10 p.m.; the ground was hard, but by the morning a good line with support-trenches had been dug and manned.

As dawn broke numbers of stragglers from the 16th Division made their way back to our line. A body of twenty-four enemy planes crossed westward; one was brought down by our fire; parties of enemy were fired upon as they made their way forward through the mist. By midday we were the front line as far as active resistance was concerned. The position was a good one, with a reasonable field of fire, as the enemy soon discovered. At 5.30 p.m. Saint received a disquieting order: the 117th Brigade on the left was being forced to withdraw and we were to conform immediately. As we left the shelter of our trenches the enemy fire quickened; Beale was killed, but in spite of the closeness of the enemy the withdrawal was made in good order.

It was a relief on reaching the so-called Green Line (six inches deep in places) to find the Black Watch and Cheshires holding it intact; and Saint was able to accommodate the Cambridgeshires partly in huts and partly in the open in support of the Green Line. But not for long; before daybreak 'D' and 'B' were sent up in close support ready for counter-attack.

At 6.30 a.m. very heavy artillery fire opened on the right, and when Bellingham arrived he reported that the 19th Corps was falling back and the Cambridgeshires and Sherwoods would fight a rear-guard action to cover the withdrawal of the Division. 'D' took up first position and were engaged almost immediately. They stayed the enemy advance, until Kemplen discovered parties of enemy working round to the rear of his left flank. As they withdrew, 'D' passed on both sides of Templeux, which was being heavily shelled. Kemplen was hit; his men put him on a stray horse to go to the rear, and then continued to withdraw. Almost immediately afterwards Clayton (F.), who had succeeded Kemplen, was hit. But 'D' were not leaving their officers behind. Clayton was put onto a hand-cart, and 'D' fought their way back until 'A', at the next position, took up the fight.

'A' and then 'C' took in turn the brunt of the enemy attack, but by midday the Cambridgeshires were able to withdraw through the 116th Brigade at Bussu. They had a short rest and then marched back to the Somme at Halle, where the 118th Brigade was forming a new defensive line in conjunction with the 66th Division on the right, and the 117th Brigade across the river on the left.

Saint reported that no event of any great importance on the Cambridgeshires' front took place on the 24th, 'but the enemy were advancing in strength north of the Somme all day and were engaged with Lewis-gun, rifle- and machine-gun fire. He implored the Brigade to get guns into action but nothing happened'—not knowing that the supporting Field Artillery Brigade had already lost 75 per cent. of its guns. The position was tantalizing—masses of men moving across the front, out of range of rifle-fire, and in the far distance, to Bouchavesnes, battalions and even brigades drawn up in close formation with masses of transport, and not a British gun firing upon these targets.

The night was quiet; no attack developed on the morning of the 25th on the Brigade front, but continuous firing was taking place on the right flank towards Éterpigny. As Saint returned from the Companies to Battalion H.Q. at noon, he was met by Wood with the news that the enemy had crossed the Somme Canal away to the right flank at Éterpigny; furthermore they had already taken La Maisonnette Ridge immediately on our right. Saint moved Battalion H.Q. up to the centre of our line, and sent two platoons of 'A' to cover our flank and the remainder to reinforce 'C' in Biaches.

Towards the evening the gravity of the situation increased each minute. The 66th Division on our right had withdrawn, and our Companies in Biaches were being attacked in strength by enemy who had crossed the Canal from the south. They were holding these attacks, but were in grave danger of being cut off. 'B' had met with disaster; they had been attacked from both flanks, and what men were left of that Company were putting up their last fight, surrounded on all sides. Regimental Sergt.-Major Matthews, who had taken up a party of 'details' to the assistance of 'B', had fallen to a machine-gun burst and was only got away through the courage of Bowers, his batman.

Saint reported the situation to Brigade, and at 10 p.m.

Major Saint inspecting sentry posts in the trenches, 1915

orders were received to withdraw to Herbécourt, some three miles in rear. This hazardous operation was carried out with great skill under Saint's and Wood's supervision. 'A' provided the rear-guard, and by 4.30 a.m. on the 26th the Cambridgeshires were occupying a new line in front of Herbécourt, with the Cheshires on the right and the 117th Brigade prolonging the line northwards to the Somme.

Worse was to follow. At 7.15 a.m. the line to the right gave way and the Cheshires were involved. Leaving Wood to look after the Cambridgeshires, Saint tore across to the Cheshires, who were now minus Battalion H.Q., and succeeded in reorganizing them on a line slightly in rear of their original position. He returned at 9 a.m., just as Wood came in from the left with the news that the 117th on our left had been forced to give ground to repeated attacks. Saint's report gives the bald statement that 'through the whole of the day the Battalion fought rear-guard actions until they finally arrived at the next selected position on the line Vauvillers–Proyart'. Yet 26 March, 1918, was one of the most trying days experienced by the Cambridgeshires during the whole campaign. It would only be fair to pay tribute to the skill and daring of the enemy for the determined manner in which they pressed the series of attacks; but this was not a simple rear-guard action, as at no time in the day were flanks ever secure. Even woods and copses which seemed to offer a rallying-point for reorganizing the tired men were found, on approaching, to be in enemy hands. The distance between the two positions, a matter of seven miles, was doubled by the détours and distractions that occurred during the day. Parties under those stubborn fighters, Lacey and Wright, became detached, and had perforce to fight for three days alongside other units until they were able to rejoin.

It was a Lewis-gunners' day; 'artists' like Lance-corporal Muffett and Private Bonnett took up positions with a store of drums and waited for the oncoming hordes. They never had

to wait long; their stay was limited by the number of drums
their overheated guns could fire. Both these performers
staggered back after dark carrying their guns, but many
nameless Lewis-gun crews were heard firing long after the
enemy waves had surged past them. A crescendo of fire, or
a gun obviously beginning to misfire through overheating—
then silence.

Yet throughout the day Saint and Wood, working together, kept the Battalion in existence as a fighting unit.
Towards evening, more dead than alive, they marshalled the
attenuated Companies and platoons into the selected position.
By this time the Black Watch and the Cambridgeshire
platoons were intermingled and a joint H.Q. was formed.

But before nightfall yet another effort was required of the
weary officers and men. It was found that the enemy were
already endangering the line in front of Framerville, and a
counter-attack had to be carried out before the position was
reasonably secure.

The attack was successful, the enemy being driven back
two hundred yards into the village. A support line was
rapidly organized. Pooley arrived with rations and small
arms ammunition, but the exhausted N.C.O.'s and men
hardly waited to eat: they dropped asleep with mess-tins in
their hands.

There was no rest for the officers. Few had returned from
leave with Hollis, and had found the Battalion after fifteen
hours' tramping from Amiens. He records how at a conference that night officers fell asleep standing, whilst making
their reports.

At 6 a.m. on the 27th the enemy attacked along the whole
of the line but were beaten off. At 10.30 a.m. the Brigade on
the left commenced to withdraw. Saint called upon Clerk
of the Hertfordshires to move up and reoccupy the position,
which they did very quickly. The success of this operation
was, however, practically neutralized by the left Battalion of

the 118th Brigade withdrawing and leaving a gap north of the Amiens road; unfortunately this example was followed by the troops on the other side of the road. The Cambridge-shires and the Black Watch south of the road remained steady, and Saint, with the help of Major Marsden, R.E., reorganized the withdrawing troops and led them back into position.

These determined efforts proved of no avail in steadying the general position. The enemy had crossed the Somme in rear of the left flank, and this fresh threat necessitated the Cambridgeshires and the Black Watch covering the with-drawal to the Morcourt–Harbonnières line.

The enemy was conducting his operations with amazing tactical skill, but attacks on the new line were beaten off, and a counter-attack by the 8th and 50th Divisions further stiffened the resistance.

Fresh troubles arrived thick and fast. At 2.30 p.m. the 16th Division on the left gave way, withdrawing from the Morcourt Ridge. Wood doubted whether the enemy had occupied the Ridge, and as a result he and Saint went out to the flank to reconnoitre. They saw the 16th Rifle Brigade on the Ridge in rear and signalled to them to advance. The advance was successful and the Ridge was reoccupied.

There was a general sigh of relief; although enemy shelling was heavy, attacks had ceased and the immediate front was intact. The general position, however, was alarming. 'At 10 p.m. information was received that the enemy had cut our communications at Lamotte, and were now on three sides of us.'

Bellingham and Armytage (the latter was Brigadier of the 117th Brigade) held a joint conference with the C.O.'s of the two Brigades to decide upon a course of action. Few gives a graphic description of this meeting. 'The Germans had crossed the Somme three miles in rear; we were practic-ally surrounded. One young C.O., wearing a leopard skin over his tunic, reported only five men left in his battalion, and actually went to sleep whilst standing making his report. (This was becoming a common occurrence.) The majority of the survivors had reached the limit of endurance. The discussion was interrupted by the arrival of a German orderly with his officer's horse, enquiring whether he could be directed to his C.O.! We all thought it was a woman, and the escort were directed to take the prisoner outside to investigate—gently. We had guessed wrongly!

'Alternative schemes were discussed; we were cut off from direct communications with Divisional H.Q. Finally, two officers were sent off to try and make their way through, to report that, failing orders to the contrary, the two Brigades would endeavour to withdraw at 2 a.m. in a S.W. direction.'

Before this message reached its destination Divisional H.Q. received orders from the 19th Corps that the present line was to be held to the last. Lieut. Rorke, R.E., and a despatch-rider on motor cycles dashed through the enemy and delivered this message. As a result, at 2 a.m. the withdrawal was cancelled; the troops would hold on and wait for the promised counter-attack.

At 4 a.m. Corps phoned to the Divisional H.Q. that the counter-attack would not be forthcoming and that the two Brigades must be withdrawn at once. The two officers who had made the journey back from the Brigade were sent on the return journey in a car and somehow they got through. The only route for the two Brigades was southwards via Harbonnières to Caix, and then north-west to Ignaucourt—and it was already getting light! The 117th Brigade moved first, their withdrawal being covered by the 118th. 'Silent marching in earnest; a light rain was making the fields and pathways greasy; we had an awful job with the loaded stretchers.' (Cooper.)

By 7 a.m. it was fully daylight, and the enemy spotted what was happening and put down a heavy barrage, but there were few casualties. Bellingham and his Brigade Major were captured whilst supervising the right flank guard, and to add to troubles the enemy advanced into Harbonnières. The luck held, and eventually the remnants of the Battalion were met by General Feetham (G.O.C. 39th Division) at Cayeux.

'The men were exhausted from lack of sleep, want of food and water'; for the first time since Ypres 1915 rations had not got through. Pooley had started off early the previous evening with his limbers. He reached Lamotte, only to find it held by the enemy, but he managed to steal away without loss of men or vehicles. He tried détours, but all ways were blocked, and eventually he played fairy godmother to Carey's Force who were then without rations.

The two Brigades were rapidly reorganized into two Battalions, one under Few and the other under Clerk of the Hertfordshires, the whole under Saint as Brigadier. The G.O.C. ordered an advance to the Marcelcave–Wiencourt railway (N.E.); Few's Cambridgeshires and the Black Watch formed the advance-guard; these weary men extended and moved forward. They crossed the Luce, and then their advance was slowed down by machine-gun fire from Hill 90, north of Cayeux.

An opportune sunken road allowed the attacking troops to get wind whilst preparations were made for the assault of Hill 90. Cooper (complete with fixed bayonet, primus stove in sand-bag, and other culinary equipment) states that the attacking troops numbered about 150. 'Half the party were to attack on each side of the road. The adjutant of the Black Watch was in command of my party, and when he saw the men hesitate to leave the sunken road he sprang to the top and waved us on. The enemy opened fire, many Cambridgeshires falling, also the Black Watch officer. We worked forward by section rushes and drove the enemy back to a small copse, where they suddenly opened fire with more machine-guns. We were in the open lying flat, sweating profusely and

11-2

vainly trying to shovel up soil in front of us. I quite expected we should be annihilated, when suddenly a miracle took place. C.S.M. Betts rose to his feet with a blood-curdling yell and ran forward straight towards the machine-guns, which ceased as if by magic. We all followed, but Betts arrived first and chased about thirty of the enemy towards a dug-out. He laid out six with his bayonet before we arrived, and would have gone for the rest of them if Mr Driver had not arrived and ordered them to surrender. Betts had to comply with this order, and about twenty were made prisoners, Betts relieving the officers and N.C.O.'s of their field-glasses, which he festooned over his equipment.'

Meanwhile the forces, under Wood and Saville, attacking the other side of the road had taken their objectives, but it was evident that no further advance was possible. Although in touch with the 117th Brigade on the left, the position of the right was 'decidedly worrying us. The French on the right packed up and withdrew without warning us'. Saint scoured the countryside for troops; he found a party digging on the side of the Luce and sent them up to guard his right. He commandeered a party of 50th Division machine-gunners to guard the exit to Cayeux. In the meantime Few and Wood had their hands full; attacks at Cayeux and Hill 90 were beaten off, prisoners being captured in each case. During the evening it was learnt that there was no possibility of support troops being sent to help in holding the exposed position. To remain in it was to risk almost certain isolation, and at 10.30 p.m. both Brigades were withdrawn to a position in rear, which was being extemporized with the aid of Carey's Force.

The troops had to be reorganized once again, but it was trying work; they had reached the limit of endurance; they were almost too tired to eat the rations which Pooley had brought up. Saint went back for a few hours' rest at transport lines, absolutely whacked; he had started a week ago with an old pair of boots, now the soles were hanging loosely to the uppers. Few was comparatively fresh, having rejoined early on the 26th; Wood, 'who had earned a dozen D.S.O.'s' (he never received one), declared that a shave and a sleep were all that he required. Wood had been slightly wounded, but Saville, Driver and the others were unhurt.

Those who took part in the fighting on 28 March declared that it was the longest day they had ever experienced.

A few hours' rest—which seemed like minutes—and before daylight on 29 March Battalions and Companies were re-sorted and endeavours made to clear up the situation on the flanks. Marr arrived to take up duties as Brigade Major. 'Most of the day seemed to be spent in stopping men in groups marching west. All had the same tale, that a Staff officer had ordered it. Later, orders came through that any Staff officer ordering a withdrawal was to be shot at sight.'

The remnants of the Division were concentrated in support to Carey's Force. The day was comparatively peaceful. Wright and Lacey rejoined with remnants of platoons, 'after having fought with every Division in the 5th Army'. A con-ference was held to enable General Feetham to outline the general position. Soon after leaving the meeting he was fatally wounded; there was now only one General Officer left with the whole Division.

Early on the morning of 30 March successive enemy attacks had forced back the troops in front, until the Cam-bridgeshires, the Black Watch and the Hertfordshires were once again the front line. By 10 a.m. the 66th Division on the right had withdrawn, leaving that flank in the air. Once again a successful counter-attack was undertaken, but the line was found untenable, and orders were received to with-draw to the Hangard–Villers Bretonneux line. That evening the 39th Division was at last relieved by the 18th Division.

The pitiful remnants of what had been a strong Division were concentrated at Longeau. Roads were picketed; bodies of troops were sorted out into units and given a hot meal. The events of the last few days began to appear in proper focus in the dazed minds of officers and men: Riddell on a horse leading his Brigade in a charge; Bowes 'with a collection of clerks and what-nots digging like Hell'; Pooley's nightly (except on the 27th) appearance with rations and S.A.A.; the gallantry of the Battery Commander who worked the last gun with the help of his B.S.M. and then limbered up and got away when the enemy were only three hundred yards distant; Col. Tebbutt in a car sent out to locate H.Q.'s of Divisions, and his proud remark, 'I have never met a Cambridgeshire straggler minus rifle and full equipment'. But pervading all, the general feeling of complete mental and physical weariness.

Our losses during the eight days' fighting were 13 officers and 370 other ranks.

Chapter XXIII

THE LAST OF THE 39TH DIVISION

31 *March*—5 *May* 1918

M. C. C.

LUDENDORFF'S thrust towards Amiens had been
brought to a standstill, and the debris of the Division
that had borne the brunt of the fighting were withdrawn.

The Cambridgeshires moved back by easy stages to Eu
near Le Tréport. 'It seems like Paradise after the Somme,
especially when you have Philip Cutlack as Area Commandant to make things easier for you.' Drafts were beginning to
arrive. 'We were informed that we should have three weeks'
refitting and training.'

Ludendorff, however, had no intention of allowing the
B.E.F. to gain its second wind. Before the week was out he
had launched his new offensive in the north, and one of the
consequences was that the 39th Division found themselves
detraining near St Omer on 10 April. Within a few hours
came orders to reorganize as a composite Brigade of four
Battalions (the 39th Divisional Composite Brigade), and then
a hurried journey into the Salient near Hill 60. To give these
units time to shake down, the 2nd Army decided to employ
them to improve and man the second main line of defence
running at the foot of the Messines Ridge, and No. 4 Battalion
under Saint, which included the Cambridgeshires, the Black
Watch and the Cheshires, was allotted to the defences in and
around Voormezeele.

When I left Aldershot I was dubious as to my chance of

getting back to the Cambridgeshires. It was already well
supplied with S.O.S. officers, Saint, Few, and Wood having
passed through the school, and it was a relief when the
Division wired for me at the base. A journey quite out of the
ordinary—a large draft, many still in bandages, picked up
on the railway line at Calais; the stream of refugees fleeing
with their goods and chattels; our arrival at Hazebrouck, and
its deserted appearance; frantic stoking of the engine to get
the train back clear of the advancing enemy; and our return to Watten with an enemy squadron trying to drop bombs
on the train.

Here I found the spare transport of the Division; and
whilst sappers laboured preparing canal locks for demolition,
we endeavoured to teach musketry and fire-tactics to trans-
port-drivers and cooks. This was a hair-raising job; 'England's
last hope', as the force was irreverently called, had unortho-
dox views regarding the safety of fire-arms, and it was just
as well they did not go into action!

My stay at Watten was short; I was ordered to Voormezeele. Here I found Naden in command of No. 4 Battalion.
Saint had been sent down the line; he was far from well. Eric
Wood was Adjutant and Few commanded the Cambridgeshire Company.

Back at Brigade H.Q. Marr gave me a résumé of the
situation—a skeleton force holding the Messines Ridge might
be pushed off it any moment, preparations were being made
to evacuate the Ypres Salient (Shades of Passchendaele!),
and whilst every effort would be made to hold the Ridge, it
was quite possible that within a few days our main line of
resistance would be Kemmel–Voormezeele–Ypres. 'We have
no reserves, everything is in the shop window, and if the line
goes so do the Channel ports.'

The Brigade sector was held by three composite Battalions,
with the fourth in support. Voormezeele, the centre sector,
was regarded as a fortified village. On the right we joined

up with No. 1 Battalion in front of Scottish Wood, and up by St Eloi we joined hands with No. 2 Battalion, which held the Spoil Bank sector.

I spent the three following days in becoming acquainted with the defence scheme and counter-attack routes. Our H.Q., in an old dressing-station at the cross-roads in the village, was strong enough but completely blind. Naden agreed to my constructing an observation-post on the roof with several tons of loose bricks (fortunately we never completed it). Things went quietly on our immediate front. 24 April was most peaceful—too peaceful for my imagination. I was convinced that an attack was imminent and went to bed early in a tin hut near H.Q. At 2.40 a.m. I was awakened by the sound of a single gun. 'Now we're for it, Doc.; let's get to H.Q.!'

We raced down the path, clutching our belongings. The darkness was already lit up with the flash of many guns, and the first gas shells were swishing overhead. Wood was already on the phone. Naden had gone out a few hours previously, no one knew where.

I just had time to tell Marr on the phone that we were standing-to and then the line to Brigade went west. It was an armoured cable buried six feet deep in the ground and a chance shell had cut it in the first five minutes. The village was being drenched with gas; it was still dark; we could see nothing; about 10 per cent. of the shells were 5·9's, the rest were gas, both mustard and phosgene.

As it grew lighter the shelling somewhat diminished; the signallers went out on the broken lines, and Hollis was despatched to No. 2 Battalion to see what Robinson knew of the situation. I clambered onto the roof to see what there was to be seen on the Messines Ridge. Shells were falling all the way down the village street. Suddenly Clinton espied another American doctor dodging his way along the street; he raced up to him:

'Say—how long have you been in Yurrup?' (One 5·9 arrives.)

'Oh, maybe five weeks.' (Two 5·9's.) I heard an audible snort from Clinton.

'Well, let me tell you, Siree, I've served over here for SIX MONTHS.' And then Clinton skipped back into his aid-post.

Standing on the roof—our observation-post was not finished —my laughter was cut short by the arrival of a dud 5·9 which hit the observation-post fair and square, and deposited the bulk of it into the street below. I was smothered in brick-dust and lime and beat a hasty retreat.

The enemy was prodigal in his use of gas shells. I got rather a large dose, and whilst I was being realistically sick Naden arrived. He had been back to see some gunner friends, and said that the whole area was drenched with gas for two miles back, and several batteries were already out of action.

Hollis returned; Robinson at Spoil Bank reported that the troops on his front had been pushed back, and he thought that things were going badly away to the right; he was better placed for observation than we were.

Clinton was busy with several shell casualties, and many men had their clothing drenched with mustard gas.

'Had we any spare pairs of "paants", or did the British Army expect men to fight in their shirt tails?'

No. 1 Battalion on the right reported that the front-line troops had been blown off the Ridge in front, and that the main defensive line was now being attacked. It was evident that something was seriously wrong at Kemmel, which was held by the French, as shells were already falling on Voor-mezeele from that direction.

I went along the road towards St Eloi. Through my glasses I could see that the enemy had gained the summit of the Ridge, but were being held up. As I hastened back with this information I glanced towards Vierstraat. Heavens! the enemy had already descended the Ridge and were trying to work round No. 1 Battalion's front posts. I could see the enemy dribbling down the Ridge in twos and threes.

I made my report, which Naden went out to confirm. Darkness came; I was ordered to report back to Brigade H.Q. at once, taking my batman and kit with me.

An hour's stumbling through the darkness and I blundered into Brigade H.Q. The G.O.C. was worried about the position in front of Ridge and Scottish Woods. I was to go up immediately and assume command of the troops available for the defence of that sector. I protested vigorously; to take over an involved position in total darkness, with several posts already surrounded, would be unfair both to me and to the men I had to command. I had got another dose of gas coming down, and to emphasize my protest I went out and was thoroughly sick again.

Marr backed me up, and it was agreed that I should have a sleep and go up fresh in the early morning. I was awakened early; a shell bursting on the roof of the farm-house brought down about half a ton of tiles with a crash onto the tin roof beneath which I was sleeping.

It was nearly light, with a thick mist. Marr was on the phone to Robinson of No. 2 Battalion; they were trying to get the guns to open fire in front of the Spoil Bank. I took up a spare receiver and heard the drama. Robinson, cool as ever, was telling Marr that his H.Q. had been rushed in the fog and the enemy was at that moment fighting its way into Robinson's H.Q.; then there was silence, and we could get no further reply. One officer and two men fought their way through; the rest were never heard of again.

We had breakfast whilst Marr explained the position. The French had definitely been forced off Kemmel and the whole of our area was now under direct observation. A battalion of the 21st Division might or might not be available for counter-attacks; the situation in front of Ridge and Scottish Woods would have to be cleared up. The Brasserie would

have to be held, and I must comb out what supports I could
in case I needed them for counter-attacks.

Curtis collected some rations for us, and we started off on
the way to my new H.Q. at Scottish Wood. As we approached
it a perfect tornado of shells was sweeping it, and the barrage
was heavy all along the Ridge. Curtis, who always looked on
the bright side, mentioned that quite a number of Wisbech
men were buried in that vicinity. I abruptly told him to save
his wind for the sprint we should probably have to do through
the barrage.

I found No. 1 Battalion H.Q. established in an ice-house
behind the Château. Whitfield, stout-hearted as ever, was
looking tired and drawn. He had been out all night trying to
clear up the situation in front. He had managed to disengage
some of his posts which had been isolated, but his officers
and men were exhausted, and, in default of his being able to
mend the gaps in his line, he had been forced back to the old
G.H.Q. line which ran in front of Scottish and Ridge Woods.

Simultaneously with my arrival the enemy attacked this
new line. They were repulsed everywhere except on the right
flank, where they took the Brasserie, from which they were
able to enfilade our line. The remnants of the Sussex were on
the right. I ordered an immediate counter-attack, but I dare
not ask if they had enough troops to do it. It was a relief
when forty minutes later they reported that they had retaken
the Brasserie, together with prisoners and machine-guns.

I went along the length of our position. I knew it well; the
digging of it was the first job performed by my old 'C'
Company in March, 1915. The field of fire had been somewhat broken up by buildings and horse-lines erected since
then, but it was a strong position; its great disadvantage was
that it was sited on the forward slope and was a good target
for the artillery.

The men were weary and dispirited. I told them that it
would have to be a fight to a finish. I felt rather dramatic,

but, as I pointed out to them, Dickebusch Lake ran along our rear half a mile away, and quite apart from it being cold for bathing, even a strong swimmer would not stand much chance with the enemy taking pot-shots at him.

The position was not any too choice on the right at the west of Ridge Wood. We were supposed to keep in touch with the 9th Division; we did, but only at intervals. There was no continuous line there, and an enemy advance at either end of the line would see us cut off with the Lake at our backs.

I went to the left and saw Eric Wood; No. 4 H.Q. had been moved back into Voormezeele into line with ours. The village was now a shell-trap; attacking waves had lapped up to and around it, but had been beaten off; casualties were rather heavy, mainly through shelling. I told Wood how we were fixed. He had a telephone test-box in a dug-out behind, and a line to Brigade; this might be useful, as our own line could not be kept going for more than a few minutes at a time.

When I got back, Whitfield had combed out two lots of supports—some Hertfordshires for the centre and right, and a platoon of Gloucesters behind the Ridge on the left.

Shelling was getting heavier. In answer to my appeal Marr had sent up a miscellaneous collection of sappers, etc., to dig some fresh defensive posts behind our line in case the line at Ridge Wood was broken. There was no rest at H.Q.; we had nothing to do, but all night a battery was firing salvoes of 4·2's, which burst thirty yards outside the door at intervals of ninety seconds. Every time the blast of the explosion puffed out our candles; finally we sat in complete darkness.

Dawn was heralded by a storm of shelling. I could hear the rattle of Cambridgeshire Lewis guns at Voormezeele, but there was no attack on our front. The Black Watch had been driven off the mound south of Voormezeele but had retaken it. Both Wood and Few had been wounded. Naden's line now ran up to the Canal lock; he was not afraid of the attacks on the village, but was unhappy about the line between the village and the Canal. He had just heard that No. 4 was to be relieved that night (the 27th) to give them twenty-four hours' rest at Dominion Camp.

The relief duly took place, but the incoming Battalion had not enough troops to take over all the frontage, with the result that the left Company, consisting of Cheshires, Gloucesters and a few Cambridgeshires under Lumsden, had to be left. This unfortunate Company when finally relieved had only 35 men left out of 117.

No. 1 Battalion was left in the line, coming under the 30th Divisional Composite Brigade (another Division rolled up into a Brigade).

Except for incessant shelling 28 April was uneventful, but I was getting worried about the state of exhaustion of both officers and men. They had never really recovered from the effects of the Somme, and the last seventy-two hours of attacks and constant shelling were beginning to make them dazed and listless. They were worn out, but could not sleep, and an order had to be repeated several times before they got its meaning.

I was still fairly fresh, but my Adjutant would doze off in the middle of writing a message. Whitfield still kept going in some miraculous manner, but he could not last indefinitely, and Company Commanders spoke of the difficulty of preventing sentries from dozing.

Eventually I had to tell Brigade that I could not accept the responsibility for the line any longer; twenty-four hours' rest and it would be a different matter, but things were getting impossible as they were. Luckily a battalion of the 30th Division was available, and a relief was arranged, but it took most of the night to effect it. We did not move far, only to the reverse side of the Ridge into support, with H.Q. on the Lake side.

29 April was another wild day; shelling was heavy and

continuous. The King's Liverpools, who relieved us in the
front line, had a bad time of it, but the line held somehow.
I was glad to hear that No. 4 (Cambridgeshires, etc.) was
being kept out of the line in reserve, but No. 1, although in
support, was being badly knocked about by shelling. I
shared H.Q. with the Lincolns, who were a support battalion
for the 21st Division. They were in the same state as ourselves,
everyone at exhaustion point.

Marr phoned me early on the morning of the 30th:

'A real sticky job for you; Voormezeele Mound has been
lost again. The Division say that we are to retake it before
we are relieved. You are detailed for the job.'

He also told me that Naden had been hit, and that if the
present process of elimination continued I should soon be
commanding the Division.

I sent warning orders to a Company and then went up to
reconnoitre. Although we were supposed still to hold the
Switch Lines on either side of Voormezeele, the village was
full of the enemy. I tried to work my way forward, but there
was a fusillade every time I raised my head to look. One
Company, even a strong one, would not suffice; it would need
two to make good as far as the Mound, and then another
Company to carry out the assault. Furthermore, as soon as
we had taken it we should inevitably be shelled off it.

I went back and phoned Marr that it would be an in-
excusable waste of lives to make the attempt; finally, between
us, we convinced the Division of the futility of the scheme.
The Company who had been warned for the attack were
lying in a ditch further back. I sent them back again, and
told them that we expected a relief that night.

The relieving battalion was late, the relief was slow and
held up by shelling, and dawn was breaking as I left Dickebusch Lake with my Adjutant and a couple of runners. It
was broad daylight as we got to Ouderdom, and we had still
some distance to go. Our pace got slower and slower, and

at last we sat down for a rest, when all four immediately fell asleep, to be awakened by a battery opening fire within a few yards of us. The last half-mile took an awfully long time. At last I spotted Pooley coming to meet me, with a beaming smile; we were sharing the same camp; No. 4 was already in and asleep, and we soon followed suit without waiting to feed.

I was awakened half-an-hour afterwards by two runners; they had tried my Adjutant, but could not keep him awake long enough to read the message. The four Composite Battalions were to be reorganized into three; the other two would go up in support that night, mine would stay in reserve.

A few hours' sleep works wonders; by 5 p.m. I felt like a different being, and went to see the Cambridgeshires and the Black Watch before they went up the line. The fleeing peasants had left many things behind them, and Cooper had sucking-pig on the menu; the survivors of the litter were running about under the mess table. I was chaffing Stewart about having to go up that night when a message arrived that the three Composite Battalions were to be reorganized into two. I was to command one and Wilkinson (Gloucesters) the other; and both would move up in support that night. In effect the 39th Division was now organized as two battalions, and I wondered what would happen at the next reorganization.

Reorganization was a comparatively simple matter. Stewart became my second-in-command, Hollis was adjutant, whilst Pooley and the Cambridgeshires and the Black Watch provided the first-line transport.

As soon as it was dark we moved up to our position. Fortunately this time it was north-west of the Dickebusch Road near Hallebast, so we were out of the stricken area. The position consisted of slits dug in the fields of growing corn; plenty of fresh air and no gas. No shells either, until parties started to move across the open; then there would be a salvo of 5·9's to remind us that we were under direct observation.

Clinton came the next day and asked to be allowed to hold a sick parade; there were numberless cases of men off colour, gas sickness and blistered feet. I told him I thought it doubtful policy; we might have the whole Battalion parading sick. Eventually I agreed.

But Clinton misunderstood me, and proceeded to hold a sick parade in the middle of the afternoon; men in twos and threes came hobbling across the fields to the farm-house where Clinton had his aid-post, until he had a parade of sixty.

I was just about to send him a message to alter his arrangements when a 5·9 burst in the roof of the house. A moment later the blind, the halt, and the lame were fleeing in all directions at top speed back to their Companies, and Clinton had a blank sick report.

Life was comparatively pleasant. We were always being warned for counter-attacks, but they did not materialize. On 3 May we were informed that we were to march back that night to entrain. Pooley's transport were stopped when near the station and sent back; the move was cancelled; we could not yet be spared.

The next day, however, for the very last time during the war we left the Ypres Salient. Three years before to the day I had quitted Ypres for the first time on a stretcher; now I was leading half the 39th Division out of the last battle it would ever fight.

We arrived early next morning at Watten. The assembled Divisional transport met us at the station; the officers rode home to billets in two ambulances, the men in limbers and waggons; there was enough transport for all to ride.

Chapter XXIV

THE REBUILDING OF A BATTALION

May and June 1918

M. C. C.

OUR fears that the 39th Division had come to the end of its fighting career proved only too true. The 39th Division, together with seven others, had to be written off as fighting units owing to the shortage of reinforcements. Out of the mass of conflicting rumours emerged definite orders. Whilst the New Army Battalions were to be reduced to training cadres for American troops, the four Territorial Battalions of the Division were to be transferred elsewhere.

Blacklock, the new Commander of the 39th Division, sent for me on 5 May and broke the news:

'Well, Clayton, the Cambridgeshires are to join the 12th Division and absorb the 7th Suffolks. I believe your new Division is somewhere near Albert. I understand that the Boche is busy mounting the father and mother of attacks there, so you look like arriving just in time.'

The next day we marched out to entrain at Audricques. Our friends the Black Watch announced that they would see us off; their pipes arrived as we were falling in. I naturally thought that they would play us out for the first mile or so and then return to their billets. But the Black Watch never did things by halves. Their pipers struck up as we marched off, and they played every step of the eight miles to Audricques. Here we found Stewart and the rest of the Black Watch officers, together with the Brigade Staff.

It was the parting of the ways, as the Black Watch was already under orders to join the 15th Division. The war was responsible for many friendships, but none stronger than that which existed between the Cambridgeshires and the 4/5th

Black Watch. It had been cemented in blood at the taking of the Schwaben Redoubt. The fighting at St Julien, Tower Hamlets, and the events of March and April, 1918, had only served to strengthen those bonds.

Another wrench that I personally felt perhaps more than the others was that this was the parting of the ways as far as Marr and I were concerned. In the early days of 1915 Marr had been one of my subalterns in 'C' Company. For many weary months he had commanded 'C' Company; at the head of his Company he was one of the first to reach the enemy trenches at the Schwaben Redoubt; and when Battalion H.Q. had all become casualties he commanded the Battalion in that desperate affair until the Cambridgeshires were withdrawn. Latterly, as Brigade Major he had done everything in his power to make smooth the path of his old Battalion; his long service as a Company Commander was of inestimable value in seeing the point of view of the man in the front trench, and we felt we were parting from a staunch friend.

We steamed out of the station to the strain of the pipes, the Black Watch waving their bonnets, and Marr, resplendent in a new brass hat, running alongside for a last handshake.

Early the next morning we detrained at Raincheval, and marched to Lealvillers, coming under the 12th Division. The new Divisional Commander (Major-General H. W. Higginson, D.S.O.) had only assumed command a few days previously. The Division consisted entirely of New Army units. The 35th Brigade comprised the 7th Norfolks, 9th Essex, and 7th Suffolks. We were to absorb the latter battalion as soon as it could be relieved from the line.

In the meantime the Division was only too thankful to have an additional, though attenuated, Battalion to act as Divisional Reserve and to find working-parties for the defence lines which were being feverishly constructed in the rear of the battle-position.

12-2

The next day I reported to the Brigade Commander, Berkeley Vincent. I saw at once that we were fortunate. Vincent had Cavalry and India stamped all over him. Coupled with many years of Staff experience he had a profound admiration for, and a sound understanding of, the man in the ranks. Of his long period of service he had spent a dozen years on active service in various campaigns.

The details of the absorption of the 7th Suffolks were quickly arranged, and on 19 May we took over 11 officers and 408 other ranks of that Battalion, and the next day moved into the support-line east of Mailly-Maillet and the Auchonvillers Ridge. In name a Battalion, it was obvious that it would be some time before we could settle down into a smooth-working, fighting unit. The threat of an enemy attack was ever with us, and it was with a sigh of relief that I welcomed Saint on his return from leave to reassume command.

The settling-down process was greatly helped by the 12th Division being drawn into G.H.Q. reserve at Raincheval. It also enabled us to size up our opportunity. The officers were good; for probably the first time since landing in February, 1915, the Battalion strength was up to establishment, and the N.C.O.'s and men were experienced. In the main they consisted of slightly wounded men returned to duty after the Spring battles. Saint set to work, with all his boundless enthusiasm, to fashion a fighting battalion out of the material so generously provided. Platoon, Company, and even Battalion training became the order of the day. True, we had obstacles, one of which was the necessity for all battalions in G.H.Q. reserve to gird their loins at dawn each morning and be prepared to move off with all our goods and chattels at one hour's notice. We discovered that we had inherited 'some' band. Only in February the 7th Suffolks had absorbed the 8th Suffolks, and had also taken on the strength a large proportion of the Band boys of the Regular Suffolk

battalions, who had been left at home at the commencement
of the war. The March and April battles had left the Cambridgeshire Drums woefully thin; the pooling of our resources
enabled us, on occasions, to turn out a band of fifty-two
drums and fifes.

These were strenuous but enjoyable days. Saint and I
spent most of the day in the saddle, and long hours at night
discussing training-points and exercises. These all had one
object in view: to weld the new battalion into an effective
fighting weapon, and give it the essential qualities of self-
confidence and *esprit de corps*. We did not overlook the fact
that the British soldier dislikes changing his cap-badge and
shoulder-titles. The amalgamation of what were in effect
three battalions might easily have given rise to petty jealousies
and questions of seniority and promotion. All these points
had to be carefully considered. We told the men we had one
object in view: to make the Cambridgeshires the happiest and
best fighting battalion in the 12th Division.

I overhauled the interior economy of the Battalion. We had
received several thousand francs as our share of the surplus
funds of the 39th Divisional canteen; we spent it in improving
the messing. After a few days we sensed a new spirit in the
Battalion; an ex-Suffolk writing home said: 'These Cambridgeshires are a very regimental lot; they expect a great deal
from us, but they seem to know their job, and we are getting
a straight deal'.

The culmination of our training in open warfare was field-
firing, first by Companies, and then by the whole Battalion.
We wanted to demonstrate the enormous fire-power of a
battalion with thirty-two Lewis guns when it is properly con-
trolled. We finished the exercise by a burst of fire in which
every rifleman had to fire ten rounds rapid, and each Lewis
gun one drum. The target chosen was a chalky outcrop at
the foot of a steep hill. The effect obtained was well worth
the expenditure of ammunition, for we had convinced the

Battalion of its power. Unfortunately the whole of the Battalion did not direct its fire onto the selected target. That evening I had to attend an inquest, with the Claims Officer as Coroner, to investigate the mysterious death of three cows, which were grazing one thousand yards away to the flank of the target. Charles Warwick, the Battalion butcher, who conducted the post-mortem, declared that their deaths were due to 'syncope', but I afterwards learnt that they were not unconnected with side-bets of twenty francs on the part of two rival Lewis-gun teams in one of the Companies!

At the end of a fortnight the Cambridgeshires returned to the line, first in reserve at Hédauville, and then in the line east of Martinsart. Constant patrolling was carried out, and endeavours made to obtain enemy identifications, but without success. Parties of American officers and N.C.O.'s came up to gain line-experience; they were all fearfully keen, but it was evident that their enthusiasm had far overstepped their standard of training. A new R.S.M. arrived in place of Matthews (wounded) in the person of Benton from the 2/1st Battalion. He was an old friend, as he had been a permanent Staff Instructor for several months prior to mobilization.

On 9 July the Cambridgeshires, with the rest of the 12th Division, were relieved and moved back to Hérissart. At this time Marshal Foch was mounting his counter-stroke on the Marne front, and four British Divisions were placed in reserve astride the Somme, in rear of the junction of the British and French armies. This necessitated on 13 July the move of the Cambridgeshires by bus through Amiens to Rumigny in support of the French 30th Corps.

The fortnight which ensued was spent in training for offensive operations. At the same time the front held by the French and the routes thereto had to be thoroughly reconnoitred.

The French Corps in the line prided themselves on being one of the crack corps on the Western Front. Certainly their defensive plans and dispositions were very thorough.

Saint and I took coffee after lunch at one of the Regimental
H.Q. This was served in delicate porcelain cups; the officers
were attired in spotless uniforms, with starched linen cuffs
complete. I always made a point of not airing my French
except when absolutely necessary; that day, however, Saint
was incorrigible, until he came across a machine-gun post
manned by bearded Frenchmen. Speaking pidgin French
he demanded particulars of the field of fire covered by that
post. The corporal in charge suffered in silence and then
commenced, 'Waal, I guess—'. We all rocked with laughter;
the Company to which that post belonged consisted of
Yankees from New York who had joined the French Army
as volunteers.

As Saint had gone to the Brigade H.Q., in the absence
of Vincent on leave, the dual responsibility of supervising
Battalion training, and at the same time of performing reconnaissance duties, gave me little time for leisure, but I
managed to see all I could of the French troops. French infantry, and Algerian and Moroccan cavalry were all in
strength behind this vital point of the line. The Colonial
Cavalry seemed more picturesque than useful, but I was
greatly impressed with the pains taken to avoid hostile observation. Reconnoitring parties were limited to three
officers, and the opening of a map anywhere within three
miles of the line caused consternation. One afternoon I
entered a wood near Boves. There must have been the greater
part of a Division there; men were lying on the ground smoking and playing cards. One sentry sufficed along the whole
eight hundred yards of the eastern edge of the wood. I
thought this was a good example of the difference in temperament between the French and British troops. The former
were moved to the wood and 'stayed put'; British troops, on
the other hand, would have wanted to kick a football about
in the open or wander about collecting firewood. But if the
wood had been shelled they would have stayed there until

ordered elsewhere, whilst the French would probably not have waited for orders.

In view of the way the fighting was developing on the Marne, information was received that the Cambridgeshires would probably remain at Rumigny for some time. Steps were taken to improve billets, and the Medical Officer (Clinton) endeavoured to teach some of the first principles of sanitation to the native population. This was, of course, asking for trouble: and I was not surprised when Walker burst into my room at 7 a.m. one morning with the news that we were to entrain at 10 a.m. at a station six miles distant for an unknown destination.

That afternoon we detrained at Canaples, a village northwest of Amiens. The next day being 31 July and the first St Julien anniversary, we held a swimming gala in the reservoir, which went off with great éclat. The first of August found officers again reconnoitring a fresh line at Buire-sur-Ancre and Ribemont. We returned in time to attend a large singsong, in which the principal honours went to a comedian singing a Yiddish song, 'Oie, Oie! Vat a game it is! Oie, Oie!' This was a favourite catch-phrase for weeks afterwards. That night was to prove the last time that most of us were to sleep under a roof for twelve weeks; for many it was their last.

The next day we moved up to support trenches at Ribemont. These were sited in fields of growing corn, ready for cutting. Harvesting parties were out every night, cutting, tying and loading the sheaves onto A.S.C. waggons for carting to the rear. Battalion H.Q. was in dug-outs on the side of a wooded slope. We were bombed most evenings, happily without casualties, until R.S.M. Benton dashed out after bombs had fallen to see if the sentries were unhurt, only to fall a victim to another bomb which inflicted injuries from which he died the next day.

In the meantime Saint had returned, and I confided to him my views that an offensive was imminent. Additional batteries were moving into position every night and parties of Tank Corps officers were in evidence. Saint, however, knew nothing, and we were left guessing.

The enemy made the first move. I was awakened in the early morning of 6 August by a heavy enemy bombardment, and soon afterwards we learnt that a Brigade of the 18th Division in front of Morlancourt, on our immediate right, had been attacked and driven out of about eight hundred yards of trenches. At midday Saint was summoned to a Brigade Conference. He returned looking thoughtful; in answer to my enquiry as to whether we were to perform the inevitable counter-attack he replied, 'As far as I can gather, the whole B.E.F. is going to counter-attack'.

Chapter XXV

MORLANCOURT

7–19 *August* 1918

M. C. C.

THE expected counter-attack on the last trenches was to be merged into an infinitely larger scheme, already in train, to take place at dawn on 8 August. The Australian and Canadian Corps were to attack south of the Somme, with the Cavalry Corps going through. North of the river the 3rd Corps, consisting of the 58th, 18th and 12th Divisions, were to attack with the north boundary of the attack coinciding with the left of the 35th Brigade front. As far as our Brigade was concerned, the Cambridgeshires were to be in support to the Norfolks and Essex.

At 3.30 p.m. on 7 August Saint sent for me: 'The Brigade front has been extended southwards. We are to attack the trench line in front of Morlancourt. I shall have to go straight away with the Company Commanders to reconnoitre and frame orders. You must see to all administrative details and get the Battalion into position to-night'.

Water, rations, S.A.A. and bombs, all had to be arranged and the rough details of the scheme explained to Platoon Commanders. The C.O. of the Field Ambulance arrived to discuss arrangements for evacuating the wounded. Padre Walters was packing his 'battle kit'; it appeared to consist of biscuits, water, field-dressings, a Bible, and innumerable packets of cigarettes. Pooley was the next arrival. We wanted a hot meal served late in the evening, after Companies had moved into position. I had to go and find that position and see that platoon guides knew which routes to take. Somehow it was done, but I never knew how Saint managed to carry out his reconnaissance in time to formulate details of his orders. To complicate matters the enemy chose to put down an intense gas-bombardment from 10 p.m. until 12.30 a.m. One gas shell burst amongst Brigade H.Q. as they were moving up, Vincent's eyes were severely affected (he had to go to hospital two days afterwards), and Cooke, the Brigade Major, was badly burned with mustard gas. Yet, in spite of it all, arrangements were completed, extra S.A.A. and bombs were issued, a hot meal was served, and by 1 a.m. the Companies were in their assembly positions. The only thing left was for Battalion H.Q. to move into position at 4 a.m. I said good-bye to Saint; an order was in force forbidding seconds-in-command sharing the same battle H.Q. as the C.O., and I traced my weary steps to rear Brigade H.Q., hoping and praying for the best.

I was awakened by the opening crash of our bombardment at 4.20 a.m. It was the dawn of 8 August, the day described by Ludendorff as 'The Black Day of the German Army in the history of this war'. I did not get up, for I knew that the Cambridgeshires were not to attack until 6.20 a.m. At this hour the bombardment was to be intensified, and 'A' Company (Hay) and 'B' Company (Baynes Smith) were to advance to the assault. I lay for some time listening to the guns; I thought I was inured to the sound of a sustained bombardment, but at last I could stand it no longer. Pulling on a coat I went outside, where I found Scott-Murray, the Staff Captain. We could see little; there was a thick mist, pierced at intervals by the flashes from near-by batteries. A faint smell of gas drifted down from the line; it seemed as though the enemy's shelling was concentrated mainly on the Cambridgeshires' front. This turned out to be largely the case. The enemy had no intuition of a British attack on an extended front, but he was naturally expecting, and prepared for, an attempt to recapture the lost trenches on the Cambridgeshires' front.

Suddenly our guns redoubled their rate of fire. I looked at my watch; it was 6.20 a.m.; the time for assault had arrived.

'Better get something to eat', muttered someone; 'we may be wanted shortly.'

If anyone wants to experience a feeling of suspense let him be placed in H.Q. immediately in rear of the line where his battalion is fighting. We had no telephone forward; we were forbidden to approach the line or Battalion H.Q.; our sole source of information was derived from the rumours and scraps of news from stretcher-bearers and walking wounded. As morning progressed we could see Morlancourt Ridge through the rifts in the fog, but it was impossible to discern what was happening. Once through my glass I saw a tank lumbering over the Ridge, with shells bursting all around; at another time one of our aeroplanes diving down to within a few feet of the ground, firing at the enemy trenches and then 'zooming' up again for another attack.

Gradually the rumours crystallized into certainty. The two Corps south of the Somme had burst the line and let the cavalry through. On our immediate front the troops on either flank of the Cambridgeshires had taken their objectives; our assaulting Companies had failed to reach their objective and were lying in the open, short of the enemy position. Here they were being subjected to a hail of shrapnel and gas shells, and casualties were mounting up rapidly. Walters, leading a gas-blinded man down to the aid-post, was met on arrival by the C.O. of the Ambulance:

'Your bloody Cambridgeshires, Padre, came to this Division with a hell of a fighting reputation; they have let the Division down badly in their first show.'

However, there was no bitterness in the line; the neighbouring battalions saw what had happened. Meanwhile Saint was busy; he moved up 'C' and 'D' Companies behind the Ridge and asked for a barrage to fall at 12.15 p.m.

Once again the guns took up the chorus, and 'C' (Hollis) and 'D' (Wallis) moved up, changing direction half right, and lay down waiting for the barrage to lift at 12.28 p.m. The time arrived and the leading wave charged the position. They were followed by the second wave which charged through and completed the capture of the support line. The surprise was complete; about 30 of the enemy were killed, but the rest of the garrison surrendered, causing great embarrassment; there were only 140 Cambridgeshires, while the wounded and unwounded Wurtembergers numbered 316. The only thing to do was to propel them out of the way of the Ridge to Battalion H.Q. so as to allow preparations to be made against possible counter-attacks. Here they were shepherded by runners and signallers. It was obviously desirable to get this large body away before they changed their minds, and no time was lost. Sergt. Cox was put in charge; his height was considerably less than his rifle with fixed bayonet:

'Now then you—Quick march!'

As they reached the metalled road Cox commenced barking out the step, and soon they were swinging along, most of them not having quite comprehended what had happened. As they approached Brigade H.Q. the Brigadier came up the steps; his sight was rapidly failing, and he stood at the entrance shading his eyes from the sun.

'March at attention', yelled Cox; 'Battalion, eyes right!'

They may not have understood the language but they understood the command!

There had been a complete change for the better in the situation. The expected counter-attack did not materialize; the captured position was safe. In addition to the 316 prisoners there were 14 machine-guns and 10 trench-mortars accounted for. 'A' and 'B' had, however, suffered severely. Cobham and Twelvetrees and 13 men were killed; Hay, Aldrich, Wilson, and 186 men were wounded, of whom 141 were suffering from gas. When the wounded had all been evacuated, Walters, weary though he was, was seen plodding away to the Ambulance. 'Where are you going, Padre?' was the shout. 'I am going to ask the C.O. of the Ambulance to apologize for what he said about the Cambridgeshires this morning.'

The attack had progressed on both flanks of Morlancourt, and Saint was ordered to draw up details of a fresh attack, which would mop up the village and throw our line forward to the Ridge eastwards. In view of the exhaustion of all concerned it was decided to defer this attack until late in the following afternoon. In the meantime Vincent's sight grew rapidly worse, and he was evacuated to the Ambulance, Saint taking his place as Brigadier, whilst I was sent up to command the Cambridgeshires.

Walker greeted me at Battalion H.Q.; these consisted of a few slits dug into the side of the hill, covered with waterproof sheets. The shells from a solitary enemy gun were hitting the ground about fifty yards in front, and at intervals a clod of soil would fall with a plop onto the roof. Saint, with his usual thoroughness, had worked out all details. Whilst the 37th Brigade attacked north and south of Morlancourt, 'C' and 'D' Companies were to advance behind the barrage and make good the village, afterwards occupying a line east of Morlancourt until such time as the converging attack of the 37th Brigade enabled our two Companies to be withdrawn.

Three tanks were detailed to assist in mopping up the village, but as they would have to cross the Ridge in full view of the enemy their chances of ever reaching it were doubtful.

I left Walker at H.Q. and crossed over the Ridge to the Companies on the far side. The enemy on the opposite slope made no attempts at concealing their presence, and amused themselves by taking pot-shots at my two runners and myself. I found Hollis and Wallis elated over their success of the previous day. They seemed to be fully conversant with details of the attack, which was timed for 5.30 p.m. I left them about ten minutes before it was due and made my way back; as I reached the Ridge I was annoyed to find that, as on the way up, the enemy had substituted sniping with a 77 mm. gun for rifles. It was only on reaching the summit that I discovered I was not the target. The enemy had spotted the only tank of the promised three to materialize. Presently there was a metallic clang and a sheet of flame. There would be no tank to assist the Cambridgeshires in overcoming enemy machine-gun nests.

At that moment the first shells of our barrage streamed over the Ridge. I saw 'C' and 'D' Companies clambering out of their trenches, and then the landscape was blotted out by the bursting shells of the enemy reply. I was disturbed to hear heavy machine-gun firing from the south end of the village; our guns evidently were not numerous enough to stifle opposition from that quarter.

And so it turned out that both Companies soon found that further advance would bring them into direct enfilade from the nest of machine-guns firing from the southern end. Without hesitation Betts, who was C.S.M. of 'D' Company on the right, dashed off alone. Taking advantage of a hedge running across the front, he worked his way resolutely forward until 'D' Company had lost sight of him. When he reappeared he was in rear of the enemy position which was causing all the trouble. There were about thirty of the enemy all engaged in firing at 'C' and 'D' Companies. Superior numbers had no terrors for Betts; practically single-handed he had re-captured a position in March, 1918. With a blood-curdling yell he dashed in with his bayonet at the nearest machine-gun crew. This unexpected attack from the rear was the last straw; those who had survived Betts' frenzied onslaught meekly surrendered, and were handed over by him to some men of the Buffs who happened to arrive before the astonished enemy had regained their wits.

The cessation of firing from this quarter had allowed the two Companies to continue their advance, and all objectives were captured, together with 47 prisoners, 19 machine-guns and numerous trench-mortars. We had under a dozen casualties, but they included two more officers, Rayner being killed and Chambers mortally wounded.

The success of the whole operation was mainly due to the gallantry and initiative displayed by Betts. A typical fen-man, hailing from near Wisbech, he had served in the Battalion from the commencement of the war. At the age of twenty-one he was C.S.M. and held the D.C.M. and Bar, and for his services in this action he was recommended for the V.C. The award of a Military Cross was announced later; unfortunately he never lived to wear the decoration, as he was killed on 22 August.

Owing to a gap in the line on our right, two platoons under Jackson had had to be left in the line, but the remainder of the Companies were withdrawn during the evening to the sunken road west of Morlancourt.

Here we remained in reserve until 16 August, when Saint returned to command. Vincent's eyes were still bad, and he had been sent to England, another Brigadier arriving in his place.

Whilst the Cambridgeshires were in reserve at Morlan-court other units of the 12th Division worked forward in successive stages to the old Amiens defence-line, about one mile beyond Morlancourt. This completed the first phase of the 4th Army operations, during which the 12th Division had acted as the left flank of the attack.

Apart from the gain of ground, prisoners and material, the moral effect of what became known as 'The Battle of Amiens' was profound. Ludendorff ascribed to it the later defection of Bulgaria and the general discouragement of Germany's allies. On the other hand it had a heartening effect on the

French and British, and enabled the strategic Amiens–Paris railway to be freed for future operations.

The tour of duty of the Cambridgeshires in the front line during the period 16–19 August was uneventful, and on the evening of the 19th they were withdrawn to Buire-sur-Ancre to prepare for the next attack.

Chapter XXVI

TIME FOR REFLECTION

19–20 *August* 1918

M. C. C.

TWO days were allotted for our stay at Buire-sur-Ancre whilst preparations were made for the next attack. Our depleted ranks were filled up. The newcomers comprised a dozen officers, some fresh, others well known, like Spicer, who twelve months previously had lain in his hospital bed reading his own obituary notice in *The Times*; and a large draft of men, mainly Cambridgeshires and Suffolks— a good useful lot, but many had spent too long under Base Depôt conditions, and were not looking as hard and bronzed as the remainder of the Battalion.

Buire was quite a pleasant place, with good bathing-pools in the Ancre. Fine warm weather and good food would have given us a summer-holiday feeling if our stay had been longer than forty-eight hours and if we were not working against time for the next attack. Saint and the Company Commanders spent most of the time reconnoitring; Walker and I, the 'maids of all work', found a day of twenty-four hours rather too short to get through our share of the work.

The change in the character of the fighting gave added importance to several points. The first was the careful selection of the 'Battle Surplus'. This important body has to be chosen with a view to facilitating the reorganization of the battalion after heavy casualties. In previous fighting an infantry battalion could reasonably count upon not having to take part in a further attack until after a month or so had elapsed. In view of the possibility of the same battalions having to attack at intervals of a few days, the importance of an adequate and immediately available reserve of Company and Platoon leaders, Lewis gunners, and Signallers became of much greater importance.

A routine order laid down that the C.O. and the Second-in-Command should never share the same battle H.Q., and that one or other should remain behind with the Battle Surplus. As one intimately concerned with this point I suggested a compromise—that Saint or I, as the case might be, should remain at a rear Battalion H.Q. I did not press this point with any mistaken idea of being indispensable. Saint and I both knew that in active operations the C.O. is the hardest worked man in the battalion, and an under-study who could step in and afford the C.O. four or five hours' uninterrupted sleep is often a boon both to the C.O. and the well-being of the battalion.

Incidentally I pointed out that on three occasions during recent months I had had to take over command of a battalion during active operations, and a ten- or twelve-mile ride up was not a good preparation for the task. The Brigadier was adamant; I was to report to the Brigade my arrival at Transport lines by 10 p.m. on the evening previous to the attack.

Another difficult question was the establishment of a forward transport section. In open and semi-open warfare S.A.A., extra Lewis guns, water, rations, and even officers' chargers might be required at a few minutes' notice. We had our own ideas on this subject, and from 21 August until the Armistice we ran a species of rear Battalion H.Q., usually located about a mile in rear of Battalion H.Q. proper.

The day before the attack I met Higginson, the Divisional Commander, on the way to the line. He was disturbed at the large proportion of officer casualties, and asked whether I thought it advisable for officers to be dressed similarly to the men. I pointed out that in the 1917 Ypres battles the officers had worn men's uniforms with rank-badges on the shoulders, but it did not prevent casualties among the officers mounting up as high as 80 per cent. (The Hertfordshires lost 100 per cent. at St Julien.) The officer, whether he be dressed as such or as an 'imitation soldier', must always lead; it was his duty, and it was the leaders, whether officers or N.C.O.'s, who suffered most. The wearing of a soldier's tunic hampered the officer in his duties; his men found it hard to recognize him, even those with whom he was in daily contact.

As an instance of this, Riddell and I, attired in tommies' tunics, were in the front line one day at Ypres in September, 1917. We were not talking; we were engaged in trying to spot a troublesome machine-gun post. A Battalion H.Q. runner passing by accosted Riddell with the remark: 'Got a match, Chum?' Riddell gravely handed the man his lighter, who returned it with: 'Thanks, Chum'. It was only when I made a chance remark to Riddell that the man realized our identity and made confused apologies.

This was merely an amusing incident which afforded us all a hearty laugh, but it would have been another matter if it was a question of giving a dangerous order; there was always the loophole, 'I did not recognize him as an officer'. Many unfortunate incidents in the March 1918 withdrawal would have been obviated if certain Divisions had not dressed their officers as tommies, especially in the later stages when the fighting was being carried out by bodies of men belonging to several different battalions, often under strange officers. To sum up, it was unfair on the officers and the men they had to command. We did, however, insist on officers wearing trousers and puttees instead of creations known as riding-breeches.

What I did stress to the Divisional Commander was the unsatisfactory routine whereby officer-reinforcements so often arrived on the day previous to the attack. Forty-eight hours afterwards I could have mentioned the case of three officers who never really saw in daylight the platoons they were supposed to command. They joined their Companies a few hours previous to assembly, and were wounded at dawn in the first few minutes of the attack.

In answer to the enquiry as to the remedy, I suggested that the Battalion should be allowed a larger number of officers, so that they might have at least a few days to get to know and to be known by platoons before they had to lead them over the top. An increased number of officers available would also have lessened the unfortunate procedure whereby the same officer, with increasing odds against him, had to take part in a number of successive attacks, until at last he figured in the casualty list.

At this juncture Haig issued a noteworthy order of the day, which had an important bearing upon future operations. After reciting that there was a complete change in the out-look, Haig stressed the necessity for exploiting local successes to the uttermost, though often they had been obtained on a narrow front. A striking passage was the one wherein it was stated that 'risks, which a month ago it would have been criminal to take, must now be incurred as a matter of duty'. The British nation and Press have always been ready to bestow laurels on Marshal Foch, but it must not be forgotten that Haig was the first to sense the impending change in the character of the fighting. He was the apostle of the converging attack which broke up the German Army, and it was Haig's insistence on the possibility, nay necessity, of finishing the war in the Autumn of 1918 that won over Foch, in spite of the threatening telegrams of the British War Cabinet.

Chapter XXVII

THE BATTLE OF BAPAUME

21–27 *August* 1918

M. C. C.

HAIG'S plan of campaign included the extension of the
front of attack to include the 3rd Army, and the latter
attacked on 21 August in the Arras sector. The attack
of 22 August in which we were concerned necessitated an
advance of about 2,500 yards to the Bray–Méaulte road. We
were the right Battalion of the Division, the 47th Division
was on our right, and the 7th Norfolks on our left. 'B', 'C'
and 'A' Companies were to attack with 'D' Company in
battalion reserve.

Dusk was falling as Walker and Warren set out to tape the
assembly-lines for the three Companies. I had to report my
arrival at Transport lines by 10 p.m., so I set out on my
seven-mile ride with Hughes, my groom, my pockets full of
lists of oddments to be sent up, and letters 'to be posted in
case—'. The enemy was filling the valleys with gas, and the
mists rising from the Ancre made the ride a cheerless one.
I was dead-tired, and Pooley's kindly smile and the hot meal
he had ready were a welcome sight on my arrival. I had not
been seated five minutes when the Brigade came through on
the line to know if I had arrived. I had already had one
strafing from the Brigadier for being present at Battalion
H.Q. during the evening, and my reply to the Staff Captain's
enquiry was rather terse. Scott-Murray, best of Staff Captains and kindest of men, had to speak in parables, for fear
of the enemy telephonists overhearing by means of induction,
but the gist of his message was:

'Well, I am sorry, but you will have to report back to

Brigade H.Q. at once. The Brigadier has been taken ill, Saint is to command the Brigade, and you must take over the Battalion. The assembly is proceeding, but the Boche seems to expect an attack and is shelling and gassing the whole area.'

I meekly replied: 'Oie, Oie! Vat a game it is! Oie, Oie!'

Bolting my supper I set off on my return trip. In view of the gas I decided not to take a horse but a bicycle. The valleys were full of gas, and I and my runner had a new experience in push-biking while wearing gas helmets. The ride proved both exhausting and exciting; we found several shell-holes.

It was 2 a.m. when I found Saint at Brigade H.Q. The Brigadier had a bad attack of fever, an Indian legacy, but thought he would be fit again within the next few hours. I told Saint I should make a bee-line for Battalion H.Q., and left without further ado. Another mile and I was passing along the line of Companies in shell-holes and an old ruined trench. The hostile fire, but for one persistent machine-gun, ceased; except for the sentries and a few officers all seemed to be asleep. It was fairly light, one could discern faces, and I passed the sleeping form of my batman, Curtis, who had asked permission to join in the attack with 'C' Company. The men had no overcoats; these had been dumped, not to be reissued until the end of September; their places in the men's packs were taken by extra bandoliers of S.A.A.

Battalion H.Q. were in a dug-out in the front line; fortunately there were two entrances, as one was blown in soon after the attack started. Walker was there with maps and message-pad laid out on a rough table. I asked the signallers if their lines were O.K., and spoke to Brigade to make sure. The signallers, linesmen and runners were sitting in a group on the floor talking in low tones. Suddenly there came a crash, our candles went out, and our lungs were filled with acrid fumes. We heard a low moan outside; one of the runners tore up the steps. 'Nipper's hit!' he shouted down the entrance. As one man the runners and signallers made a bolt for the steps.

'Stop', I shouted. 'Two of you will do; there is no need for the next shell to get the lot.'

Someone relit the candles. The signaller on duty looked at me appealingly. I nodded. He tore off his ear-phones, thrust them into the hands of his relief, and disappeared up the steps. He returned in a few minutes biting his lip, and readjusted the ear-phones. I did not speak; we all knew how much he and 'Nipper' meant to one another.

The Brigade rang up to know if Saint had arrived. I went up the steps; there was a thick mist. The air was full of the droning of our planes flying low to drown the noise of the approaching tanks. On the left I could hear muffled sounds of equipment being tightened up, and Lewis-gun drums slung over shoulders. There was no sign of the tanks which were to subdue the troublesome machine-gun posts.

'Only five minutes to go', said Walker as I groped my way into H.Q. 'Where's Saint?'

The C.S.M.'s of 'A', 'B' and 'C' reported their arrival. All four C.S.M.'s were to remain at H.Q. until the situation was clarified, to be used if needed to pull together Companies depleted of officers. Betts of 'D' Company had not arrived. Where was he?

Just as the first gun of our barrage barked its challenge at 4.45 a.m. Saint slid into H.Q. with his orderly. He had not seen the tanks; we could do nothing further for the present. The enemy counter-barrage was beginning to fall heavily all around H.Q.; between the crashes we could hear machine-gun fire, a bad omen for 'B' Company on the right.

The mist cleared a little. Messages indicated that the mist and smoke made direction difficult, and Companies had suffered severely in the first hundred yards from machine-gun fire. Now better progress was being made, and by 6 a.m. Companies were within reach of their objective, but the right was in difficulties from machine-gun fire somewhere in the 47th Division area.

Saint decided to move H.Q. further forward. The present H.Q. was being badly strafed; one entrance had been blown in, and in any case it was now too far back to enable him to control the situation. I was to remain there to act as report-centre to the Brigade. The signallers laid out a new line as they advanced; our line to Brigade held good.

The C.O. of the Essex stopped for a minute to gather news as his battalion went up in artillery formation to continue the attack. Saint reported the position of his new H.Q. and then the line went. We found the break a few yards forward of our dug-out and restored communication. Some bunches of prisoners were passed back. Baynes Smith of 'B' Company was still having difficulty on the right. The battalions on his right had run up against Happy Valley, which was bristling with machine-guns.

I found out why C.S.M. Betts had not reported to H.Q. with the other C.S.M.'s. Just as the attack was starting, an enemy machine-gun opened up only a short distance in front. Impulsive as ever, he could not resist the challenge and sprang over the parapet, doubtless intending to work round and take the machine-gun from a flank. He had only gone a few yards when he fell, and with him Cambridgeshire lost one of its bravest sons and the Battalion a devoted and fearless warrant-officer.

From the wounded who passed to the dressing-station I gathered scraps of information which I pieced together and passed on to the Brigade. What I saw through my glasses confirmed the information; our left had reached its objective and was fairly comfortably dug in, but our right was held up a few hundred yards short of the road, with little chance of continuing the advance. Company officers were suffering severely. Hewer and K. H. Clayton were killed and 10 others had been wounded.

An exclamation from my orderly made me turn round. I could hardly believe my eyes. Two squadrons of Corps Cavalry were advancing at a trot, apparently unscathed by the shelling. When about one hundred yards away from me, they formed line and drew sabres. I heard the shouted command of their leader on a big plunging chestnut, and away they went at a canter straight for the centre of all the trouble. I had no chance to tell them to make towards the left where there was more chance of exploiting our success. The enemy shelling had increased; they seemed to bear charmed lives; and I was fascinated by the sight. When they had gone about one thousand yards they topped a slight rise. There was a crescendo of machine-gun fire, and down they went like a pack of cards: odd riderless and wounded horses were careering back, but the two squadrons had ceased to exist. That was the only cavalry charge I ever saw; I never want to see another.

A voice hailed me from the path one hundred yards on my right; it was that of a Cambridgeshire officer propelling himself along with a stake. I ran across and found that it was Winfield, now a professor at Cambridge. He had only joined the Battalion on the previous day and apologized for the shortness of his stay. He was in considerable pain but refused to let me send a man with him; he said he was safely bound up and could find his way.

I went forward to see Saint. He had established H.Q. in a captured machine-gun nest, which his spare signallers were converting into a strong point under Walker's supervision. Saint was satisfied with the progress made, but anticipated counter-attacks from the right flank and was leaving nothing to chance. I did not tell him about Betts; he had troubles enough without adding to them.

On the way back I overtook a wounded N.C.O. with his arm around the neck of a slightly wounded man, being half supported and half dragged along. I stopped him. It was Bonnett, a mere boy, but wearing the honourable blue and red ribbon of the D.C.M. It was heroic but fatal kindness; Bonnett was shot through the stomach. In spite of his protests we put him on a stretcher, but I knew it was too late; the damage had been done. I thought of Spicer at St Julien, shot through the stomach and left for twenty-four hours as a hopeless case, but the delay in moving him saved his life.

The sun was now shining brightly, but the shelling hardly lessened. At 2 p.m. the 47th Division on our right was counter-attacked, and 'B' Company became involved, their posts east of the Bray–Méaulte road having to be withdrawn to the line of the road. Towards 7 p.m. the shelling increased, and we hunted for Lewis guns in case we had to defend rear H.Q.; but the Division had the situation in hand, and soon afterwards the reserve Brigade moved up in artillery formation, preceded by tanks, and our anxieties were diminished.

Later, rations arrived—with water and S.A.A., both badly needed—and a hot meal was ready for the Companies. Both that night and the ensuing day (23 August) were quiet and uneventful. During the evening the Cambridgeshires were relieved, and by 2 a.m. were concentrated back in a sunken road east of Morlancourt. Our casualties were less than we thought: only about 60, but they included 12 officers. Sergt. Clements and his cooks had a hot meal ready for the exhausted men. The necessary sorting out and reorganization were rather difficult; the men simply slept where they had fallen out, and some hours elapsed before the completion of this task.

Meanwhile the Brigades in the line were gaining ground, and at 6 p.m. on the 24th the 37th Brigade reported that the enemy were withdrawing and that they were following them up. There was every indication of semi-open warfare developing, and we brought up our forward transport section, which had been planned in readiness for such a happening. At 2.30 a.m. on 25 August Saint received orders to move to position on the left flank five hundred yards south-east of Méaulte. The Cambridgeshires set off without delay, and as soon as I knew of the feasibility of so doing I moved rear Battalion H.Q. up, and the men had breakfast direct from the cookers. A fog was very helpful in shielding us from observation.

The 36th and 37th Brigades had already gained three thousand yards that morning. Mounted troops and cyclists were pushing forward, meeting only with slight opposition. The 35th Brigade was concentrated in the valley behind the Fricourt Ridge. The orderly-room limber was needed for new supplies of maps, for a map covering a few square kilometres no longer sufficed. I joined Saint and Walker on the summit of the famous Ridge with its yawning craters. To the east small bodies of advanced troops were trying to push forward, but the enemy evidently meant to hold the Carnoy Ridge. Behind in the bright sunlight the whole landscape was alive with troops moving forward. In the foreground the Cambridgeshires and Norfolks were waiting orders to take up the advance.

A machine-gun section with its limbers arrived to be attached to the Cambridgeshires; Saint ordered that they should take up a supporting position at the summit to cover our next advance; the Companies were moved close up to the Ridge. We were to advance at 3 p.m., our objective being the Mametz–Carnoy Ridge.

Shrapnel was now bursting over the Ridge, and I decided to move the forward transport to a sunken road further to the left. As I cantered across, a shell burst somewhere behind, and my steed, probably stung by a spent shrapnel bullet, commenced to buck and rear. The men shrieked encouragement at my frantic, but successful, efforts to remain mounted. It was good to hear them laughing again. As I reached the transport the leading Companies of the Cambridgeshires and Norfolks breasted the Ridge. Immediately there was a tornado of shrapnel, and the ground all around the transport was peppered with spent bullets. The only thing to do was to clear out quickly, and we did a very successful imitation of a Royal Tournament Musical Ride with our limbers across the fields, until we reached the shelter of the sunken road.

The barrage of shrapnel and machine-gun fire which greeted the leading waves of the Cambridgeshires on the summit of the Fricourt Ridge served but to hasten the advance. It was only natural to charge down to the bottom of the valley, where comparative shelter could be obtained, and casualties in this part of the advance were few. It was not until the Battalion commenced its attack up the next Ridge that the advance began to slow down. The enemy machine-guns were skilfully posted in the ruins of the old trenches, and eventually both flanks of the Battalion were held up. Walker, on his own initiative, immediately went forward, and succeeded so effectively in infusing new life into the attack of the centre that eventually the centre Company reached its objective on the summit of the Ridge. The success of the centre made it possible for the two flanks to continue their advance. Ultimately the Battalion held a line just short of the summit, with patrols pushed out to the north and east of Carnoy.

At dusk I took the limbers up to Battalion H.Q., which was an old dug-out on the road at the foot of the valley. I could but wonder at the way the Companies had succeeded in securing a hold of the Carnoy Ridge. Saint had been worried when the attack hung fire, and a serious situation might have developed but for the initiative shown by Walker and the resolute way in which Hollis led his Company. Saint thought the enemy intended to make a stand on the Ridge.

Torrents of rain were falling as I returned to rear H.Q. on the far side of the Fricourt Ridge. I was wet through and hungry, and found all rations had been sent to the Battalion.

Curtis produced a ration biscuit and a tin of lobster; I only learnt afterwards that he had given me his own supper. The rain, if anything, grew worse; I spent the night with my back against a bank, and a waterproof sheet over my tin hat in a vain endeavour to shoot off the bulk of the rain.

I was awakened at 4 a.m. by our barrage. The Sussex and Berkshires attempted to carry the line further forward without much success. The small progress achieved by the latter was nullified by a counter-attack which developed at 9 a.m., and the Companies in the line had to hold on tightly to their gains. Shelling was heavy all day. We had 50 casualties but only lost one officer, A. F. Gray being unfortunately killed.

Next morning the 37th Brigade took up the attack, and after preliminary failures the line was at last carried forward to one west of Maltz Horn Ridge. Saint moved the Cambridgeshires in support to the Maricourt–Montauban road; and, in view of the cover afforded there, I decided to close rear H.Q. and transport on to the Battalion. I led the transport down into the valley behind the Battalion; we were trotting, as we had been under observation for a short distance. I was using an old, worn track made by the enemy batteries, and was just approaching a track junction when I was held up by a sapper waving his arms and shouting. We pulled up thirty yards short of a carefully mined portion of the track. Once it was pointed out, the miniature mine-field was obvious, with its carefully raked soil and the detonators showing through like small mushrooms. After that we kept a sharp look-out!

Saint had not had a night's rest for a week, so we prevailed upon him to take a day off. He was very annoyed because, during the night, someone, probably a passing gunner, had scrounged the Cambridgeshire H.Q.'s flag, which was stuck in a bush on the road below H.Q. Driver, the signalling officer, back from leave, had brought out a fresh one by Saint's instructions, but it was back at transport in his kit.

I went round all Companies. The men were trying to dry their clothes, as far as it was possible, in a line of shell-holes and disused gun-pits. Coles of 'D' Company had an awful cold and was looking the picture of misery, despite the efforts of Harding-Newman, who was trying to cheer him up by comparing the relative dangers of the Stock Exchange and the Western Front. I went back and told the cooks that they must prepare the biggest and hottest evening meal they could provide, and at dusk it was taken round to the Companies in hot containers on pack mules.

No further orders from Brigade had arrived and we all turned in early to make up arrears of sleep. At 11 p.m. orders arrived that the Cambridgeshires were to attack Maltz Horn Ridge early the next morning, with the Royal Fusiliers on the right and the Essex on the left.

It was likely to prove a difficult operation. The deployment necessitated an advance of over a mile in broken country in pitch darkness, with a ridge a little further on, strongly held by machine-guns, as the ultimate objective. The officers and men were worn out by the fighting of the previous three days; no reconnaissance of the objective had been possible and none could now be carried out. Saint's orders condensed down to this:

'At 4.50 a.m. a barrage will open on the Ridge. You will at once advance. Soon after crossing a road you will descend into the valley. Cross this valley, and you will come to a steep Ridge held by machine-guns. Climb the Ridge, capture the machine-guns, and consolidate a position on the far side of the Ridge.'

Saint left Walker and myself to warn the Companies and get them up to the assembly position, and he tore off with a few runners to consult the C.O. of the Battalion in the line and choose a H.Q. for the operations.

The first streaks of dawn were appearing as I retraced my steps to my H.Q. There were still a few minutes before zero hour, and I paced up and down the road wondering how the Companies would fare on that steep, chalky Ridge.

Suddenly the whole of the western horizon was lit up with the flash of many guns, to be followed a second afterwards by the whine of the shells on their way overhead. The neighbouring 18-pounders joined in, and a few seconds afterwards the shells bursting on the Ridge were interspersed by a dozen coloured S.O.S. rockets.

The enemy's artillery reply was relatively small, but I heard the ominous splutter of many machine-guns. As the minutes passed these gradually decreased; it was a good sign.

About half-an-hour afterwards I descried some sixty prisoners being marched to my H.Q., whom I took over from the corporal in charge. I was the only one present who knew the position of Brigade H.Q., so summoning my batman and one of the cooks I put myself at their head and set out. I marched with a bespectacled, lantern-jawed German officer at their head. We conversed in a mixture of broken English and German. He seemed to be nursing a complaint; the attacks we were delivering in such rapid succession were not according to the rules of the game! I gave him a cigarette, after which he started collecting maps and scraps of messages out of his pockets with the intention of destroying them. I politely removed them out of his hands, and after that relations were rather strained, so I casually loosened the flap of my revolver case.

Our arrival at Brigade H.Q. caused embarrassment; they were very busy and suggested that I should take the prisoners elsewhere. Cooke, the B.M., was sitting up in bed in his pyjamas with a telephone at his side and maps spread out on his knees. I turned the prisoners over to some Brigade details and did a bolt back to my H.Q.

Taylor and Gibbons came down wounded, followed by Lumsden carried on a stretcher by two prisoners.

'How goes it, Lummy?'

'Rotten; I'm chock full of machine-gun bullets', he gasped.

I saw him into the Ford Ambulance on the road behind, and wondered whether he would ever again wield the bat in far-off Natal. He did recover, but his cricketing days were over.

I made my way up to Battalion H.Q. Saint was up on the Ridge, and Clinton and the Padre were doing all they could for two critical stretcher cases. H.Q. was in the Briqueterie, a disused brick-yard. A hole in the ground was covered over with corrugated iron, supported on railway metals. Cooper and Churchman were contriving a meal on two wooden shelves which also served as beds. Walker and Driver were at a wooden table, the four legs of which consisted of posts sunk in the ground. Five yards away, in a similar erection, the signallers had their instruments, and the two runners next for duty were sitting in the sun at the door.

Walker gave me the details of the morning's happenings. The Cambridgeshires got well away, with 'D' on the right, 'C' in the centre, and 'A' and 'B' amalgamated on the left. Casualties were slight when crossing the valley, but as soon as they reached the foot of the Ridge they mounted up. It was essential to capture the summit in the half light; the holding up of the attack half-way up, with no possibility of digging in the hard chalky hill, would have led to disaster.

The leaders, both officers and N.C.O.'s, were magnificent. Hollis, bearing a charmed life, went up and down his line, urging the sections forward. There were not many machine-guns left, but those still firing were well posted and difficult to locate. Suddenly fortune favoured the Cambridgeshires. The enemy machine-guns commenced firing belts with A-A tracer bullets; these showed up not only their positions, but the areas swept by their fire. There were a few minutes of confused bayonet work, and then the Companies swept over the Ridge to some ruined trenches at the foot of the eastern slope.

Shelling on the Ridge was still heavy; I did not envy Saint and those who had to establish communication with the Companies. Several small shells were falling round H.Q.; I thought they were probably 'overs' firing at the Ridge in front. I told Walker that I was worried about the position of H.Q.; I had an unhappy feeling about it all the time I was there.

Walker said it was the best that could be managed at the time. I had to agree that, if the shelling were, as it seemed, the 'overs' fired at the Ridge in front, anywhere in that area would be just as likely to receive shells. We were to be relieved that night by the Norfolks, and the pros and cons of selecting another H.Q. would be put to them.

On relief that night the Cambridgeshires were to withdraw to their original positions grouped round rear H.Q. I arranged for hot meals to be served when the Companies arrived. By 9 p.m. I could only keep awake by walking about; I suddenly realized that it was eight days since I had had a proper night's sleep: so I decided to turn in for an hour, to be called as soon as the relief commenced.

I was awakened by a white-faced runner shaking me violently. He bore a verbal message from Walker that 'a shell has dropped right into Battalion H.Q. and wiped out practically the lot. Saint is seriously wounded; please come up'.

I gave the man a drink and questioned him as my fumbling fingers laced my boots. Driver and the Signalling Officer of the Norfolks were killed; Saint was evidently very bad. When the runner left, Clinton and Walker were tying up the gallant Saint, who persisted in giving final instructions to Walker about the relief. Several of the runners and signallers were killed or wounded, and Sergt. Cooper was also a casualty.

By the time I arrived the ambulance had taken Saint away. To the last moment he kept Walker by him, questioning him to see that he understood the details of the relief, and asking whether I had arrived. As he was carried away he was heard muttering, 'Oie, Oie! Vat a game it is! Oie, Oie!'

I found Walker in consultation with Scarlett of the Norfolks, who had had the sense to give him a stiff drink. Walker declared that he was all right—only a few flesh wounds, but Clinton told me he was dubious about the after-effects.

I had only time for a glance at the wrecked H.Q. Saint, Driver, the Norfolk S.O. and Walker had been sitting round the table working out the relief. Cooper and Churchman, assisted by some of the runners, were packing up ready for moving. Clinton and the Padre had just gone across to the aid-post. The shelling, which had lasted all day, had been quieting down, and only one gun was still firing, but at increasing intervals. The very last shell to be fired that day crashed through the roof and table, and exploded in the ground. How Walker and the other survivors escaped was a mystery.

There was no time for reflection. The signallers had already re-established the broken lines; I was in command of the line until we were relieved by Scarlett's Companies. The indomitable Walker, covered with iodine, was parading the guides who were to conduct the Norfolk Companies to the positions on the far side of the Ridge. As each Company arrived they were despatched back to rear H.Q., where rations and hot food awaited them. Last of all, 'D' Company reported relief complete.

'Well, I think that is all', I said to Scarlett, who nodded in reply. Brigade were notified by code word, the Cambridgeshire signallers disconnected their instruments, which were replaced by those of the Norfolks, and we set out into the darkness, picking our way over the mile of broken ground back to the Battalion.

A few hours later we were engaged in the inevitable reorganization. Walker, in spite of all his protests, was packed off in the ambulance; it was obvious that he needed a complete rest; he was, however, absent exactly forty-eight hours!

Meanwhile the 37th Brigade were gaining further ground towards Combles, and at midday we were ordered up again in support at Maltz Horn Ridge. That evening I had to go up in a hurry to reconnoitre towards Le Forest, but we were not required, and the next morning the 47th Division passed through and relieved the 12th Division. Maltz Horn Ridge was now a 'rest area'.

The next day we moved to the huts in Favière Wood, only a few yards away. We were to have four days' breathing space; we needed it. Not only were we all spent both bodily and mentally, but the whole Battalion had to be reorganized. 'A' and 'B' Companies needed completely rebuilding, and all sections of the Battalion had sorrowful gaps to be filled.

Chapter XXVIII

THE TURNING-POINT

1–3 September 1918

M. C. C.

THE first week of September 1918 may not unjustly be regarded as the turning-point in the great autumn campaign. The British 3rd and 4th Armies, in conjunction with the French on the right, had, in the battles officially known as the Battles of Amiens and Bapaume, broken the German forward lines of resistance, and the enemy, fighting savage delaying actions, was slowly but surely being forced back to the outer defences of the Hindenburg Line. In the north the battle of the Scarpe was in progress, and the Drocourt–Quéant line was broken at last.

The Cambridgeshires, as part of the 12th Division, had helped by continuous fighting to drive in the German line to a depth of fifteen thousand yards, and there were already signs of the German Army cracking under the strain. As a fighting Battalion we were proud of our record, but we had suffered severely. In three weeks the following had been killed or wounded: C.O., Adjutant, S.O., R.S.M., 24 Company officers, and 397 N.C.O.'s and men.

To our great sorrow Saint had died of his wounds; perhaps I felt his loss more than that of anyone else in the Battalion. He and I were the last two pre-war officers to serve with the Battalion, though Cutlack and Bowes were still serving somewhere on detached duty. Saint had enlisted in the Battalion as far back as 1900, being gazetted to a commission in 1906. When the Cambridgeshires landed in February 1915, Saint was O.C. 'B' Company, and his Company was the first to come into action at St Eloi. After a spell as second-in-command he was brought home to command the newly-raised 4/1st Battalion. A home command was unsuited to his temperament, and he took the first opportunity to return to France, eventually attaining command of a Service Battalion. He poured into his new command all his enthusiasm and powers of leadership, only to have a setback. Through no fault of his own, Saint's Battalion met with a reverse, and he uncomplainingly took upon his shoulders the blame for other people's shortcomings. He returned to the Cambridgeshires, keenly sensitive but uttering no complaint against the injustice meted out to him. After attending the S.O.S. at Aldershot he returned in October 1917 to take Riddell's place as C.O. The award of the D.S.O. for his outstanding leadership during the March 1918 battle was tardy recognition of his gallantry.

When the news of his death was received I was informed by the G.O.C. that, but for his death, he would have received a further decoration for his work in August. I protested, pleading earnestly for this to be granted, but in vain; the regulation forbidding the award of posthumous decorations (except V.C.'s) was very definite, although it was continually disregarded by most C.O.'s, whose sense of justice rebelled against not honouring a gallant deed because the soldier died at the moment of victory.

I was given command of the Cambridgeshires, in which I had served for eight years. As a youngster who had just had his 26th birthday I suppose I should have felt elated, but the feeling uppermost in my mind was that I had just parted with some of the truest friends, both officers and men, that I should ever know. 'When shall we see their like again?'

A further blow was that Roger Tebbutt—another 'original', whom I had seen a few days previously—had been killed whilst serving with another battalion in the advance on our left flank. Roger hated the war, though he was a very brave man. Of a scholarly temperament, he was the complement of

his brother Oswald, whose death at St Eloi cut short a career
which would have ended as a General Staff officer. The third
brother Charles was then on his way to rejoin the Cambridgeshires, whilst Colonel Tebbutt, after his strenuous days in the
March retreat, was now an area commandant further north.

Sergt. Cooper, fortunately only wounded, would be sadly
missed at H.Q. Few men lasted three-and-a-half years at a
Battalion H.Q. on the Western Front. Cooper was as gallant
a performer with his rifle and equipment as he was with his
primus stove. Riddell had found at the Schwaben that he
was quite capable of carrying on Battalion H.Q. when all
officers were casualties. Few, if any, other battalions in
France produced a mess cook who, in addition to his normal
duties, could also act as Adjutant or R.S.M., and when
needed could guide a party in darkness to any point on the
map.

It was the turning-point in more ways than one. I was in
touch with the Reserve Battalion at home and knew what
officers we could expect in the near future. Tebbutt, Fison,
and 'Jock' Dunlop were on their way, but the majority of the
future officer-reinforcements were untried and unknown.
There is no aspersion in this. Hitherto it had always been
possible for new officers to have a turn of trench duty to
enable those above and those under them to assess their
value. Now the newly-joined officer was expected within a
few hours of joining to lead his men over the top. I still had
a number of tried officers in the Battalion, but the 27 officer-
casualties in August included, to name a few, experienced
officers like Saville, Spicer, Jackson and Hay. That old
warrior Baynes Smith still declared he was only temporarily
out of sorts, but Clinton insisted on sending him down.
Walker had no right to be there, but I could not spare him,
and the same applied to Hollis.

Turning to the others: they were a gallant lot, and had
earned the confidence of their men, but at that period we

had to budget for the loss of anything up to a dozen officers in one attack, and the position worried me. As regards the men, I had received drafts amounting to 350. About 50 of these were old hands, including several good N.C.O.'s, but the other 300 were boys called up in the Spring. Their average length of service was about fifteen weeks. They had fired a musketry course but knew nothing about Lewis guns. They had come straight from the base and had never been under fire.

On the other hand I had about three hundred men who had been through some or all of the attacks of the preceding month, and the framework of the Battalion—H.Q., and Company, Platoon, and Section leaders—was sound and reliable.

The *blasé* attitude taken by these veterans towards the war interested me profoundly. Officers reported that immediately a position was captured, consolidated and sentries posted, the men made a hearty meal and promptly went to sleep, oblivious of the shelling.

The usual superstitions were prevalent. Nobody would think of lighting three cigarettes with the same match, and it was unlucky to volunteer for a job. I also discovered, quite by accident, the existence of a system of classifying officers and N.C.O.'s as 'luckies' or 'unluckies'! One night, as I lay awake, with no intention of eavesdropping, I overheard the whole cult explained in detail. I was duly gratified to discover that I was a 'lucky', as was apparently Walker. If you were detailed to accompany a 'lucky', endeavour to walk on the same side of the path, and if you have to dive because of a shell, endeavour to get in the same shell-hole.

Light dawned on me. One day during an advance I fixed my compass on a gatepost to take a bearing; I then crossed the road to get a better view with my glasses. The four men with me also crossed over. When I recrossed they did the same, until I sternly ordered them to sit down until I had finished.

It was very fortunate to be considered a 'lucky', but at the same time it was bitterly unfair on some of the finest Company officers that they should be considered 'unluckies', and it might have led to disastrous results. Hollis was considered a 'lucky', which explained a puzzling occurrence at Maltz Horn Ridge. Hollis reported that during the attack he had to cross from the right to the left flank of his Company, and was amazed to discover that most of the right flank were following him; he led them back and corrected their direction, only to find that the left flank were following suit.

Nothing offends men quicker than mocking at their cherished beliefs and superstitions. I said nothing, but I made a mental note to watch out for undesirable developments.

As I write now, in these prosaic days, all this sounds very futile. It probably was, but at the time of which I am writing I doubt whether anyone was really normal. These discursions, however, present a sidelight on the attitude of the men to whom it fell to finish the war, and to a certain extent perhaps they explain the feeling I often sensed of the men trusting me, even when things went wrong. It had not lessened my sense of responsibility, but I do not deny that it was helpful to know that I was a 'lucky'.

Chapter XXIX

NURLU

4–6 *September* 1918

M. C. C.

THREE days' respite was a very short time for the Cambridgeshires to shake down before engaging again on active operations. We were, however, in similar condition to the rest of the 12th Division, and we were needed in the line.

At midday on 4 September I rode forward with the Company Commanders—Johnson 'A', Orbell 'B', Boyd 'C', and Harding-Newman 'D'—leaving Walker to embus the Companies at 3.30 p.m. *en route* for Frégicourt. We were blessed with fine, hot weather, and the ride up the valley via Combles was most interesting and gave an idea of the relentless pressure on the retreating enemy. Our destination was the north-east corner of St Pierre Vaast Wood, where we were to take over the Brigade Reserve position from the Royal West Kents in the 18th Division. The Norfolks and Essex were to take over the front line, which was, according to the information then available, 'somewhere in Vaux Wood, and possibly by now it includes Riverside Wood on the far side of the Canal du Nord'. The whole line was in a ferment, with parties of the enemy still in Vaux Wood. Through gaps in the trees I could see the line of trees indicating the main road through Nurlu village two-and-a-half miles away.

We rode back to meet the Battalion and guided the Companies at dusk to their posts. Relief was quickly completed; we had an easy task compared with that of the Norfolks and Essex. I went up to the latter to see what information I could glean. Further reconnaissance, however, was impossible owing to the nature of the ground, Vaux Wood being impassable owing to the undergrowth, except along certain narrow paths.

During the evening the eastern horizon was dotted with the glow of burning dumps, and when at 11.30 p.m. I was summoned to Brigade I knew what it meant, and told Walker to send out warning orders and collect Company Commanders to meet me on my return.

An hour later, when I returned, we went through the details of the intended operation. The enemy was withdrawing to the strong Nurlu position in a desperate attempt to stay the advance. He was believed to be clear of Riverside Wood (he was not quite clear, as it turned out), and an attack was to be made on the Nurlu line at dawn before he had time to settle in.

Whilst such an operation would normally require heavy artillery support, the time-factor would not allow us to wait for the guns to be brought into position; in short, we should be dependent on the number of guns that could be got into position by dawn.

The 36th Brigade was attacking on our right and on our left the Norfolks and Essex, the attack of the Cambridgeshires being directed onto the village of Nurlu itself, and timed for 7.45 a.m., one hour after the main attack. To make up for the deficiency in artillery support I was given a section of machine-guns.

The first problem to be tackled was the approach-march to Riverside Wood. One guide only was available, a machine-gun officer, who had been down to the bank of the Canal during the evening by a path through the Wood barely 2 ft. wide in places. The only method available, therefore, was for me to lead the Cambridgeshires in single or double file, with the guide accompanying me at the head of the column. This had the disadvantage of stringing the Battalion out over a distance of about one thousand yards, but it could not be helped, so we set off at 1.30 a.m.

Soon after we entered the wood the enemy put down a dense gas-shell barrage. We had no casualties from the shells, but the dark wood reeked of gas and masks had to be worn. For the next hour we made slow progress, wearing masks. It was necessary to make frequent halts to enable the rear to close up; over two hundred and fifty of the men had never been up the line before!

By 3.30 a.m. we were able to remove the masks, and presently we came up against a formidable obstacle. On either side of the narrow path the undergrowth consisted of dense thorn which was impassable. Fifty yards ahead the enemy was bursting salvoes of 4·2's with maddening accuracy. We timed the salvoes; they came every thirty seconds. I dared not run the gauntlet with my thousand yards of men. We waited and watched for twenty minutes; the shelling still continued. In vain we sought for ways round the danger spot; there were none; the enemy had chosen the place well.

It began to get lighter, and I discovered with a shock that we were on the top of the slope running down to the Canal, and that if the mist suddenly cleared we should be visible to the watching machine-guns on the opposite Ridge. Walker agreed that there was no alternative; Clinton and his stretcher-bearers would stay where they were in case of trouble; Walker would marshal the Battalion in small parties and set them off every thirty seconds, immediately after a salvo. A sprint, remembering the burdened men, would carry them just over the danger area before the next salvo.

I took the first half-dozen men, and as soon as the crash had come we sprinted. We kept on sprinting, hoping for a crash behind us to tell us that we were clear. But it never came; Providence decreed that the enemy should cease firing at that very moment.

By the time we reached the Canal Bank in the valley a

thick ground-mist enveloped everything. I thanked our guide, who had brought us to the limit of his knowledge, and crossed the shallow Canal by a plank bridge. A machine-gun was firing at the bridge, fortunately a few feet too high to cause damage.

The next obstacle, the narrow but deep Tortille river, was crossed by a bridge which Walker discovered, but neither of us could find Riverside Wood. We checked our position as well as we could with our maps, but though we wandered round in circles in the half light, whilst the Battalion waited, the Wood was not to be found; furthermore, we could not discern any large trees in the locality.

Eventually I found a small quarry—yes, according to the map there certainly was a quarry on the Canal side of River-side Wood. Then we tumbled to it: we were at our destination. Riverside Wood, although shown as such on the map, had been cut down and now consisted of a coppice, three or four feet in height.

I lined the Battalion under the steep bank and told them it was breakfast-time. As a matter of fact many of the new draft by that time were being realistically sick, due to a combination of phosgene gas and nervous strain.

My tunic reeked with gas. Suddenly I laughed, and Walker looked enquiringly at me; my thoughts had gone back to a pitch-black night in February 1915. We were behind the lines near Mt Rouge, and I was directed to lead 'C' Company home by compass over two miles of enclosed country. I had got them to their objective all right, but my route led them through a three months' accumulation of manure adjacent to some cavalry horse-lines! The laugh did me good; I felt happier than I had felt for a week. The Battalion could not be in too bad a trim after all; the last four hours would have been trying at any time; the veterans were playing their part magnificently.

Taking an escort of runners I hastened up the slope. The

scene was weird; rolling banks of fog occasionally lifted, showing parties of the enemy feverishly digging, whilst to the
south could be seen elements of the 36th Brigade moving up.
Sometimes it was impossible to discern friend from foe. For
a few seconds the fog lifted, showing the village of Nurlu and
in a neighbouring field a German officer in a long blue cloak
peering through his glasses; then the fog descended and all
was blotted out.

I sent for the Company Commanders. 'C' was to remain
in reserve, 'D' to attack south-east across the valley and to try
to enter Nurlu from the south. I did not know, for we could
not see, that it was guarded by an unbroken belt of wire ten
yards in width. Nor were we to know that the line of trench
so clearly marked on the map, which seemed to offer a haven
in the event of the attack being held up, was only spitlocked
out to a depth of six inches.

In the centre 'B' were to attack the western face of the
village; not much wire, but they must not dally on the level
plateau on this side of the valley.

On the left Alec Johnson's 'A' had the best line of advance,
but there was a considerable amount of wire to be faced in the
later stages. I left the Company Commanders to complete
any further reconnaissance and hastened back to the Battalion. Walker had despatched a party to help our attached
machine-gun section which was in trouble; a shell had caused
several casualties, and there were not enough men to bring
up sufficient belt-boxes.

I got hold of the machine-gun officer and gave him final
orders.

At 6.45 a.m. the barrage, very meagre, fell on the Nurlu
Ridge, and the troops on our right and left advanced. I
should have preferred to attack at the same time. It would
have been better if I had done so, but I had definite orders
not to attack until zero plus sixty minutes. It was a great
temptation, as the fog would have blinded the garrison in

the village; but it would have subjected us to our own second barrage, timed for 7.45 a.m. I could not consult the Brigade, who were two-and-a-quarter miles away, and so far they had run no line to us. So we should have to carry on according to orders; my only hope was that the fog would persist.

We moved the Companies up to assembly positions, 'A' and 'D' to the two flanks, and then 'B' under Orbell, with Nock bringing up the rear and smoking an enormous cigar.

Through my glasses I could see the 36th Brigade to the south. Their attack seemed to be progressing; they had, however, not yet gained the Ridge, and the barrage on their front was dying down; the guns were preparing to switch onto Nurlu for our attack; it was nearly 7.45 a.m.

The whine of shells directly overhead told me that the hour had arrived. The barrage was miserably thin and, worse still, the fog was rapidly clearing. I saw 'D' Company go over and disappear in the valley. Johnson was well away on the left, but the Company on the plateau were already having casualties—not many, but enough to make those youngsters who had never been under fire wonder whether things were going to plan.

We had lost sight of 'A' on the left, but I could see 'D' climbing the Ridge south of the village. They were trickling up to a line just below the summit; they were held up and were scratching in on the hard chalky slope. Walker went off to see if the machine-guns could do any more to smother the fire from the village. Two runners came panting in from Johnson; he was held up five hundred yards short of the village, but on a line with the Norfolks and Essex on the left. They were in a maze of old trenches, and were fairly happy, but the runners said that the journey back was Hell.

Another couple arrived from 'D'; they were held up by wire and were being enfiladed from their left and had to 'go to ground'. Still no word from 'B'. I was getting worried, and went forward with Walker. As we passed a clump of bushes we heard a noise and saw two Germans coming towards us. I pulled out my revolver, but they held up their hands, having thrown down their arms. We pointed to the rear, and they ran like scared rabbits in the direction of H.Q.

There were a number of walking wounded coming back from the plateau shepherding a dozen prisoners of the 6th Dismounted Cavalry Division, a miserable lot; I asked them when they had come into the line—apparently it was only last evening. There was a pause (I was not thinking about them) which they misconstrued, because they commenced pulling out their watches and souvenirs and offering them to me, all the time eyeing my revolver. I saw Banyard coming down wounded, and left the prisoners to continue their journey, and hastened to him. He had been hit on reaching the far edge of the plateau. A wounded batman came down; he told me that Orbell and Huckle were both killed. I gradually pieced the story together. On approaching the eastern edge of the plateau 'B' was caught in a barrage of machine-gun fire. There was a fatal moment of hesitation; casualties mounted up; Nock found himself the only officer left. 'Come on,' he shrieked, and dashed down the slope.

Of what happened after that nobody seemed to be able to give a connected story, but it was evident that the Company had suffered severely.

I told Walker that he had better go back and make out a report for the Brigade, and I set out with a runner to size up the situation. We breasted the plateau, and the enemy immediately spotted us. I had to advance in ten-yard rushes— things grew worse—eventually we lay flat on the ground, absolutely winded, and watched with a sickening fascination the machine-gun bullets kicking up spurts of soil all around us. It was hopeless to get further forward by that route.

I thought of Johnson's report about the ruined trenches on the left, so we crawled back about fifty yards and then struck out to the left. We still had to progress by nicely timed rushes.

As I lay on the ground I wondered what I should do if my runner got hit; he was a good fellow, but my errand was important. Eventually I spotted some of 'A' Company in a trench fifty yards ahead. Alec Johnson's voice hailed me: 'For God's sake, sir, don't cross there. Work round to the left'.

At last I reached Johnson. His men were fairly happy, but a wired strong-point fifty yards ahead was holding them up, and the Norfolks and Essex were similarly placed. We worked to the right, where I could see the edge of the village. There were a few khaki forms with Cambridgeshire shoulder-badges lying in the open fifty yards short of the Ridge, but there was no movement there.

As I worked my way back across the plateau, the stretcher-bearers, oblivious of the machine-gun fire, were at their merciful task. Wing, a hefty farm labourer hailing from Emneth, was tenderly lifting onto a stretcher a boy shot through both legs.

'That's all right, sonny; you're for Blighty. What do you mean by wasting your jam like that?'

This boy, under fire for the first time, had been lying wounded on the ground when he espied a German plane flying above him. He concluded that the plane (which was probably directing artillery) was going to fire at him, so he groped in his pack, spread his towel beside him, and smeared on it a Red Cross with the tin of jam he carried as part of his rations! Although I have mentioned Wing by name, he was but typical of the rest of the stretcher-bearers; they carried on regardless of danger. Only a few days later Wing died of wounds; he was one of several to be hit whilst performing an errand of mercy.

When I reached H.Q. Walker and I pieced the information together. With 'A' and 'D' both stuck fast on the flanks it would have been futile to reinforce them with 'C'. In the centre 'B' had to be written off as an effective force for the

time being. They had suffered severely, but the remnants of
their platoons were dug in in the valley in front of the
field, where we could not reach them. A section under Sergt.
Ransome was lying under two abandoned field-guns with a
few prisoners. They could neither advance nor withdraw, and
friend and foe lay there all day until dusk, when Ransome
duly delivered the prisoners to H.Q.

It was evident that nothing further could be done until
darkness allowed the necessary reshuffling of Companies.
'D' ought to be withdrawn; their way was barred. Grose,
who came down wounded during the afternoon, said that
they were just short of an intensely thick belt of wire with the
enemy in strength on the other side. Their withdrawal would
not affect the 36th Brigade on our right, and I determined to
get them back as soon as it was dark.

We had not been visited by Brigade, nor had they yet put
us into telephonic communication. As a result of this I received a message by runner at 6.50 p.m. to co-operate in an
attack with the 36th Brigade at 7 p.m. It was out of the
question.

At the same time the Essex on our left were counter-
attacked and had to give ground slightly. It was obvious
that our next effort would have to be made in the early
morning, and I arranged for the withdrawal of 'B' to reserve,
'D' to come back to act as a screen in case of a counter-
attack from the western side of the village, whilst 'C', which
had been in reserve, would probably be required on the left
flank.

During the evening definite orders were received to attack
again the next morning. I sent orders to 'D' to withdraw,
and sent Wallis up to collect and bring back the remains of
'B', a task which he carried out with great skill.

I discussed plans with Boyd ('C') and Johnson. We decided
that 'A' should attack the strong-point in trenches one
hundred yards to their front, and that 'C' should then pass

through 'A' and carry the Ridge, whilst the Berkshires attacked the village from the south. The assault was arranged for 8 a.m. next morning (6 September). This reshuffling of the Companies was carried out smoothly and quickly, and by 1 a.m. I found that for the first time since the morning of the 4th I had a chance to have a sleep.

Curtis arranged my Burberry and pack in a slit dug in the ground at the foot of a tree-stump, and I turned in to get a few hours' sleep. I was unable to discover any reason for my waking an hour afterwards; all I know was that I felt an irresistible urge to go up to Scarlett's H.Q. to talk things over with him. There was no real need for this as everything was cut and dried, but the fact remains that I felt I must go and see him.

Leaving my kit in the slit I went up the edge of Riverside Wood taking with me a runner who said he was too cold to sleep. When I had gone a short distance I remembered that I had foolishly omitted to warn anyone of my departure, but I did not expect to be away for any length of time.

Only occasional shells were coming over, but when I returned to H.Q. I found an excited group of Battalion H.Q. who were feverishly digging with their hands, clawing out the loose soil which filled the slit in which I had been resting. I heard Curtis exclaim: 'Here's his cap!' Then I arrived behind them and asked what all the trouble was.

Shortly before I returned a solitary shell had scored a direct hit on my 'slit' and blown my waterproof sheet, etc. into smithereens. But I never knew really why I went up to see Scarlett. Nor did Curtis nor the rest of H.Q. But the runners and signallers decided that henceforth the R.S.M. must be classified as a 'lucky'. He had been sleeping in that slit until Curtis awakened him and claimed it for me!

It was bitterly cold, so we decided to have breakfast, and then we established a forward H.Q. in the sunken road behind 'A' Company in readiness for the attack. My brand

new Battalion H.Q. flag, which marked the position for incoming runners, had already been torn by several jagged
pieces of shell. Some idiot was sticking it in the top of the
bank instead of the side; luckily we spotted it just in time.

Our attack at 8 a.m. was a complete success. 'A' charged
the strong-point in front of them; the garrison, except for one
man who surrendered, did not wait but fled. 'C' Company
passed through; I followed behind the last wave in their
thousand yards' advance, accompanied by Newman carrying
a basket of carrier-pigeons to enable me to send reports back
to Brigade.

The enemy bolted, and we occupied the Ridge with only
two casualties. We pursued them with Lewis-gun fire until
they took up position on the next Ridge eight hundred yards
to the east. They had evidently no intention of making a
further stand, and the troops detailed for pursuit gained the
line Liéramont–Sorrel soon after midday.

Battalion H.Q. was brought up closer in case of a move at
short notice. We were not, however, required, and the 37th
Brigade passed through us at 8 a.m. next morning and pursued the enemy to the Epéhy position. The 12th Division was
relieved by the 58th, and the Cambridgeshires moved back to
Riverside Wood for 'rest'.

Our casualties in the Nurlu action consisted of 3 officers
killed, 3 wounded, 25 other ranks killed, 70 wounded, and
5 missing.

Padre Walters, engaged with the Band in the sorrowful
duty of making a Cambridgeshire cemetery at Nurlu, found
the bodies of Nock and several of his men within a few yards
of Nurlu. It had been a valiant effort, typical of the gallant
Nock; had 'B' Company had a larger proportion of 'veterans'
they would doubtless have carried the village at the first
attempt.

I could not, however, but admire the way in which these
two hundred and fifty youngsters had carried out their job;

it was a baptism of fire such as might have dismayed more
experienced troops. As long as they had leaders they kept
steadily on, but when, as in 'B' Company, the officers (all
four) and the platoon sergeants became casualties they
quickly lost cohesion and were scattered in depth, to become
victims of their inexperience in how to make use of ground
and cover.

We mourned the loss of these lives, but I felt confident that,
given breathing-space and opportunity for training, we could
weld this new material into a weapon which would add
further to the reputation of the Cambridgeshires.

It would not be unfitting to close this chapter on Nurlu
with the text of the message sent by the Corps Commander
to Divisional H.Q.:

'Many congratulations on your occupation of the Nurlu
Ridge. The advance of the troops yesterday after the heavy
gas-shelling, and their progress both yesterday and to-day
in overcoming the stubborn hostile resistance, merit high
praise.'

Chapter XXX

PREPARING FOR THE HINDENBURG LINE

6–17 *September* 1918

M. C. C.

WE settled down in Riverside Wood. The men constructed brush-wood shelters housing about a section each, and these served admirably for the first week, as the weather was fine and warm. When later we struck a rainy patch we had to invoke the aid of the sappers to produce roofing, but only a limited amount was available.

The swift-flowing Tortille river provided a bathing-place on our doorstep. The proximity of the river had its disadvantages; the enemy knew that the river-line was the ideal position for horse-lines, of which there were miles, containing thousands of horses, and every night his planes were over with bombs. For several nights we watched the 'Archies'' attempts to hit the planes when caught in the beams of the searchlights, but without success. The position got serious; hundreds of horses were being killed or maimed each night; a neighbouring battalion lost sixty, and those not actually killed had to be shot.

The next evening the tables were turned; our searchlights caught the two bombing-planes in their glare, but no guns fired. What was happening? Thousands of onlookers watched the drama. Suddenly behind the bombing-planes we saw a gleaming fighting-plane; a distant crackle of machine-gun fire, and the first plane was falling in flames. As it fell the frenzied airmen released their bombs, which crashed in the open country, followed a few seconds later by the plane itself. The second bombing-plane met the same fate as the first, and a wave of cheering passed all down the crowded banks on either side of the valley. The same thing happened next evening, and after that our horses were safe.

We had brought up our battle-surplus and incorporated them in the reorganized Companies. We had a week's intensive training; the youngsters daily grew more like the hardened veterans. Hollis took up his former rôle of Battalion Lewis-gun officer. We made a L.G. range and did great work until the sappers a mile away sent a polite note praising our efforts, but suggesting that either they must move their camp or we our range!

Major R. G. Royle, D.S.O., of the K.O.Y.L.I., came as second-in-command and lightened the burden on the shoulders of Walker and myself. Johnson, Wallis, Boyd and Coles were to be the Company Commanders in the next show; I brought up the newly arrived 'Jock' Dunlop to help as well.

In the meantime the Divisions in the line were closing up to the outer defence of the Hindenburg Line. The enemy was putting up a fierce resistance. The 58th Division managed on several occasions to get into Epéhy, only for the enemy to emerge from the numerous deep dug-outs to cut them off.

The 12th Division were warned that their next task would be the Epéhy line; the Cambridgeshires were allotted the village of Epéhy itself, unless it fell in the meantime. The Brigade worked out their scheme: the Essex and Norfolks would attack Epéhy from the south-west and pass through to a line on its eastern side. We were to follow and remain in the village to mop up the numerous dug-outs and strong-points, and to prevent any smouldering opposition breaking out into flame.

I made myself a perfect nuisance. I demanded detailed plans of the Epéhy defences and air-photos taken from varying angles. Dunlop constructed a large-scale model, about twenty feet in length, on which the position of every known centre of resistance was marked, together with the platoon which would be responsible for it. The N.C.O.'s of every Company paid continual visits to the model, until everyone knew the part he would have to play in the attack, if, of course, things went according to plan. I had never heard of an attack in which everything had gone according to plan, and the only way to provide for this contingency was to keep one Company in reserve for eventualities.

Training and preparations for the next attack kept us hard at work. If any incentive had been needed, it lay in the fact that we were detailed for what might prove to be one of the most difficult tasks in the history of the Cambridgeshires. If the enemy would stave off defeat on the Western Front he must hold the Hindenburg Line, of which the Epéhy Line formed the Western defence, and it was unlikely that he would leave anything to chance.

There was evidently some idea on the part of the Higher Command that the enemy might attempt a counter-stroke before our attack was mounted. At any rate one afternoon I received an urgent order to reconnoitre the routes to, and a defensive line in front of, Tincourt Wood, five miles distant across country. The order allowed of no delay; we might be required that night, so I hurriedly detailed one officer of each Company to report mounted to me at once. We set off straight across country; fairly easy going, with only a few fences and banks. We had no time to lose, and arrived at our destination in very respectable time. It was only when I saw the pitiable state of 'D' Company's representative that I realized that something was amiss!

'But I thought you could ride,' I said; 'I detailed you because you had been in the Yeomanry': to which I received the amazing reply that he had never ridden a horse before. It was a striking instance of the 'theirs not to reason why' attitude which was the characteristic of the average subaltern at that period of the war. It was an astounding feat, but it caused much suffering for several days to the victim!

The attack was finally fixed for 18 September, and the previous afternoon I rode up to complete final details. Royle, who was to conduct the assembly of 'C' and 'D', brought up the Battalion after they had had tea on the Nurlu road. Whilst halted there they were addressed by the G.O.C. He was right in telling them that they had got to live up to the reputation of the Cambridgeshires as a fighting Battalion; but I was annoyed to hear that he also told them that they would have an easy task, when I knew that probably the very reverse would be the case, and had spared no pains in impressing upon them the magnitude of the rôle they would have to play.

Walker and I had a good look round and chose a dressing-station for Clinton close to H.Q. I left Walker with the signallers who had just arrived, and went back to meet the Companies at the point where 'C' and 'D', under Royle, crossed the valley to their assembly-position south-west of Epéhy, whilst 'A', who were to attack the western edge, and 'B', for reserve, moved up via Battalion H.Q.

There was a certain amount of congestion on this track-junction, mainly due to the belts of wire through which gaps had been cut. It was commencing to rain, and the enemy was dusting the area with shrapnel. This congestion was intensified by a mule which became entangled in the loose wires in a gap and then chose to sit down. I had issued a routine order that all pack-animals must carry wire-cutters, but it would not have helped much in this case as the mule, though equipped with cutters, was sitting on them. Other cutters were quickly available, but I spent an anxious ten minutes until the road-junction was clear.

I retraced my steps to H.Q. just in time to hear some unadulterated American 'cussing' flying in the air. Clinton had taken some heavy sheets of iron to roof over the trench that he was converting into a dressing-station. He was underneath sorting out his supplies when, in the darkness, his roof was mistaken for a trench bridge by the drivers of an 18-pounder and limber which were being brought up for duty as a forward gun. Happily the roof did not collapse, but Clinton was very annoyed.

H.Q. was in a dug-out consisting of a corrugated iron shed let into the ground, with a light covering of soil to stop shrapnel. It was built on the reverse side of a slight rise, which prevented direct observation from Epéhy. In front of this ridge were 'A' and 'B', there was a large gap on our left, then came the 58th Division, who were to attack the Pezière end of Epéhy and work down to meet us at the fortified strong-point in the centre of the village, known as Fisher's Keep.

After seeing 'A' and 'B' I returned to H.Q. to find that Royle had reported 'C' and 'D' in position some fifteen hundred yards across the valley on our right. I tested the two lines to Brigade; these were 'T'd' in, so that I could also speak to the Norfolks and Essex.

Both lines were in order; the stage was set.

Chapter XXXI

EPÉHY

18–30 *September* 1918

M. C. C.

IT was a wild, dark morning; the rain had been falling intermittently all night, and was now being driven in sheets by a strong wind. The enemy artillery had been comparatively quiet, but was now tuning up; they were evidently expecting an attack.

At 5.20 a.m. the western horizon was lit up with the flash of our guns, to be followed within a few seconds by the German reply; guns of all calibres firing, and a torrent of machine-gun bullets skimming the friendly ridge in front. It was the quickest reply I had ever known.

It was impossible to see anything that was happening. Although my line to Brigade was holding, those to the Norfolks and Essex had 'gone west' in the first few minutes. After about twenty minutes the light improved; I wrote a message to Wallis at 'B' Company: 'Can you see what is happening in front of you?'

The runners returned within a few minutes and stated that Wallis with his runner had gone forward into the valley and would report on his return.

'What,' I shouted; 'they have gone into the valley?'

Feverishly I turned up the carbon copy of my message; the wording was clear: '*Can you see* what is happening in front of you?'

I went up to 'B' in the trenches over the ridge. The C.S.M. confirmed the runner's report. 'The captain has gone into the valley to find out what is happening.'

I groaned. We had been warned that in previous attacks

this valley was swept incessantly by machine-guns, and must be avoided at all costs, and Walker had gone to the length of putting a warning about it in operation-orders.

I returned to H.Q. There was serious news from Sergt. Read of 'A'; he reported that their three officers, Alec Johnson, Keating and Carter, had all been killed; they were held up on the edge of the village and had not reached Fisher's Keep.

Meanwhile news had arrived from Coles which made me send two platoons of 'B' under Bond to reinforce him, by a route which kept them south of the bullet-swept valley.

On the right Boyd and Coles led forward their Companies behind the second waves of the Norfolks and Essex. It was their rôle to follow the two Battalions attacking Epéhy, and whilst the two Battalions passed through to the far side to continue their attack, 'C' and 'D' were to mop up the numerous posts and strong-points in the southern part of the village.

Rain was falling in torrents; it was dark, and the burst of shells gave little indication of the line of the barrage, as the German shells from the right were bursting in the same area. The slippery ground fell away sharply to the east; small wonder that the two Battalions, aided by the slope of the ground, eased off in that direction, missing the village. 'C' Company following behind on the right eventually found themselves engaged in a bitter fight by the railway embankment on the south-east side of the village. Boyd was wounded and Warren left in command.

Meanwhile Coles with 'D' had kept wonderfully accurate direction, but instead of fulfilling his allotted task of mopping up a portion of the captured village, he reached the edge to find it intact, and its strong-points manned by determined garrisons of the Bavarian Alpine Corps.

The village was not organized in definite lines of defence, but with a series of well-placed strong-points complete with deep dug-outs and alternative machine-gun posts, many of which consisted of manholes connected by underground passages, formed by knocking holes through adjoining cellar walls. The ruined houses, many of which had garden walls about four feet high, were described by one of 'D' Company as 'a nest of —— surprises'. Coles continued to make progress, but slowly, and in answer to his appeal I had already despatched two platoons of 'B' to assist in his attack.

If I had not had any responsibility, but had been merely a spectator, I could have found plenty to interest me in the view from Battalion H.Q. Taking advantage of the cover afforded by the rise in front of us, batteries of 18-pounders were moving up into the advanced positions. I noticed that, in addition to his flag, Clinton had a man posted to prevent his roof being used as a bridge again. Turning round I was amazed to see one of the reserve Battalions in artillery formation coming straight towards the rise and the bullet-swept valley. I sprinted across, shrieking to the C.O. who was directing the advance, and trying to raise my voice above the sound of the shelling:

'Where the Hell do you think you are going?'

'That's Lempire, isn't it?' he shouted, pointing to Epéhy.

'No,' I cried, 'it's Epéhy; and if you get over that rise fifty yards in front your Battalion will know all about it.'

He switched his Battalion off at an angle of forty-five degrees and disappeared with them into the smoke and mist.

Several wounded came in from 'A', with a few prisoners taken from a trench on the outskirts of Epéhy. These prisoners were tall and well set up, very different from those we took at Nurlu.

'A' could see the 58th Division to the left in the northern part of Epéhy, but Fisher's Keep was still holding out.

Coles was still progressing, and had dug sixty prisoners out of holes and cellars.

Hart and Bond with their platoons were engaged in a

gigantic rat-hunt, with the 'rats' biting back and causing casualties all the time. Fuller had been killed, whilst Woor and Burton had been wounded. Warren on the right had the enemy on three sides of him, and S.A.A. running low. Later on, when his S.A.A. was exhausted, he had the mortification of seeing about fifty of the enemy slipping away escorting some prisoners, and could not raise a finger against them.

I went across to see Coles. On the way I passed the body of a Cambridgeshire runner, with a small hole drilled in his forehead, still grasping in his left hand a message form, and in his right a half-burned cigarette. Coles, brave as a lion, but looking as miserable as Hell, had nearly reached his limit. I told him that the Berkshires were being sent up from the south-west to finish off the job; words could not express my admiration for the work he and his men had done. Taking a couple of runners I went up to the main street of the village; we made our way in the shelter of the houses and garden walls. I found a place which should have had a Lewis gun in position in case of trouble, and sent back one runner to tell Coles to send up a section to that point, and then continued my tour towards the eastern edge of the village. Coles despatched the section with the runner as guide. As they came up the street a Bavarian popped up a machine-gun out of a hole, fired a burst, hit every man of the section in the legs, and then dived down, to reappear at another point some distance away. That was typical of the fighting in Epéhy.

I lost my way and got too far to the right. I soon knew all about it, and beat an undignified retreat in a series of dives from shell-hole to shell-hole.

The Berkshires had arrived, and their additional weight enabled the southern end of the village to be cleared; but Fisher's Keep held out until 7.45 p.m., when only eleven men remained out of the original garrison of forty-six; the Bavarian Alpine Corps were tough fighters. Coles had sections in various positions in the village, and withdrew the rest of the men to posts on the southern edge. Later in the evening Cropper Post was found to be occupied, and it fell to 'D' Company to deal with this outbreak.

When I got back to H.Q. Walker told me that the bodies of Wallis and his runner had been found in the fatal valley. Walker got 'A' Company concentrated again; we still had the remainder of 'B' in reserve; and Coles had the two other platoons and his 'D' on the southern edge of Epéhy. We could not locate Warren and the remainder of 'C'. Brigade warned us that we should be attacking again some time during the next day. I left Walker to piece things together; I needed a couple of hours' sleep if I was going to keep a clear head.

The early hours of the morning brought me warning orders for the next attack. I left Walker with instructions to keep 'A' in reserve and move up 'B' and 'D' and any parts of 'C' that were available, and I went forward to reconnoitre.

The position on the eastern side of Epéhy was involved. The Sussex of the 36th Brigade had their H.Q. in Princes' Reserve Trench, with remnants of their Companies holding a line of trenches five hundred yards to the east across the Malassise valley. On their left were two Companies of the 5th North-amptonshires, and further still to the left the Berkshires. On the right were troops of the 37th Brigade, which had taken a line just forward of Malassise Farm.

The enemy were in strength in Room and Ockenden trenches, which had a clear field of fire up the valley, and prevented any bodies of troops moving up to the front line of the Sussex in daylight.

The objective of the attack at 11 a.m. was to be the line of Room and Ockenden trenches. The attacking troops could only be brought up under cover in daylight as far forward as Princes' Reserve Trenches, which meant that they would have to do an advance over the open of five hundred yards before they cleared our front-line troops. After that there would be an advance of eight hundred yards before they could rush the enemy position.

The Sussex were to stay in their present position until after the attack, which would be undertaken by the Queen's on the right, then the Cambridgeshires, two Companies of the Northamptonshires, and the Berkshires on the left—a miscellaneous force and a complicated manœuvre.

As was constantly the case, I found on arrival that there were no telephone lines run forward to connect us with either the Brigade or the guns. The two Companies of the Northamptonshires were there in readiness, but there were no signs of the Queen's. I expected and hoped that they would turn up, but I knew that the scheme was being carried out at short notice.

We did not get the Cambridgeshire Companies into position until ten minutes before zero. Coles with 'D' was on the right, 'B' under Bond on the left, and in the centre some platoons and sections of 'C' under C.S.M. Howard.

I had barely enough time to point out to the leaders their objective and give verbal orders. The Queen's had not arrived, and I had seen no officer belonging to them. Our line of attack lay straight down the valley, but I relied upon the two Northamptonshire Companies on the high ground on our left to prevent us from being taken in flank from the north. 10.55 a.m. arrived and still the Queen's had not turned up. What did arrive was a message from the Brigade that the Northamptonshires were not to attack but would be withdrawn to join their battalion.

I glanced at my watch; it would be impossible for me to reach both Companies in time to stop them; furthermore, if I could stop them it would mean the Cambridgeshires advancing down the valley with no troops on either flank. One's brain works rapidly on these occasions. I thought of the countless times Riddell had repeated to me that paragraph in Field Service Regulations about the recipient of an order

The Maltz Horn Ridge

Imperial War Museum photo.

Epéhy: prisoners being marched back

THE FINAL ADVANCE, 1918

disobeying it if he was certain that the issuer was not aware
of the circumstances prevailing at the time of its receipt.
Walker scribbled a reply to the Brigade saying that I had not
withdrawn the Northamptonshires, and then the barrage fell
and the Cambridgeshires advanced.

On the right, Coles, who had led 'D' Company consistently
well in a series of attacks, received a nasty wound, from which
he eventually lost a leg, and C.S.M. Howard dropped into
H.Q. to have his wounds dressed. The platoons, now mainly
commanded by N.C.O.'s, advanced steadily over the Sussex
line and fought their way forward but could not gain the line
of their objective, and the Northamptonshires were similarly
placed. We could make no further advance until dusk.

My reserve was augmented during the day by the arrival
of Warren with his exhausted men, who had been cut off in
the advance of the previous day. Thomson of the Sussex had
lent me a captured 'V'-shaped pair of artillery glasses mounted
on a stand. (I hoped he would forget about them, but he
did not.) These enabled me to see with great clarity what
was happening. Our men had dug in in the low ground short
of their objective, where they were suffering from sniping and
machine-gun fire from Ockenden Trench. We still had no
telephone back to Brigade, but Walker produced Stamper,
a battery Commander. I pointed out to him our trouble;
could he help us?

Of course he would, only too delighted. His signallers ran
out a line, whilst he moved a section of his guns further left
behind Epéhy to enable him to enfilade Ockenden Trench.
One or two ranging shots, rather close to 'B' Company, and
then he got the exact range. He was an artist at his job; he
burst shrapnel only a few feet high over the trench; he traversed
the length of it; he lifted the range a few yards to encourage
the Boche to remount his machine-guns, only to switch back
onto the trench.

Another battery Commander arrived; this time it was Case,

an old schoolfellow. He had heard I was in trouble and came to see if he could help, but Stamper was doing all that was necessary, so Case switched his guns onto the limbers and guns which the enemy was trying to extricate further down the valley.

About 6 p.m. Walker grasped my arm: 'Look; the Boche is clearing out!'

Away on our left, through our glasses, we could see parties of the enemy trickling away down a sunken road.

'That means,' I replied, 'that he is clearing out of the trench in front of us. Stamper, can you order your battery to cease fire fifteen minutes from now and prevent other batteries firing on Ockenden trench?' Stamper replied that it should be attended to. I grabbed the first man I came across, who was Brown, the H.Q. sanitary man, and we raced up the valley. As we approached our men lying in the valley they scrambled up and came back to meet me, doubtless thinking I was coming up to withdraw them. I told them the enemy had evacuated the trench in front and we were going to occupy it. As we pressed forward our numbers were increased; now we had a line of about thirty, including Bond, Hart, Wilkin and a few of the Northamptonshires.

Suddenly a naked feeling came over me, akin to that experienced when one wakes up dreaming that one is attending a garden party in scanty attire plus spats. I had nothing in my hands; my equipment and revolver were hanging outside H.Q.

I grabbed a rifle with fixed bayonet and a bandolier which were lying on the ground, and caught up the advancing line. There was not a sound; we breasted the slight rise. Merciful Heavens! the previous tenants were still there; they had not left, and for some unknown reason had not spotted our advance. There were a few in the trench, but the majority were crawling back to the trench through the long grass in the rear. A tall Bavarian and I fired simultaneously at one another; we both scored misses, but the man on my right brought him down. I gave a yell, and we jumped into the trench, and opened fire at the enemy behind. Out of the corner of my eye I saw a Bavarian three traverses away to the right.

'Bond, quick!' I shouted; 'have you got a bomb?'

'I am very sorry, sir, but we are completely out of bombs', he replied in his best City manner. A Northamptonshire on my left without a word handed me a bomb out of his haversack in the interval between opening his breech and ramming in another clip. I pressed the bomb into Bond's hands, told him to get a bayonet man in front of him, and work towards the right as fast as he could.

A few seconds later clattering footsteps came up the wooden floor-slats from the right. The bayonet man arrived first; going round a corner in the approved style, with Bond carrying the bomb behind him, he ran head first into an enemy couple approaching from the opposite direction. Both startled bayonet men turned and stumbled back over their bomber, and our bayonet man was followed by the dishevelled Bond.

Bond was really angry; he told his bayonet man what he thought of him, and then, preceded by Sergt. Roper, he returned to the charge, but the enemy had fled, and we established a stop some distance down the trench. At the same time Hart had made progress along the trench on our left, and with the enemy disappearing from our front I thought they would be able to hold on until I pushed up further reinforcements.

I told Bond that before I left H.Q. I had told Walker to send up 'Jock' Dunlop, who had been brought to H.Q. He was fresh, and the very man to deal with the situation.

Going back I met Jock half-way with his runner. I told him what had happened, and pointed out the limits on our flanks in the captured trench. I told him I would push up some more men to garrison the trench better and he left me with a cheery smile.

We had just parted company when the enemy put down a heavy barrage across the valley, so heavy that we both had to take shelter in holes, and by the time it quietened down it was rapidly getting dusk.

I got back to H.Q., thanked Stamper for his help, and went down into the signal dug-out to report to the Brigade. A few minutes afterwards Walker propelled a panting runner before me. It was Jock's runner; in the rapidly increasing darkness they had struck Ockenden Trench too far to the right, where the enemy were still in occupation. Jock had been hit, seriously the runner thought; tragedy had followed close on the heels of comedy. Walker was very distressed, and organized a party which went out and brought Jock in about an hour later. I saw his was a bad case, and his death the next day deprived us of one of the best leaders the Cambridgeshires ever possessed.

We held our gains that night, and the next day Warren was able to make further progress down the trench to the right, until we held the whole of Ockenden Trench on that side of the valley.

That morning the Brigade received a very welcome reinforcement in the return of Vincent to resume command of the 35th Brigade. We were all glad to see him recovered from his injuries. His experience, skill, and the support he afforded his C.O.'s through thick and thin were worth an extra battalion to Brigade at that juncture. He took in the situation at a glance; his little pat on the back for our efforts during the two days' fighting did a lot to dispel the feeling of weariness and strain from which we were all suffering.

The Cambridgeshires were now organized as one composite Company in the line, whilst the supports consisted of two composite platoons and Battalion H.Q. details under Crosher, who had served throughout as Intelligence Officer.

Maps and air photos indicated the existence of a trench parallel to, and further forward of, our present front line. Walker and I explored this and found it unoccupied, and we pushed our advanced posts into it on the 21st, materially strengthening our position thereby. In the meantime the 36th and 37th Brigades were having a bitter fight to capture the enemy posts on the high ground on the right. In one attack the Royal Fusiliers lost 10 out of 13 officers and 270 other ranks. We did not take part in these attacks, but our area shared in the general liveliness and retaliation which they provoked.

The night of the 23rd saw us at last relieved, after six days of effort and strain, and the weary men were brought back to a position on the embankment east of Epéhy. We brought up the battle nucleus and reformed the Battalion into four weak Companies, each of three platoons, but it was a difficult matter to provide enough officers. The irrepressible Charles Tebbutt arrived, for which I was thankful. Officers like him were a godsend at a time like this.

Crosher's batman, Gosling—civilian occupation a poacher —produced a twelve-bore gun and crept about the broken ground, slaying some of the coveys of partridges, which were plentiful, and provided a welcome addition to our rations. I went out one evening and did quite well until I got caught in a barrage in the valley and had to beat a hasty retreat.

The Official War Diary notes that on the 26th we moved into support at Little Priel Farm. This laconic statement covers a move which was part of the immense scheme for the historic capture next day of the Hindenburg Line. Although we had no attack to make, our job was to guard the left flank of the operations which were to sweep through the hitherto impregnable line and seal the fate of the German Army. Immediately on our right the attacking troops were two American Divisions, supported by the remnants of the Australian Corps. The G.O.C. and the three C.O.'s of the

35th Brigade in effect held a watching brief, and we might be called up in certain eventualities to take a hand in assisting the American C.O.'s.

My poor Companies at Little Priel Farm got a good deal of the shelling and had twenty odd casualties, but they were cheered by the sight on their right. Sitting with Vincent on the embankment, we watched the spectacle through our glasses. Through the burst of the shells and smoke-screens we could plainly see our tanks fighting their way up the slope, whilst British gunners fired the barrage.

For a time things did not go well with the Americans, and Clinton spent his time parading up and down the road in rear of the American H.Q., telling all and sundry that he belonged to the British Army although he wore an American uniform. He made himself extremely unpopular by offering to show some of their officers the way to the front line, but at length even Clinton had to admit that his fellow-countrymen were delivering the goods.

It was unlikely that we should be called upon in the immediate future for a further attack. We were played out; in twelve days our casualties had mounted to 6 officers killed, 6 wounded, 36 other ranks killed, and 152 wounded.

On the night of 30 September we were at last withdrawn to a position west of Epéhy, to be taken back in buses the next day. As the Padre, Walker and I were walking back through the ruins of Epéhy my thoughts turned to the Forty whose sacrifices had made our efforts successful. We left them sleeping on a slope close to where the Twelfth Divisional Memorial now commemorates those battalions which fought and suffered in the historic battles of Epéhy and the Hindenburg Line.

Chapter XXXII

THE ADVANCE FROM VIMY RIDGE

1–10 *October* 1918

M. C. C.

AFTER a night spent in the shelter of banks and hedges between Epéhy and Guyencourt, buses moved us back to Proyart, and we stayed that night and the next day in bivouac on the banks of the Somme.

Next day we had a train journey in a real train, the first we had seen since the end of July. True, we only moved to Aubigny, a matter of thirty miles as the crow flies, but it took from 5.25 a.m. until midnight for us to arrive at our destination.

Aubigny was rail-head for the Vimy Ridge sector, one of the few places where the line had not already moved forward. Villers-au-Bois, to which we marched, provided us with a hutted camp, where we spent the day preparing for a move into the line.

The reorganization of the Companies had already been carried out. Three of the Company Commanders, Tebbutt, Hollis, and Harding-Newman, were experienced, whilst the fourth was a stout fellow.

Clinton insisted that Walker must give in and go down to a Casualty Clearing Station for a complete rest. Bowers took his place as Adjutant, and it was decided that Royle should command the Battalion for the tour of duty in the trenches. I badly needed a rest after the events of August and September, and Royle was naturally anxious to take his turn.

I stayed at transport, partly because I wanted to explore the Vimy Ridge, which I had never seen before. Another reason was that, like the majority of C.O.'s at that period, my rank of Lieutenant-Colonel was an acting one. If I left the Battalion and went down to a C.C.S., a sudden influx of casualties might see me transferred to the base. In this case I should run the risk of some clerk in the War Office discovering the fact, and of my being obliged to relinquish my acting rank, and of having to complete a further fifteen days in command of the Cambridgeshires on my return, before I could resume my rank. This may seem rather mercenary, but there had been several cases of C.O.'s who, during their fifteen days' re-qualifying period, had become casualties and suffered accordingly.

Royle took the Battalion by bus to Thélus on 5 October, and the next morning they took over the front line between Fresnoy and Oppy. I spent a couple of days sightseeing on the famous Ridge. The eastern horizon as far north as Lens was black with the smoke of burning dumps, and a heavy pall hung over Douai on our right. It was evident that the enemy was preparing to retire in this sector.

When the transport returned from taking up rations on the night of the 7th, they brought a message from Royle reporting that they had had a trying day. The Higher Command, in view of the enemy's intended withdrawal, had initiated a system of sending out battle-patrols consisting of platoons to test the strength of the enemy and where possible to occupy tactical points. Royle had been ordered to send out four platoons that day under a barrage, and they had had bad luck, as the enemy was holding the line in force.

Hopkins, one of the last-joined officers, had been killed with the 'A' Company platoon, which was unable to reach its objective. 'C' Company platoon had been driven back at first, but on advancing again up the communication trench three gas shells had burst in the middle of the platoon, killing two men and drenching the rest with gas. The two platoons from 'B' had gained their objective, but were counter-attacked from three sides and eventually driven back, leaving McNish and several men cut off.

I went up next morning to see Royle who had things well in hand. The Padre had also come up, and on enquiring about the men who were killed by the gas shells learnt that they could not be brought back, and their bodies had been covered over with a light covering of soil. Unknown to me, the Padre had worked his way out along the communication trench. He recovered the personal effects of the two men and gave them a decent burial—a dangerous proceeding, but typical of Padre Walters.

I told Royle before I left that the Brigadier thought that I had better take a few days' leave, but that I should not be going before the 12th. Things were quiet in the line that day, but the patrols pushed out early next morning found the enemy had gone. Royle occupied the enemy's front line with 'A' and 'B', and later in the day these Companies pushed on a further two thousand yards without meeting serious opposition.

The next morning 'C' and 'D' passed through and reached the sunken road in front of the famous Quéant–Drocourt line, but met with greater opposition than on the previous day. Tebbutt's Diary mentions how their spirits rose when they saw the progress they were making:

'The rest of the 10th was passed quietly except for the first issue of rum for the winter, with the result that my C.S.M. started practising bombing, with live bombs, in the trench we were holding. The Company H.Q. cook disappeared over the parapet towards the enemy before I could stop him. Explanation was given by my servant that "he wanted to have a game with that there machine-gun"; he came back an hour later very muddy, complaining, very soberly, that "that there machine-gun had had a game with him".'

The 11th of October was always a 'moving-house' day at home: the Quéant–Drocourt line received some new tenants that day in the shape of 'C' and 'D', but the next day saw even more astonishing happenings—the Cambridgeshires were moving forward in artillery formation after the retiring enemy.

I was to go on leave that afternoon, and rode up to Brigade to get my warrant and see the Brigade Staff. Vincent was up the line, but Cooke told me that we were following up the enemy, who were withdrawing to the line of the Haute Deule Canal. I felt like a schoolboy going on holiday, and putting my warrant in my pocket I rode up to the next rise to have a look at the view. A wide level grass plain led up to the Flers–Hénin-Liétard road with its miners' model villages and pit-head heaps of refuse, or fosses as they were called. Through my glasses I could see infantry and guns moving forward; on my left a field battery was limbering up in readiness. My contemplation of the panorama was disturbed by a remark from Hughes: 'The Brigadier seems in a hurry, sir'. Vincent was galloping across the plain, leaving his mounted orderlies far behind him. I waited to say good-bye to him.

'Clayton, you are just the man I was coming for. Royle has established his H.Q. by that fosse; as I was talking to him a machine-gun opened fire and Royle was hit. Go up at once and take command.'

I galloped across to the Cambridgeshires to find Tebbutt commanding. For sentimental reasons, if nothing else, I would have liked to have seen him commanding the Cambridgeshires; one might almost say it was his right both by patrimony and service.

Tebbutt had H.Q. in a big culvert under the road, and although he had only taken over an hour before, his Companies were all disposed in good positions. I saw nothing that required altering. On the left the Essex were attacking Courcelles, advancing by short rushes. They eventually cleared it, but were unable to make further progress; the enemy had a strong position behind the Canal.

A mile and a half to the right was the village of Auby, on the western bank of the Canal; we were the right Battalion of the 12th Division. The 2nd Northamptonshires of the 8th Division were trying to force an entry into Auby, which was surrounded by a level plain on three sides.

I saw the Northamptonshires work round to the west and north, but they were held up about two hundred yards short of the village. Machine-guns on the west and the strong wire-netting of a prisoners' cage on the north had stopped the advance, and that evening they were withdrawn and Auby was added to my frontage.

Curtis had come up with rations, and had had the sense to bring up my equipment and working clothes, and I changed into them from my holiday attire. The retreating enemy were leaving plenty of excitement behind them; the whole area was well provided with dug-outs, but 'booby traps' were common. Delayed-action mines were blowing up for weeks afterwards; the loose board in a floor, or a helmet hung on a peg, might be the means of detonating a mined dug-out, and the sappers had a busy time discovering and rendering safe these traps.

Further advance was impossible until Auby was in our hands, and Harding-Newman with 'D' was detailed to make an entry into Auby by patrols working along the railway embankment under cover of the early morning mist.

The present H.Q. was badly placed now that we were responsible for Auby, so Bowers went up with signallers to form a new H.Q. in one of a row of miners' cottages behind Fosse 7. I arrived as it was getting light. Our new H.Q. was the first since July which had had a tiled roof intact over it. Bowers had chosen No. 2 in the terrace; the signallers had just finished sweeping it out and were connecting their instruments in the cellar, into which I went down; there was nothing wrong with the house, but I had a feeling that I did not like it, and issued peremptory orders to move into the next house.

As I stood peering over the garden wall in the direction of

Harding-Newman's patrols the signallers were moving into
the new H.Q.; I overheard one of them grousing like fury at
my fickleness: 'There was nothing wrong with the other place;
if the C.O. didn't like it, why didn't he leave the signallers
there and run a line into the next house instead of messing
them about like this?'

I went down into our new H.Q. to see if they had got
through to Brigade. As I came down the steps a 5.9 dropped
through the roof of No. 2 and exploded in the recently
evacuated cellar, and for the next few seconds there was a
perfect rain of broken tiles and bricks.

Silence reigned; the signallers looked at me in awe; the
signaller on the instrument turned round to the grouser and
said: 'You bloody well ought to have been left in that cellar'.

The mist still held; I was hopeful that 'D' would get into
the village in time to let the other Companies get up before
the mist disappeared. Standing at the corner of the garden
wall I heard a few rifle shots and the crackle of a machine-
gun. A few minutes afterwards I saw Harding-Newman
running along the embankment towards H.Q.—Harding-
Newman, immaculate as ever, as though he were going for a
walk down Bond Street. As he ran alongside the fosse a 5.9
burst on the bank, enveloping him in a dense cloud of coal-
dust. When he emerged from the cloud, still running, he was
a Kaffir, black from head to foot. I rocked with laughter. He
registered a formal protest at youth laughing at the misfor-
tunes of the aged and infirm (he was about twenty years my
senior in years) and then reported on the situation. Auby was
strongly held; his leading section had bumped into an enemy
post, of which there were several; Myer had been wounded,
not seriously, but the enemy made a sortie and they could not
get him back before he was captured.

I told Harding-Newman to withdraw to the Flers Road
whilst the mist still held, a task which he accomplished with
a few minutes to spare.

It was finally decided to attack Auby under a barrage on 14 October. The Cambridgeshires were to attack the northern part and push through to the banks of the Canal, securing the crossings if possible. The 1st Worcesters of the 8th Division would attack from the south and join hands half-way through the village.

During the evening the 8th Division reported their belief that the enemy was abandoning the Canal line, so at 10.30 p.m. Tebbutt, accompanied by Bowers, moved up his Company towards his assembly position and sent a platoon forward to reconnoitre. When still one hundred and fifty yards short of their position a machine-gun opened fire from a point which was supposed to be held by the Worcesters. No casualties were incurred, but Tebbutt very properly moved his Company back, and Bowers came back to report to me so that we could notify the gunners. Forming up for the assembly two platoons of 'B' lost their way, and only Hoole and one platoon of 'B' took part in the assault under orders of Hollis. The gunners had warned me that their barrage would be a tricky business; not only were their guns badly worn, but most of the creeping barrage had to be fired from a flank, a difficult operation at any time.

Tebbutt's report on the assault gives a good description:

'Directly the heavy shelling commenced it became clear that something had gone wrong with the gunners; the barrage resembled more closely an "area shoot", the assembly positions being well within the "area". Shells fell in, behind, and immediately in front, of the leading Companies. H.-N. and I decided simultaneously, and independently, that shells were better than machine-guns and took both our Companies forward. This was justified in so far that the enemy were caught coming out of their cellars, and the attacking Companies reached their objective without a check.

'"D" Company on the left met with most resistance, capturing about forty prisoners. On the other hand several

casualties were caused by our own shell-fire and some by the
enemy's, which soon became pretty active. The leading Companies at once began to dig in. After a few minutes' pause
on the first objective to allow our guns to get ahead, "C"
Company moved through and took their objective, in which
only a few of the enemy were found. When, however, they
tried to get forward again, to take the third objective, "B"
Company being missing, they found themselves unable to
advance owing to heavy and accurate machine-gun fire from
the further bank of the Canal, which it was impossible to
locate or get at. The fight then became a duel between Lewis-
and machine-guns.'

During the advance Robinson of 'A' and Powditch of 'D'
were wounded, leaving Harding-Newman with 'D', Tebbutt
with 'A', Hollis, Ebbutt, and Wilkin with 'C', and Hoole
with 'B'. Directly we reached the objective the Boche blew
up a big dump in the village.

As soon as I saw we had entered the village I went up,
meeting on the way a runner with a message stating that the
Worcesters were nowhere to be seen, and that, whilst we had
reached the Canal Bank in the northern half of Auby, the
southern end was full of enemy.

Tebbutt met me on arrival; our right flank was completely
in the air. I ordered him to put a post covering the cross-
roads on his right flank at the narrowest part of the village,
and went forward three hundred yards to where Hollis was
with 'C'. His men were digging in behind hedges in orchards
and gardens just short of the Canal. I went up to one of the
forward posts which should command a light wooden bridge
over the Canal. As I arrived the bridge was blown up. A
moment later one of 'C' Company pulled me down behind
the wall just as a machine-gun traversed the length of its top,
for which I duly thanked him.

I came back and saw Hollis and Tebbutt. I told them that
they ought to hang on although our right flank was in the air,

in case the Worcesters were able to make a further advance and clear the southern part of the village. I would go straight back to the Worcesters' H.Q. to find out what had happened; meanwhile they must send out patrols to the right, and if they were threatened by an attack from that direction, Hollis would have to bring 'C' back from its advanced post to form a defence on the right of 'A'.

Immediately I had left, the two patrols I had ordered went out, very wrongly—it was not their job. One patrol consisted of Tebbutt and a man, whilst Hollis went out with the other. Both had narrow escapes. Tebbutt was fired upon from a barricade near the bridge, and had to beat a hasty retreat.

Hollis with one man proceeded down a street between two rows of houses. Round the corner he met a party of enemy; he had to bolt back up the street; the enemy soon reached the corner and commenced firing at the two retreating figures. When they had about thirty yards to go to reach cover the man was hit in the hand. 'I'm hit, I'm hit, I'm going to faint!' he shouted. 'No, you don't!' said Hollis, and delivered a well-aimed kick at the man's backside. This had a tonic effect, and they dead-heated in the race for cover!

Shortly afterwards a party of the enemy crossed the Canal by a plank bridge on 'C''s right flank. Hollis thereupon decided to withdraw and took up a position on the right of 'A'. This movement was carried out with remarkable steadiness, 'C' moving back over three hundred yards of open ground under fire until they reached the shelter of the houses behind 'A'. They then reorganized and took up a position on the flank—just in time, as the enemy were already trying to work round the flank.

Whilst this had been going on I had arrived at the 1st Worcesters' H.Q., one and a half miles away. Their C.O. (F. C. Roberts, V.C., D.S.O., M.C.) told me the reason for their non-appearance. They had had an exciting night; they had been counter-attacked after dark, involving several

Companies in fighting, and the position even then was not quite cleared up. In addition they had had a direct hit on the Battalion H.Q., which had caused severe casualties. In answer to my enquiries Roberts said he was perfectly all right himself, and hoped to get his advance going shortly; as a matter of fact we got in touch with them again that evening.

When I got back to H.Q. I found a message from Tebbutt and Hollis stating that the shells from our 18-pounders which were aimed at the Canal were hitting the houses held by 'A' and 'C', causing casualties.

The gunners told me that they had only one battery of 4·5 howitzers available, but these were substituted for the 18-pounders. The Brigade sent up a Stokes mortar, which did good work in quietening the snipers, and I obtained a further reinforcement of four machine-guns for each flank, and felt happier, especially as during the evening Hollis further prolonged his right flank and got into touch with the Worcesters at the cemetery.

The next day, except for spasmodic shelling, was uneventful, and we were relieved during the evening by the Norfolks and marched back to the model village of Hénin-Liétard.

Our casualties during the ten days since we came into the line had amounted to 9 officers (of whom fortunately only one was killed) and 107 other ranks. Considering the nature of the operations, we could feel relieved that they had not exceeded this figure.

There were several lessons to be learned from the Auby fighting. It emphasized the value of officers like Tebbutt, Hollis and Harding-Newman, especially as it developed into a Company Commander's battle. I could exercise little influence on the operations once the Companies had entered the village.

I should have liked to move H.Q. into the village to keep closer control. To have done so would have been a wrong move. On the left of Auby was a gap of several hundred yards between us and the Essex, and not only was Battalion H.Q. the channel of communication between the Companies in Auby with the guns and the rest of the Brigade, but its personnel were the only infantry available to form a screen in this gap between the enemy and our guns in the event of a counter-attack.

Auby also emphasizes another lesson—the difficulties encountered when the attack on a village is allotted to the two flank battalions of two Divisions. If the attack had been delegated to two battalions of the same Brigade, one G.O.C. would have been responsible, and the battalions would have been in close touch with one another. As it was, the 8th Division on the right of Auby must have known early that the Worcesters had enough on their hands without the further task of an attack on Auby, but this news never filtered down to me or even to the 35th Brigade. In 'set piece' attacks this difficulty was overcome by liaison officers at Battalion H.Q., but in open and semi-open warfare, with Battalion, Brigade, and gunner H.Q. constantly on the move, the problem was greatly intensified.

Finally, firing barrages on villages with worn guns and low trajectory shells is a risky business; an operation like Auby required a concentration of 4·5's—and under one commander.

Chapter XXXIII

THE FINAL ADVANCE

15 *October*—20 *November* 1918

M. C. C.

THE night of 15 October and the following day were spent in the village of Hénin-Liétard. The village had been untouched by the war; H.Q. was in a villa complete with garden and croquet lawn; luckily for our peace of mind we did not know what was underneath the villa.

Padre Walters asked to see me alone and informed me that he had received an order to join for duty behind the lines. If I wished him to do so he would go and see Brumwell, the senior Nonconformist Padre of the Division, with a view to the order being cancelled. We all hated parting with Walters, but I felt it had to be; he was not young and had gone through a harrowing time during the last three months.

Walters stood in the front rank of Padres. In or out of the line he went about his work quietly and unobtrusively. Of frail physique (he dropped dead at a football match some years after the war) he never spared himself; his M.C. was awarded for tending the wounded under fire earlier in the war. He laughingly used to say that he had forgotten the meaning of sects 'for the duration'. He used to complain about having to wear badges of rank; his idea was that it raised a barrier between him and the men he had to serve, but he was a master-hand at breaking down barriers of any description, when they prevented him from performing what he considered to be his duty.

I went across to Brigade and was duly chaffed and asked how I was enjoying my leave, to which I made suitable reply. During the night a party of the Royal Sussex had succeeded in crossing the Canal on a raft and secured a bridge which permitted the rest of the Sussex to cross over. The enemy, finding his flank threatened, had evacuated Auby, and the Norfolks had crossed the Canal and were taking up an outpost line two thousand yards to the east. The enemy was carrying out a withdrawal on a large scale.

That night we moved up to Auby, and Walker rejoined as adjutant. Brigade warned me that advanced guards might soon be the order of the day, so I put the forward transport up with the Battalion and the Drums accompanied it. They were to play on the march when possible, and to act as escort to the transport. A further duty soon devolved upon them, to pass the limbers over the many demolished culverts and bridges.

The sappers were working hard all night constructing a pontoon bridge over the Canal. Charles Tebbutt had a birthday party (bully and a bottle of 'Bubbly' between ten!). Walker in the midst of taking over from Bowers discovered that a set of maps had been left at our 'villa residence' back at Hénin-Liétard. Two cyclists were sent off; on their return they informed us that the maps were not to be found; shortly after our departure a delayed-action mine under H.Q. had exploded, with disastrous results to the villa.

When we moved off in the fog on the morning of 18 October it was by Companies at hundred yard intervals. We thought it only fitting that the Drums should play us out of Auby. The leading Company was stepping out on the pontoon bridge; suddenly I remembered that 'troops should break step when crossing pontoon bridges'! It took a lot of invective to convey the meaning of my order.

We were to move to Raimbeaucourt; ahead of us were the Norfolks as advanced guard and the Essex in support. Soon I felt grateful for the thick fog; the road was crowded with artillery which we overtook, and there was a complete jam. What a target for enemy planes or guns if only the fog lifted!

I decided that we would not add to the congestion, so we marched on the grass verge and eventually cleared the traffic jam.

The fog began to lift. Suddenly I heard yells of joy from the leading platoon—civilians, certainly only an old man and his aged wife smiling from their garden gate, but we had entered the occupied zone at last. Soon we saw crowds of civilians, including children—hollow-cheeked, with wan faces, upon whom the men started to thrust their rations. The sun broke through the fog; Brigade sent word that the enemy was in retreat, so our Drums struck up. We entered a village —flags, including Union Jacks, were flying from practically every house—and rumour declared that the day previous the enemy had sent vans round selling banners.

The civilians were raising cries of 'Vive l'Angleterre!', but they were physically at a low ebb. Suddenly a woman dashed into her house and returned rending the blossoms off a geranium in a pot. She presented the flowers to me; I gravely saluted and placed them between my tunic and gas helmet. That was a signal for a concerted rush on the part of the villagers; soon the Sergt. Drummer, the Drums and the leading platoon had anything from geraniums to aspidistras stuck in their equipment.

This all sounds like a Drury Lane spectacle, but it must be remembered that for four weary years these civilians had heard the guns but had waited in vain for deliverance.

This distribution of rations had to be stopped; we might want ours shortly; there were plenty of other troops following behind. I am afraid, however, that my orders carried very little weight; the groups of hungry children proved too much for discipline, and I had to turn a blind eye on what was happening.

A few prisoners came down from the advanced guard; they needed a strong escort, to protect them from the villagers. The shouts of welcome to us were changed in an instant to yells of hate at the sight of the detested Germans. It gave me an uncomfortable feeling, the intensity of their hate; poor devils, probably they had ample cause for it.

Scarlett with the advanced guard, consisting of the Norfolks, two batteries of guns, and a section of machine-guns, was in touch with the enemy rear-guards and progress was slower. We halted just through Raimbeaucourt. H.Q. was formally established at a cottage on the road-side, the H.Q. flag on its lance-shaft being tied against the garden fence. On the opposite side of the road a section of 18-pounders opened fire on some distant target; away in front there was a distant crackle of musketry; the civilians heeded it little—this was their day of deliverance.

The cookers came up and fed the waiting troops; the bulk of the meal issued was passed on to the civilians. I rode down the line, feeling ridiculous with my bunch of geraniums; to have discarded them, however, might have given offence.

Orders came to move forward to the village of Boujon for the night. On arrival the Companies bivouacked in farms and houses, whilst the H.Q. flag hung limply outside a deserted estaminet. This had evidently been used by the enemy as there were several wires leading into some of the windows. The R.S.M. reported a large automatic piano in one of the rooms, with wires leading into the lid. I was suspicious of it so we cut the wires, and the assembled H.Q. were warned to leave it severely alone.

Late in the evening Walker and I were poring over maps and orders, whilst Clinton was dozing on a form against the wall. Suddenly the air was rent with 'music' from the suspected instrument. Walker and I slid onto the floor, whilst Clinton rolled under his form; then there was silence, only broken by Clinton's muttered curses on that 'blarsted pianner'. We looked at one another; nothing happened; then in the passage outside a flow of invective. This was directed on two runners who had been absent when the warning was issued. We laughed when we knew what had happened, but everyone was feeling the strain.

Tebbutt arrived; he had been the recipient of an order to 'report to the War Office forthwith for employment at home on compassionate grounds'. He was furious; some relative had made an application on the grounds that he was the last surviving brother and his father was serving in France.

'I'm sorry, Charles; there is nothing for it; you will have to go.'

'Well, sir, do you mind which route I take?'

'No', I replied, 'as long as you carry out your orders.'

'Well, then, I shall strike across country to Lille, which has just been recaptured, and see my father, who is somewhere north of there.'

So Tebbutt departed next morning, saw Colonel Tebbutt, reported to the War Office, and, as soon as he had exhausted their patience, returned to the Battalion.

One or two shells arrived during the night just to remind us that we were still at war, and the next morning we moved off in support of the Essex, who were the advanced guard. It was necessary to limit the advance each day, one of the main reasons being that every day we were moving further away from rail-head. The roads across the devastated strip would in many cases be impassable to motor vehicles for some days to come, and our supply-line was getting longer and longer. Pooley, Grain and the transport slept when they could, about once every few days; every night there were rations to come up on congested roads, and every day a further move of Q.M. stores and the drawing of rations from fresh supply-points.

Our daily advances were, therefore, comparatively short, although usually in touch with the enemy's rear-guards. We halted at midday at Coutiches and then moved on to a point a mile west of Orchies. I went forward to see Johnson of the Essex at Orchies. He uttered a solemn warning; when he entered into the square a few hours previously he was surrounded by a cheering mob, with the usual flowers. In an unguarded moment he dismounted; it was a fatal mistake; in an instant he was submerged beneath a wave of females of all ages trying to kiss him. Johnson was now regaining his composure, and his men were taking up an outpost-line to the east of the town.

I rode back with Vincent. We stopped to examine a huge crater which the enemy had blown at the cross-roads; on my way up I had detailed a work party to construct a road round it to allow limbers to get past. As we returned towards the Cambridgeshires we saw the inevitable football game in progress.

'I didn't order that', I said.

Vincent laughed; 'I like to see it—does them good. By the way, what is that troop of cavalry on the left?'

'That, sir', I murmured, thinking of the countless certificates rendered that we possessed no horses in excess of establishment; 'that's my mounted infantry section'.

Vincent chuckled; 'Well, you may need that to-morrow'.

At dusk we took up a support-line in houses and farms behind Orchies. H.Q. was in a farmhouse, where the aged farmer and his wife were pathetically watching the flames from their stack and barn, which had been fired by the enemy immediately prior to their retreat.

Orders for the next day did not arrive until after midnight. My advanced guard was to consist of the Cambridgeshires, one section of guns, and some cyclists. A squadron of cavalry would be out, acting independently during our six-mile advance, and we should form an outpost line that night east of Sameon.

There was a wide front, so I detailed a vanguard for each of the two roads, which were roughly parallel—Harding-Newman's 'D' on the right, and Hardman's 'A' on the left. I told them I did not intend to use guns if I could help it; the enemy always chose his defensive positions in front of occupied villages, and unless we got up against something really nasty, I thought our own covering fire would be enough.

There was a raw mist and a slight drizzle as we passed through the outpost line. I saw the two vanguards set out and then returned to the remainder. The band was having a hectic time; bridges and culverts had been blown up and big craters formed at road-junctions. They were working like niggers, filling up holes and man-handling the limbers and guns over the difficult places.

We approached a village; in horror I observed a section forming a point marching gaily up to the entrance in close order. Fortunately it was all right; the enemy had gone and the inevitable banners were being hung out of the bedroom windows. I managed, however, to pour a few winged words into the ear of the officer who was exposing his command in such a casual manner.

As we cleared the village I heard the sound of firing ahead, which I thought was in front of 'D'. As I rode across I saw that Harding-Newman's platoons far out on the right were losing direction; they were advancing parallel to the railway, which ran thirty degrees south of our line of advance. Before I got there Harding-Newman had spotted it and corrected it.

As I galloped back, a far distant machine-gun opened fire on the mounted figures of Hughes and myself. When I regained the shelter of the road I was amused to hear 'C' Company settling up fifty centime bets made on the chance of either or both of us getting hit. In case, however, any reader of this account should consider their conduct callous, it is only fair to suggest that the men who were cheerfully laying the odds would probably have been the first to dash out if we had been hit.

We soon approached Landas. A regular fusillade broke out about a mile further ahead. In addition to attending to the battle, I had to do the polite; I was duly presented with flowers, and sat on my horse saluting, whilst the oldest inhabitant sang the Marseillaise in a quavering voice. The ceremonial was brought to an abrupt end by the arrival of a Hussar officer, who reported that his squadron had approached Sameon to find the enemy holding it strongly in front of the village, mainly with machine-guns.

Walker and I went forward to have a look. The one-and-a-half miles of open space between the two villages was perfectly flat; we could just detect the enemy machine-guns in front of Sameon—about thirty men with several guns. 'D' and 'A' had both deployed and were advancing in platoon rushes. The enemy fire was mainly directed against 'D'; the tiles of a barn roof a few yards from where Walker and I were standing were flying in all directions. 'A' were getting well ahead; 'D''s covering fire was proving effective. It would not be necessary to deploy 'B' and 'C'. The cavalry got ready to dash forward to cut off the enemy as soon as 'D' got within striking distance. I told them to wait for a few minutes; I knew what was coming. When issuing orders I had told Company Commanders that the state of training of many of their men would not lend itself to the niceties of sectional rushes under covering fire; in other words, our covering fire would probably be more dangerous to ourselves than to the enemy. I advised them to experiment with a Company in line firing ten rounds rapid and each Lewis gun one drum if they encountered serious opposition.

Harding-Newman had evidently decided that the moment had arrived. There was a roar of musketry; through my glasses I could see the tiles of Sameon clattering down in all directions; but it had done its work—the enemy was on the run, and 'D' were closing in and extricating the remaining enemy out of their posts, together with three machine-guns.

The cavalry set off at a gallop and soon disappeared on the far side of Sameon. It was as well that they had not started earlier; a line of wrecked telegraph posts and wires lying on the ground would have forced them close into the village.

'D' and 'A' were now well through the village and on the way to their outpost position a mile further east. I told Walker to go up to the village and arrange the disposition of the supports whilst I stayed behind with the remainder of the Cambridgeshires and the guns. I am afraid that it was rather unfair, but I thought that the waiting civilians might work off some of their enthusiasm on Walker before I arrived. His 'ceremonial entry' was, however, a complete washout owing to the enemy choosing that moment for an ill-mannered outburst of shelling on the entrance to the village.

H.Q. were established in the Mairie, recently evacuated by the German Town Major, and Clinton set up his dressing-station there as well. To my astonishment there were no casualties; in spite of the thousands of rounds fired by the enemy machine-guns not a single man in the attacking Companies had been hit. Later in the day, when I returned from the outposts, there was a still form lying on a stretcher, covered by a blanket; a patrol sent out from the outposts had bumped into trouble in the next village of Rumignes.

The enemy had evidently withdrawn his field-guns, so I let the Drums give a programme outside the H.Q. From the window I watched the faces of the crowd; they were intensely interested in the performance. As the band struck up the first bars of the Marseillaise I looked out of the window again. There was now no chattering or pointing at the evolutions of the tenor drummers; the crowd were standing in silence, with tears coursing down their cheeks; it was four long years since they had heard their national air played in public.

I afterwards had a talk with the Curé, a fine old priest and a man of culture. The village had had a hard time during recent weeks, and food, never plentiful, had become rapidly shorter. The enemy had removed anything they fancied in the village—furniture, carpets, and even a piano had been loaded into waggons. The church-bells—they went many months ago.

'See, Monsieur le Colonel, where they cast them down from the belfry; never will I forget the sound those bells made as they crashed onto the hard pavement; and then they made us load the fragments into carts to be sent to munition factories.'

Walker and I slept in a house adjoining H.Q.—real beds, the first since July. The enemy awakened us before the hour of 'stand to'; a high velocity gun from a long distance was using up its stock of shells before withdrawing. The first hit the garden wall, the next uprooted the vegetables below our bedroom window. We speculated whether the next would hit our mahogany bedsteads, but it sailed over the roof. Unfortunately it landed on 'B' Company's cooker and killed Strange, one of the cooks who had served in the Battalion throughout the war. It was bad luck; as it happened, he was the last man in the Battalion to be hit during the war.

The Norfolks moved through our outpost line at dawn and we concentrated in Sameon as Support Battalion. On the 22nd we moved a short distance away to Rue Balary as the Brigade was now Divisional Reserve, and here Tyte of the Royal Fusiliers joined as second-in-command.

Meanwhile the Brigades in the line were finding the advance gradually slowing down; they had crossed the Scarpe at St Amand only to find that the area to the east had been flooded. It was whilst reconnoitring for a site for a bridge that the 12th Division lost Bob Dawson of the R.W.K.'s, who had just gained the third bar to his D.S.O. An outstanding leader; as a boy from Sandhurst he had been gazetted in June 1914, by December 1916 he was commanding the Battalion, and he commanded it until the last day his Battalion was in action, when he received his seventh and fatal wound.

On 26 October I was mounting my horse to go up to re-connoitre, preparatory to the Cambridgeshires taking over the front line that night, when a message arrived to say that the move was cancelled and the 12th Division was to be relieved.

Two days' march brought us back to Raches for a period of training and refitting. We found much to interest us; the civilians were digging up their gardens and unearthing their treasures, hidden from the covetous eyes of the invaders. In the garden behind H.Q. we helped to dig up a complete set of dinner-ware, hidden to prevent it sharing the fate of the piano and carpets which had been carried off by the late German Town Major.

It was at these H.Q. that one afternoon a runner knocked on the door of the mess with:

'Beg pardon, sir; the Prince of Wales.'

This was the first time we had seen H.R.H. since we went to the 12th Division. At Ypres in 1917 he was a familiar figure, especially in that horrible area of the Canal Bank. He did a tremendous lot of good; a few words and a smile, and a dejected and tired working-party felt that things were not quite as bad as they seemed. Whether it was wise to let him cross those deadly canal bridges which were continually strafed is another question; there was always a general feeling of relief when it was known that he had recrossed in safety after his visit.

Our stay at Raches was devoted to training in open war-fare, and it did a lot of good. The recently joined drafts had begun to take on that hard-bitten look of the experienced soldier. This short spell of open warfare proved a welcome relief after attacks under barrages. War news in general grew more exciting every day, and for the first time the men in the ranks began to take interest beyond the happenings in our own immediate vicinity.

My often deferred leave came at last. Early one morning

Higginson called for me at Raches and I accompanied him in his car to Boulogne, and was thus able to breakfast in France with the Cambridgeshires and lunch in London a few hours later.

In the meantime the Divisions in the line were pressing hard on the enemy's rear-guards, but the systematical destruction of roads was making the supply both of rations and ammunition difficult. It had already been necessary for the Divisions in reserve to contribute a portion of their horse-transport to fill the lengthy gaps between supply-points and the line. In places these distances had increased to forty miles, and it was imperative that the roads should be made passable for lorries, in addition to horse-transport; the only other alternative was to call a halt in the pursuit.

The Divisions in support, including the 12th, also had to move closer to the leading Divisions; thus it fell to the Cambridgeshires when they moved up to Odemez on 9 November to stop and repair the roads *en route*. The next day they moved to Hergnies, repeating the performance. In the early hours of 11 November the fateful news was received. Tyte came in to breakfast with a message form. 'We stood in silence wondering what it all meant; then we awkwardly shook hands all round and sat down to a hurried and scanty meal. We slaved all day repairing the roads, pulling down walls and collecting material to fill the holes, and I doubt whether even at the end of the day we realized the full significance of the news.'

The next day they moved to Bonsecours, repairing roads *en route*, and I found them there on my return. After a few more days of road repairing we resumed training once again, but it all seemed very unreal.

The Sunday following the Armistice saw a ceremonial Brigade parade, followed by a thanksgiving service at the Basilica. This immense building was thronged. In addition to the Brigade, civilians crowded every inch of the edifice. Many of these had only returned from deportation a few hours previously. The organist had arrived in the early hours of the morning. He was playing his beloved instrument with every stop pulled out. The six priests entered and bowed ceremoniously to Vincent, and the service commenced. The climax was an oration from the pulpit by a venerable priest in French and Flemish; later he called and presented Vincent with the manuscript of his sermon. After the sermon the Brigade marched past Vincent and then dispersed. In the afternoon the Cambridgeshires gave a concert in the Convent on behalf of the poor. The civilians vociferously applauded every item. They cheerfully endured my appalling French when I appealed for a handsome collection, and the Sister Superior and the nuns looked on smiling with folded arms.

It was whilst inspecting billets in the Convent that day that I came across several men who were feeling off colour. That night one of them died of heart-failure due to 'flu', and fresh cases were reported every day. The cases were almost invariably men who had had a long period of service; several of them had served in the Battalion since 1915, and continued hardships seemed to have impaired their powers of resistance. They were of course evacuated to hospital at once, but for weeks afterwards I dreaded looking at Part 2 orders; they nearly always contained names of men who had borne the burden of the campaign, only to fall now that the fighting was over.

Two days' marching brought us back to Somain on the Douai coalfields. Here I learnt that yet another Cambridgeshire officer had passed over. Kenneth Gill was one of that fine body of Cambridge undergraduates who had enlisted in Bowes' 'B' Company at the outbreak of war. Gazetted shortly afterwards to a commission, he had proved a fearless officer, and his exploits whilst on patrol with Hopkinson were commemorated in Sir John French's Despatch. Upon recovering from his severe wounds he had transferred to the Flying Corps, but sustained fatal injuries in a crash a few days before the Armistice.

Chapter XXXIV

DEMOBILIZATION AND RETROSPECT

20 *November* 1918—21 *May* 1919

M. C. C.

SOMAIN was to be our home for several months. Demobilization had commenced. Meanwhile there was plenty in hand to occupy us; salvaging of war material was carried out on a large scale, interspersed with field training. Although the Armistice had been signed we were still officially at war.

Somain was an important railway-junction; the supply trains for the Cologne bridge-heads were marshalled in the sidings. Unfortunately they became subject to raids by bands of half-starved civilians. Guards had to be posted every evening, with orders to fire if necessary. We were forced to do so on several occasions, and for weeks one Company was permanently on duty at the railway-junction.

A colour party consisting of Pooley, Grain, and three sergeants repaired to Cambridge and brought out the colours, which had been laid up since August 1914. The remainder of the infantry of the Division, being New Army units, had as yet no colours. To repair this omission the Prince of Wales presented a King's Colour to each of the service battalions at ceremonial parades held for that purpose. The Cambridgeshires were on parade with their King's and Regimental colours, so were inspected at the same time. In answer to the Prince's query I told him that the Cambridgeshires' Colours were presented by King Edward in 1909 at Windsor.

'Oh, yes', he replied. 'I was there as a small boy and

remember the parade and Grandfather presenting the colours.'

During his stay with the 12th Division the Cambridgeshires were chosen to provide the guard. I wish a photo had been taken of that guard; they were picked men, not only for their physique but for the ribbons they wore, a gallant lot and worthy of the duties they had to perform. Our ceremonial march past the Prince was in fact the last time the Battalion paraded as such in France. The Cambridgeshires made a brave show with their colours fluttering in the breeze. The Drums were dazzling in their splendour; they had just carried off the Eighth Corps championship and had been placed second in the 1st Army.

Demobilization was being accelerated, drafts were being sent off daily to demobilization centres, and soon we had dwindled to 'cadre' strength of six officers and fifty men. This included the Drums and enough men to handle the transport-vehicles and stores. Our horses departed for an unknown destination; I went round the previous evening to say good-bye to 'Queenie' and 'San Fairy Anne', which had endured my indifferent horsemanship for over twelve months.

Divisional and Brigade Staffs were breaking up, several going to appointments at the Rhine. Higginson and Vincent both had kind things to say about 'their Cambridgeshires'. This gradual dissolution of Brigades and Battalions was trying for discipline; men waiting to go home, with reaction setting in after years of strain, were inclined to get out of hand, but we never had the slightest suspicion of trouble in the Cambridgeshires.

Shortly before the Cambridgeshire Cadre commenced its homeward journey I was arranging entraining details with a newly posted Staff officer. I mentioned casually that I hoped the Staff would see us off at the station.

'Well', he replied, 'we should like to, but I am just wondering whether it would be tactful. You see, the other day we went down to see the ——'s entrain and the whole lot were as drunk as newts, and had to be carted to the station and loaded into waggons.'

'My dear man', exclaimed a companion, 'you don't know the Cambridgeshires; Clayton's men will be perfectly capable of marching past in slow time with uncased Colours if he thinks fit to issue the order.'

And it was so. I possess a photograph of Walker inspecting the Cadre preparatory to handing over the parade to me for our march to the station; the ranks were steady, and each man a credit to the Cambridgeshires. As we marched into the station yard a khaki-clad individual from the Demobilization Camp was heard enquiring of a typical old sweat wearing the Mons ribbon: 'Who are them?'

The old sweat spat, and then replied: 'Take a good look at them, Chum; them's soldiers; real soldiers!'

A train journey to Dunkerque and embarkation on a ship with the Cadres of the 2nd East Lancashires and our old friends the 4/5th Black Watch were followed by a leisurely progress up the English Channel. It was a beautiful day, the sea was like a mill-pond, and the three bands took turns in playing. The white cliffs of England stood out sharply in the bright sunlight, and to the south we passed and left behind the land to whose keeping we had committed the bodies of so many wearers of the Cambridgeshire badge.

We drew into Southampton at the same quay whence we had sailed in February 1915. I was the only officer who had been present on both occasions, but this experience was shared with several of the men. The next morning we loaded our transport and stores and entrained for Sandling Camp. Here stores and vehicles were handed over, a task of several days, and at last, on 21 May, the Cambridgeshires as such made their final war-time move to Cambridge.

The welcome was worthy of a great occasion. The Lord-Lieutenant was the first to greet us; he then introduced the

Mayor of Cambridge, followed by the Mayor of Wisbech. (The latter, my father, had in his official capacity bidden farewell to my Wisbech Company in 1914.) Everyone in Cambridgeshire or connected with the Cambridgeshire Regiment seemed to be in Cambridge that day; familiar figures, strange in civilian attire, increased each moment the escort of our Colours as we made our progress through the crowded streets.

In addition to County, Civic, and University dignitaries, invitations for the luncheon had been sent to the relatives of the men forming the Cadre. It fell to me to respond to the toast of the Cambridgeshires—an ordeal: but I tried to tell them in simple words what I knew of the officers and men who had worn the Cambridgeshire badge during the long months since the Battalion left Cambridge in 1914.

That evening we escorted the Cambridgeshire Colours back to the Regimental H.Q.

'Fall out the officers!' Walker, Tebbutt, Harding-Newman, Hollis, and Bowers formed in line and saluted. For the last time, 'Cambridgeshires, Slope—Arms, Dis—miss!'

.   .   .   .

Nearly fifteen years have elapsed since I gave that last war-time word of command. Memories tend to fade, but the passage of time allows one to view the war in truer perspective, and perhaps in a more dispassionate manner.

We have tried to avoid writing a bare recital of the sequence of events. Few people read the preface to a book, but therein we have stated our reasons for writing the story in the form of a personal narrative.

We have had two major worries. The first was that we were unable to do justice to our theme; the second concerned the inclusion or omission of names of officers and men.

A Commanding Officer forming a mental picture of his command naturally sees in the foreground the figures with

Col. Clayton with Battalion H.Q., November 1918

Left to right. Front row: MAJOR TYTE, COL. CLAYTON, CAPT. WALKER
Back row: LIEUT. COPE, LIEUT. POOLEY, CAPT. CLINTON

Cambridge Chronicle photo.

The Cadre marching through King's College, 21 May 1919

VICTORY

which he was constantly in touch. Thus it happens that certain names constantly recur in the text. We are, however, keenly conscious that whilst we directed, others did the fighting. We could compile a list of at least one hundred names of those whose gallantry and devoted service merit mentioning in a book on the Cambridgeshires. To have worked in these additional names would have added to our already numerous publishing difficulties. Furthermore, if we had added this one hundred names we should immediately have been confronted with the question of whether we had not been unfair to a second hundred still omitted. We had, therefore, to adopt the general principle of mentioning whatever names fitted into the ordinary course of the narrative.

Nearly nine hundred of those whose gallant efforts are described in this book lie in those vast cemeteries across the English Channel. Upon their headstones is no mention of their achievements; merely a few brief particulars, but the whole surmounted by the Cambridgeshire badge. We who survived may not have our names mentioned, but we can hold up our heads when we say 'I was a Cambridgeshire'.

Those who joined the Regiment were not fire-eaters in any way. They were civilians; the vast majority had never touched a rifle before 1914. Some were at school or training for a career; others were employed in a trade or had businesses of their own. Many had wives and families dependent upon them. When the crisis came they armed and submitted themselves to authority. They came forward, not as aggressors, but to defend their homes against the menace of the greatest military machine the World had ever known.

At times, especially in the Spring of 1918, there was little left but Hope. It almost seemed as though the sacrifices of those long weary months had been in vain. Even in the Autumn of 1918, when the tide was definitely turning, there was no lessening of the burden. Those last hundred days cost the Cambridgeshires twice the fighting strength of a Battalion.

Few came through unscathed, but though they suffered they endured.

Victory was at hand.

The news came as the light crept in one cold, grey, November morning.

Appendix I

BATTLE HONOURS

'SOUTH AFRICA, 1900–1'

'YPRES, 1915, 1917', 'Gravenstafel', 'St Julien', 'Frezenberg', 'SOMME, 1916, 1918', 'Thiepval', 'ANCRE HEIGHTS', 'Ancre, 1916', 'PILCKEM', 'Menin Road', 'Polygon Wood', 'Broodseinde', 'Poelcappelle', 'PASSCHENDAELE', 'St Quentin', 'Rosières', 'Lys', 'KEMMEL', 'Scherpenberg', 'AMIENS', 'Albert, 1918', 'Bapaume, 1918', 'HINDENBURG LINE', 'Epéhy', 'St Quentin Canal', 'PURSUIT TO MONS', 'FRANCE AND FLANDERS, 1915–18'.

Honours printed in capitals are borne on the Colours.

Appendix II

SUMMARY OF HONOURS AWARDED

K.C.S.I. (1); C.M.G. (1); D.S.O. and 2 bars (1); D.S.O. (5); M.C. and 2 bars (2); M.C. and bar (6); M.C. (31); D.C.M. and bar (2); D.C.M. (30); M.M. and bar (6); M.M. (172); M.S.M. (5); French Military Medal (Médaille Militaire) (1); Bronze Italian Medal (1); Belgian Croix de Guerre (1); Special Promotion for Service in the Field (Brevet Lieut.-Col.) (1); Special Promotion for War Service (Brevet Major) (1); Mentioned in Despatches (27); C.B.E. (2); O.B.E. (3); Officially mentioned by the Secretary of State for War (14).

Appendix III

SUMMARY OF CASUALTIES

	OFFICERS	OTHER RANKS
Killed in Action, or died of wounds or disease	77	789
Wounded	159	3299
Totals	236	4088

Prisoners of war (all ranks) 175.

Approximately 10,000 all ranks served with the 1st Battalion in France.

The names of those who fell are recorded in St George's Chapel in Ely Cathedral, which is dedicated to their memory.

'While yet was war around us, they found Peace,
And Peace they now have, greater even than we.'

Appendix IV

A BRIEF ACCOUNT OF UNITS OTHER THAN THE 1/1st BATTALION

1914–19

The Depot

During the first week of the war 106 recruits were enlisted for the Regiment, some from a waiting-list, and on 11 August, 1914, authority was received from the War Office to pay and ration them: they were accommodated at the Girls' County School, Cambridge (vacated by the 1st Battalion three days previously on its proceeding to Romford), and were placed under the command of Capt. G. D. Pryor. He with a skeleton staff continued to enlist, clothe and partially train recruits, who were posted partly to the 1/1st Battalion (Imperial Service) formed on 1 September from the officers and 'other ranks' of the original Battalion who had volunteered and been passed medically fit for active service, and partly to the Reserve Battalion formed on the same date. The depot was shortly afterwards moved to the Battalion Headquarters in Corn Exchange Street, and in February, 1915, to the newly completed Territorial Headquarters in East Road. On Capt. Pryor being posted to the 2/1st (Reserve) Battalion, Capt. E. S. Peck was appointed to the command of the Depot, later called the Administrative Centre, and carried on the duties of this post until June, 1915, when, on being posted to the 3/1st Battalion as second-in-command, he was succeeded by Capt. J. W. A. A. Ollard of the 1/1st Battalion. He in turn continued in this post until he was followed by Major D. J. Freyer, under whom the Depot [Administrative Centre] remained until it was closed early in 1919.

2/1st Battalion

On 31 August, 1914, authority was received for the formation of a Reserve Battalion, composed of officers and men of the original 1st Battalion who had either not volunteered or had not been passed as medically fit for foreign service, and new recruits in these categories. Lieut.-Col. L. Tebbutt* was appointed to the command, but retired on account of ill-health on 6 October and Col. C. T. Heycock* was then appointed. The officers and other ranks from the 1st Battalion were on detached duties at Ipswich and elsewhere, but early in November the Battalion was suddenly concentrated at Cambridge, with headquarters at the Girls' County School, in response to an order, which was not cancelled for forty-eight hours, to be in readiness to proceed forthwith to Newcastle, where rifles and ammunition would be served out. (N.B. A demand from Eastern Command for particulars of all equipment, utensils, etc., held by the Battalion resulted in the famous NIL Return.) The field officers were Majors A. A. Howell (Indian Army) and G. B. Bowes, with Capt. G. D. Pryor as Adjutant and Capt. H. E. Verrinder as Q.M.

Just before Christmas, the Battalion moved to Peterborough, as part of the 207th (East Midland) Brigade in the newly-formed 69th (2nd line East Anglian) Division and continued to supply drafts of officers and other ranks for the 1/1st Battalion. In February, 1915, it was sent to Bury St Edmunds, taking the place of the 1/1st Battalion, which had just gone overseas, in the 54th (1st Line) Division, remaining with them at Bury and Norwich till April when it rejoined the 69th Division and returned to Peterborough. In June it moved to

* Cols. Heycock, Lyon and Tebbutt, the last three pre-war C.O.'s, volunteered for foreign service and were later employed on various administrative duties overseas, the last-named being eventually British administrator of the North part of Cologne during the occupation by the Allied Forces.

Newmarket and shortly afterwards, as the Division was then earmarked for foreign service, those officers and other ranks who were ineligible were transferred to the newly-formed 62nd Provisional (Home Service) Battalion. The 2/1st Battalion remained at Newmarket, save for a short period digging trenches at Rayleigh for the defence of London, till the summer of 1916, when it went with the 69th Division to Harrogate and other places in Yorkshire, and Nottinghamshire. In the autumn of 1917 it was sent to Ashford, Kent, to join a Brigade intended for overseas service: this was never sent, and in February, 1918, the Battalion was disbanded. In June, 1916, on Col. Heycock's retirement, Major W. P. Cutlack was appointed to the command, and on his going overseas he was succeeded temporarily by Major M. M. Eastwell, and finally by Major J. R. A. H. Paul, D.S.O., Leicestershire Regiment, who continued to command the Battalion till its disbandment in January, 1918. During the war there were on every front, including Afghanistan 1919, officers who had at some time or other been in the Battalion.

3/1st Battalion

On 17 February, 1915, authority was received for the formation of a 2nd Reserve Battalion to be called the 3/1st and to be quartered in Cambridge. The first recruits were enrolled on 25 February by Capt. E. S. Peck, O.C. Depot, and on 1 May Major A. A. Howell, who had been appointed the previous month, took over the command. From the first, one of its duties was to receive officers and men from the 1/1st Battalion returned through sickness or wounds. Owing to the shortage of officers and N.C.O.'s as instructors, help was sought from, and ungrudgingly given for some months by, the M.A. section of the Cambridge University O.T.C. and the Perse School O.T.C. The original authorized strength having been increased by 50 per cent., the Battalion continued to recruit and train at Cambridge (which was made more difficult by the men being distributed in billets) until 25 August when it proceeded 811 strong to Windsor, where it was for the first time a compact unit and was brigaded with other Battalions. From this time onwards it continued to send out drafts of officers and men to the 1/1st Battalion, and to receive officers and men who had been invalided from the front, on their being passed fit for duty. On 10 October it moved to Halton near Tring, where it remained for some two years. In 1917 it was amalgamated with the Reserve Battalion Suffolk Regiment under the title of the 'Cambs and Suffolk Reserve Battalion Suffolk Regiment', which was later sent to St Albans and became the 22nd Training Battalion. Throughout its existence, training was much hampered by the deficiency in number and quality of rifles, and from 1916 onwards by the duty of maintaining at all times a reduced establishment Battalion, mainly composed of ex-B.E.F. personnel, which was liable to be sent off at a few hours' notice in case of invasion. It is estimated that from February 1915 onwards over 150 officers and more than 2000 men passed through the Battalion; whilst the majority of these went out as drafts to the 1/1st Battalion, reinforcements of both officers and men were found for the 2/1st and 4/1st. Officer reinforcements were also found for various units in practically every part of the war area.

4/1st Battalion

The Battalion was formed under authority of the War Office 6 November, 1915, and consisted in about equal parts of officers and other ranks from both the 2/1st and 3/1st Battalions. The first C.O. was Major (afterwards Lieut.-Col.) E. T. Saint, D.S.O., who was succeeded on 4 November, 1916, by Major H. S. Scott Harden, and he in turn in April, 1917, by Lieut.-Col. G. L. Archer. It was first at Bury St Edmunds as part of the 208th (Norfolk and Suffolk) Brigade of the 69th (2nd line East Anglian) Division. In May, 1916, it moved with the Brigade to Harrogate, in October to Doncaster, and in the following April to Thoresby. Certain officers left at various times to join the 1/1st Battalion, and it sent drafts of men to other regiments. It was disbanded in July 1917, the personnel being transferred to the 3/1st Battalion.

62nd Provisional Battalion

In June 1915 officers and other ranks of the 2/1st Battalion who had not volunteered or had been medically rejected for foreign service were sent from Newmarket with similar details from the 2/4th Battalion Northants Regiment to Sheringham, to form the 62nd (Home Service) Provisional Battalion. Their duties were coast defence (hitherto performed by Cyclist Battalions), the preparation of defence works (at first under the direction of R.E.'s, but after the first fortnight without such guidance) and training. They, with similar Battalions along the coast, formed part of a Provisional Brigade, which included Yeomanry Regiments as reserves. The first commander was Major G. B. Bowes, who held the appointment till 25 October when he was succeeded by Lieut.-Col. C. E. F. Copeman, who had earlier in the year been invalided home from the 1/1st Battalion, Major J. W. Fisher, 2/4th Northants, joining about the same time. From the start, and throughout the existence of the Battalion, its adjutant was Capt. P. W. Gray and its Q.M. Capt. H. E. Verrinder. In October 1916 the Battalion was moved along the coast, being distributed over an area including Cley, Blakeney, and other places, and remained on that coast till it was disbanded, its title meantime having been changed to the 9th Battalion The Northants Regiment. During the whole period, several officers and many other ranks left it to join the 1/1st Battalion overseas.

Volunteers

On 6 January, 1915, authority was received from the War Office to call up National Reservists Class II. These were formed into No. 2 Supernumerary Company, 1st Battalion Cambridgeshire Regiment.

On 29 April, 1916, the Volunteer Force was officially recognized by the Army Council, and three Battalions of the Cambs Volunteer Regiment were formed, 1st (Cambridge) Battalion under Major H. S. Cronin, 2nd (Cambridgeshire) under Major S. G. Howard, and 3rd (Isle of Ely) under Major L. H. Luddington, the whole being under Col. T. W. Harding as County Commandant.

They were employed on various duties, such as guarding railways, bridges, munition works, wireless stations, and other places of strategic importance in the Eastern Counties.

Throughout the war the County Association, under the able chairmanship, and from October 1915, when he became Lord-Lieutenant, the presidency of Mr C. Adeane, laboured unceasingly, with the assistance of Capt. W. R. Elworthy, its indefatigable secretary, for the welfare and encouragement of all units of the Regiment.

G. B. B.

INDEX

La Bassée Canal, 37
La Belle Alliance, 127
La Maisonnette Ridge, 158
Lacy, Lieut. J. Le G., 159, 165
Lamotte, 161, 163
Lancashire Fusiliers, 63
Landas, 264
Le Forest, 212
Le Tréport, 167
Lealvillers, 179
Leinsters, 10, 15, 16, 20, 25
Leipzig Redoubt, 67
Lempire, 237
Lenninghem, 153
Lens, 248
Liéramont–Sorrel Line, 228
Lille, 262
Lilley, xiii
Lincolns, 175
Little Priel Farm, 245–6
Littledale, Capt. H. A. P., xvii, xviii, 2, 3, 5
Liveing, xiii
Liverpool Scottish, 111–12, 120–3, 125
London, 269, 281
Long Melford, 5
Longavesnes, 156
Longeau, 165
Longley, Brig.-Gen., 14
Looker, Capt. A. W., 37
Lottinghem, 153
Lowestoft, xiv
Luce, 163–4
Luddington, Major L. H., 284
Ludendorff, 167, 187, 192
Lumsden, Lieut. V. N., 174, 208
Lyon, Col. A. J., xiii, xvi, xvii, 2, 280
Lys, 277

Mailly-Maillet, 180
Mailly Wood, 50
Malassise Farm, 239
Malassise valley, 239
Maltz Horn Ridge, 206–7, 212, 217
Mametz–Carnoy Ridge, 204
Marcelcave–Wiencourt railway, 163
March, xi–xiii, 4
Maricourt–Montauban road, 206
Marne, 182, 184
Marr, Capt. F. A., 16, 21, 23–4, 52–3, 69, 77, 82–3, 86–7, 165, 168–9, 171, 173, 175, 179
Marsden, Major (R.E.), 161
Martin, Capt. R., xiii, xvii

Martin's Lane, 61–3, 69
Martinsart, 182
Matthews, R.S.M., 158, 182
Maxse, Gen. Sir Ivor, 97, 99, 102, 136–8
Mayor of Cambridge (Ald. R. Starr), 274
McMicking, 2/Lieut. G. T. G., xviii, 6
McNish, 2/Lieut. J. A., 248
Méaulte, 198, 293–4
Menin Road, 15, 18, 23–4, 151, 277
Messines Ridge, 99, 167–9
Metcalfe, xiii
Methuen, Lieut.-Col. J. A., 88, 90–2
Methuen, Lord, xv
Meyer, Lieut., 252
Mill Road, 61
Milne, F.M. Lord, 29
Miraumont, 43, 45, 51, 60, 66
Moislains, 156
Mons, 277
Mt Rouge, 221
Montauban, 206
Morcourt Ridge, 161
Morcourt–Harbonnières Line, 161
Morlancourt, Morlancourt Ridge, 185–6, 188, 190, 192, 203
Morley, xiii
Moule, 39
Mouse Trap Farm, 100–2, 106–7, 128
Moyes, xiii
Muffett, Lance-Corp., 110, 124, 159
Murray, Lieut.-Col. T. D., 87–8, 101, 130, 132–3

Naden, Lieut.-Col., 168–71, 173, 175
New York, 183
Newcastle, 280
Newman, Pte., 228
Newmarket, xii, 281, 283
Nightingale, Lance-Corp., 38–9, 47, 53–4, 56–7, 59, 60, 63, 69, 70, 74, 76, 84, 96, 100, 103–5, 111, 114, 120, 122–3, 125–7, 129, 131, 140, 142–4
'Nipper', 199, 200
No Man's Land, 9, 37, 45–6, 48, 106, 127–8
Nock, 2/Lieut. G. G. R., 223–4, 228
Norfolks, 179, 186, 198, 204, 210–11, 218–19, 223, 225, 231, 234–6, 256, 259, 261, 267
Norris, Major S. E., 32
Northamptonshires, 239–43, 251, 283

PRINTED BY WALTER LEWIS, M.A., AT THE UNIVERSITY PRESS, CAMBRIDGE

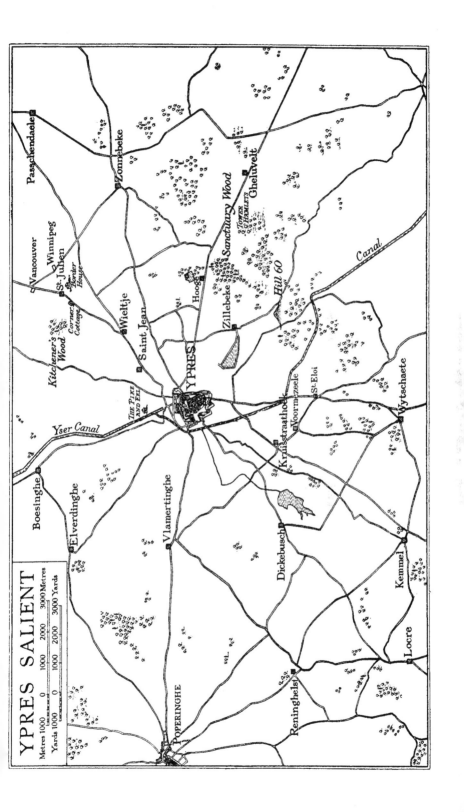

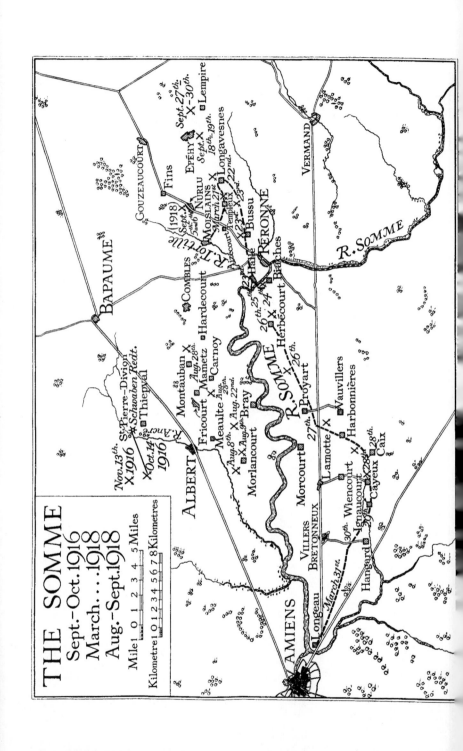

THE SOMME
Sept.–Oct. 1916
March....1918
Aug.–Sept. 1918

Mile 1 0 1 2 3 4 5 Miles
Kilometre 1 0 1 2 3 4 5 6 7 8 Kilometres

BAPAUME

GOUZEAUCOURT

Fins

Sept. 27th X–30th
EPÉHY Sept. X
Sept. X 18th–19th
NURLU Longavesnes
MOISLAINS Templeux 22nd
March 21st X X23rd–X23rd
(1918) Bussu
Sept. X PÉRONNE
5 and 6 Haie
R. Tortille R. SOMME
COMBLES Hardecourt
Hardecourt Herbécourt Brches
26th.25th 23rd
26th. 24.
Montauban X X
Aug.28th R. SOMME
Mametz Carnoy Proyart
Fricourt X 27th. 26th.
Thiepval Meaulte Aug. X Vauvillers
Nov.13th St.Pierre–Divion Aug.25th X Harbonnières
X 1916 Aug.8th Aug.22nd Lamotte X
X Oct.14 X Aug.5th Bray Wiencourt X Aug.28th
1916 Morlancourt 30th. Ignaucourt X28th Cayeux Caix
ALBERT VERMAND
Morcourt Hangard
VILLERS
BRETONNEUX
Longeau March 31st.
AMIENS

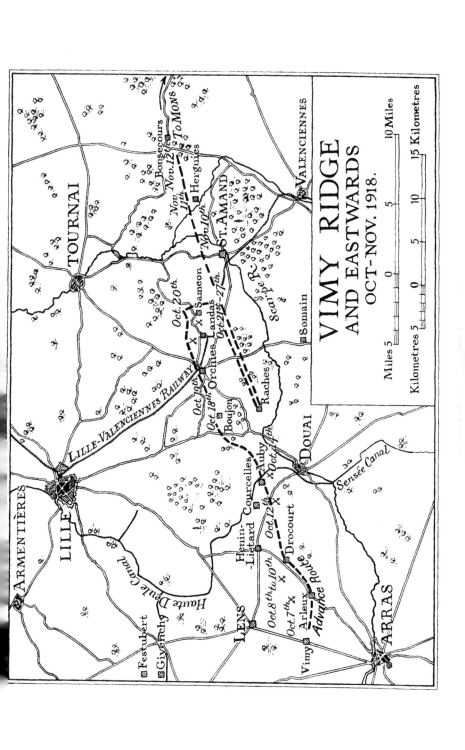

VIMY RIDGE
AND EASTWARDS
OCT–NOV. 1918.